Writers' Houses and the Making of Memory

Routledge Research in Cultural and Media Studies

Writers' Houses and the Making of Memory

Edited by
Harald Hendrix

Routledge
Taylor & Francis Group
New York   London

Routledge
Taylor & Francis Group
711 Third Avenue,
New York,
NY 10017

Routledge
Taylor & Francis Group
2 Park Square
Milton Park, Abingdon
Oxon OX14 4RN

© 2008 by Taylor & Francis Group, LLC
Routledge is an imprint of Taylor & Francis Group, an Informa business

First issued in paperback 2012

ISBN 978-0-415-95742-7 (hbk)

ISBN 978-0-415-54082-7 (pbk)

Library of Congress Cataloging-in-Publication Data

Writers' houses and the making of memory / edited by Harald Hendrix.
    p. cm. -- (Routledge research in cultural and media studies ; 11)
    Includes bibliographical references and index.
    ISBN 978-0-415-95742-7 (hardback : alk. paper)
    1. Literary landmarks. I. Hendrix, Harald.

PN164.W75 2007
809--dc22   2007007172

Visit the Taylor & Francis Web site at
http://www.taylorandfrancis.com

and the Routledge Web site at
http://www.routledge.com

Contents

PART II
Self-Fashioning

.

1 Writers' Houses as Media of Expression and Remembrance
From Self-Fashioning to Cultural Memory

Harald Hendrix

Writers' houses have meaning, even beyond their obvious documentary value as elements in the author's biography. They are a medium of expression and of remembrance. Planning, building and decorating a house provides a writer the opportunity not only to materialize his architectural fantasies and fictions, but also to experiment with a mode of expression fundamentally different from his own. To some authors a place to live, whether or not purposely created, means nothing more than a frame for his art, a tool that contributes to the making of literature. To others, a house is an object of prestige. It can express social or cultural status or the hope for it, and be a means to immortalize and remember such success. But expression and remembrance fuse most in houses created by authors as a work of art, as a parallel or an alternative to their poetry or narrative. Such places not only are thought to be statements on art, on what is expressed and how it can be best expressed. They, moreover, perpetuate these artistic assertions, being turned into monuments by the builders themselves, their heirs, or by later generations of admirers.

The transformation into monuments and museums marks a second process of memory-making characteristic of writers' houses. They attract readers that feel the need to go beyond their intellectual exchanges with texts and long for some kind of material contact with the author of those texts or the places where these originate. As material objects historically related to the cherished writers, their houses can thus grow into destinations of literary pilgrimages and other manifestations of heritage tourism. While these semi-religious rituals of worship contribute to the making of cultural memory, they do so, however, in a selective way, privileging some aspects and interpretations of the authors' work and persona over others. These cults, moreover, are highly susceptible to manipulation. Indeed, they are often the products of initiatives by persons or institutions interested in constructing a particular kind of public memory or a commercially exploitable tourist attraction.

Though recognized and revered as memorial sites over many centuries, in recent years writers' houses have grown into a major asset of heritage tourism. The number of houses turned into museums has significantly

1

risen. When a first survey of all museums dedicated to single persons was made in 1972, among the total of 475 institutions all over Europe it listed 145 places dedicated to the memory of poets and writers.[1] In 2007, France alone has some 203 *maisons d'écrivains* and a most active association specifically dedicated to this type of museum.[2] In Italy, not only can we find more than sixty writers' houses, of which almost 40% was established since 1990;[3] in addition, there are some forty literary parks, all of which have been instituted as of the same year.[4] This public interest in the phenomenon of the writer's house finds its commercial counterpart in an ever-expanding production of often lavishly illustrated guidebooks, clearly directed not only to visitors of the sites but also to a general readership.[5]

Against the background of such a remarkable increase in public and commercial interest, this book explores in more detail the significance of the writer's house as a medium of expression and of remembrance. By focusing on some fifteen cases from various periods and countries, it aims to detect and analyze some of the patterns that recur in this particular kind of literary memory making. In offering such a broad range and a comparative approach, it develops and elaborates on some of the notions introduced by the few historians and literary scholars who previously have engaged in the analysis of specific writers' houses and their functions, whether concentrating on their conception and museum-like organization,[6] their meditated iconography[7] or on their relevance to the author's oeuvre.[8] As such, it contributes to introducing and consolidating this topic as a parallel field of study to the one of the artist's and architect's house, a phenomenon that in the 1980s has attracted quite some scholarly attention, mainly from art historians writing in German.[9]

While the places built and used by artists and architects can generally be understood as demonstrations of their art or of their social status and success—from the ones created by Renaissance artists (Vasari in Arezzo, Zuccari in Rome, Rubens in Antwerp, Rembrandt in Amsterdam) to those designed by their modern counterparts (Gustave Moreau in Paris, Franz von Stuck in Munich, Theo van Doesburg in Meudon, Giorgio De Chirico in Rome, Niki De Saint-Phalle in Capalbio, Michael Graves in Princeton)—writers' houses have still other dimensions that cannot as readily be grasped. Their homes certainly can express cultural status or social aspirations, and most houses purposely built by poets and writers in fact do so. In many cases, moreover, they also are conceived to communicate their builders' position regarding his craft, as we can most often discern in the arrangement of the spaces particularly dedicated to their profession, notably the studio or the library.[10] But since by nature they cannot be straightforward demonstrations of what literature is about, they need to express such positions in an indirect way, by using a different medium which requires a shift in expression from the immaterial to the material, from the intellectual to the tangible and visible. This shift often turns out to be a blessing in disguise, as is suggested by the fact that so many authors did not hesitate to put it into practice and, indeed, to actively explore the new opportunities it offered.

For a writer, building or decorating a house in fact can be a tool to express and demonstrate his opinions on what literature may or may not be able to accomplish, or which direction it should take. Such aspirations can lead to materialized fictions, as we can witness in buildings like Horace Walpole's Gothic castle at Strawberry Hill and Alexandre Dumas's Château de Monte-Cristo,[11] where the author's world of imagination is being fixed in matter and becomes a kind of parallel expression to the literary one. Rather than being eccentric and capricious fantasies, these places suggest a fundamental dissatisfaction with the expressive power of literature, and an eagerness to surpass such restraint by experimenting with other media. Such an inquisitive disposition can develop into an even more ambitious attitude, when the house is viewed as a work of art in its own right, not any more as a parallel to, or a derivative from literary fiction, but as an alternative and even a substitute. In houses like Gabriele D'Annunzio's colossal Vittoriale on Lake Garda, we not only find the ambition to construct a new kind of *Gesamtkunstwerk* based on the integration of various media, from the intellectual to the visible, tangible and aural.[12] Here we also see the transformation of literature in matter, not only with regard to its fictional content, but also at the more fundamental level of its narrative or poetic structure. Places like these are conceived and organized as if they were poems or novels, not constructs of words alone, but with rooms and objects that by their particular design and display suggest meaning. By re-mediating precisely those devices that add symbolical, allegorical or metaphorical dimensions to texts, they explore and at the same time explode literature's intrinsic potentials of indirect expression. Such writers' houses are at the same time a critique of literature and an attempt to surpass it.

But what is the expressive surplus value of building or decorating a house when compared to another medium like literature? The Italian author Curzio Malaparte, who on Capri left us one of the most spectacular writers' houses still in existence, programmatically baptized his self-designed home "casa come me" (house like me) and provocatively stated that in none of his books he had shown his inner self better than in this house built on an almost inaccessible cliff overlooking the sea.[13] Though arguably overstated out of an apologetic drive, Malaparte's words direct our attention to the link between homes and the inner self of the persons building or decorating them, a connection not unfamiliar to literary scholars, psychologists and philosophers alike. In fact, since Gaston Bachelard's *La Poétique de l'espace* (*The Poetics of Space*, 1957) numerous critics from various detraction have underlined the central importance of spatial concepts like the one of the house in understanding the human psyche and its literary representations: "Notre inconscient est 'logé'. Notre âme est une demeure. Et en nous souvenant des 'maisons', des 'chambres', nous apprenons à 'demeurer' en nous-mêmes." (Our unconscious is 'located.' Our soul is a dwelling. And while remembering 'houses' and 'rooms' we learn how to 'dwell' in ourselves.)[14] This awareness has called for greater attention to the function of space in literature, as we can find both in the rich production of scholarly works analyzing the representation of fictional or non-fictional space in literature,[15] and in the essays dedicated to exploring the ways in which spatial elements like houses reinforce and consolidate the structure of literary texts.[16]

So what seems specific about houses as expressive media, is that they allow the persons who build, decorate or just inhabit them to link this particular space to what they consider their inner self, their emotions, memories and psychological disposition. The house, moreover, facilitates structuring this inner self, and communicating it in a coherent fashion. As such, it is ideally fit as an autobiographical technique, and in fact most of the houses that have been shaped or reshaped by writers may well be read as alternative autobiographies or self-portraits. Their orientation, however, is not primarily retrospective, but prospective instead. What they reflect is not a factual account of a writers' life or a neutral assessment of his mental disposition, but an attempt to construct and mould these on the basis of a particular kind of self-interpretation. Rather than alternative autobiographies, therefore, writers' houses are instruments of self-fashioning. They can reveal not just a writer's ideas and ambitions as to the contents and the means of literature, but his aspirations regarding his own artistic and private persona as well.

Not every house, though, built or inhabited by a poet or a novelist is to be considered and interpreted as the product of a well-meditated self-fashioning strategy, far from that. Next to Henrik Ibsen's carefully orchestrated studio in his Oslo apartment,[17] there are the many houses in Prague where Franz Kafka intermittently lived, without him ever making any substantial effort to alter or re-style these temporary homes.[18] This does not imply, however, that such places have no meaning for his literature. Their relevance is of another kind. Besides being a product of a writer's imagination or ambition, his house may also be a source of inspiration in its own right, or a material frame necessary for the production of literature. This is evident not only in the narratives specifically dedicated to writers' or artists' houses,[19] but also in those works of fiction where the description or—as in the case of Kafka—the suggestion of places may be linked to spaces familiar to the author, be it his own home or otherwise.[20] Factual spaces in various ways condition the author's mental map, and thus return, be it directly or metaphorically, on the pages of his poetry or narrative. Such spaces do not just provide a reservoir of possible descriptions. They may moreover condition the way in which an author thinks and works, by association or through memory, willingly and consciously or not. Besides being shaped by writers, houses shape the writers dwelling in them.[21]

As some of the best known writers' houses like those of Marcel Proust or Mario Praz suggest, one of the most potent ways in which spaces can be turned into tools by poets and novelists is their being used as mnemonic devices. Whether meditated or spontaneous, this strategy brings into practice one of the central concepts of the ancient *ars memoriae*:[22] the awareness that the human mind tends to remember things better when organized in spatial configurations like houses, rooms or pieces of furniture, notably libraries. Organizing private spaces equals structuring one's thoughts, mentally or materially, and fitting them into a format that allows them to be evoked at any convenience. Or, for that matter, at any inconvenience, as Proust's mechanism of the *mémoire involontaire* (involuntary memory) suggests. In this respect, therefore, a writers' house may function as a repository of memories linked to objects or spaces, as an archive which documents a person's intellectual and emotional biography, like we see in Mario Praz's Roman apartment and in his parallel book *La casa della vita (The House of Life)*.[23] But it may also become a tool that transcends the personal nature of the memories it contains, and grow into a machine able to evoke through remembrance of things past imagination of a more universal kind.[24]

Both as a technique of self-fashioning and as a mnemonic device, houses of writers originate in what is fundamentally the private sphere of the author's creativity. They offer a moldable and productive frame that enables them to organize and construe their artistic and private persona, as well as part of the imaginative world they set up in their work. But the very process of fixing these tools in concrete matter entails a transformation of the house from a flexible instrument into a stable object, and this in its turn evokes a passage from the private to the public. With this double move, the house changes from being a medium of expression to becoming one of remembrance, and simultaneously slides from the sphere of personal and individual into that of collective and cultural memory. The meanings projected onto the house, in fact, cannot any longer be controlled by the author's personal perspective, but may and indeed increasingly are being appropriated by others, who in their turn may project their meanings and memories onto the house. At the end of this process, writers' houses become monuments and museums, thus entering into the public sphere of heritage culture. But what they signify changes over the course of this process. They contain more than the expression of the writer's ideas and ambitions. In addition to that, they accumulate the various interpretations and appropriations of those ideas and ambitions by later generations, who tend to project onto the material object of the house both their vision of the writer and some of their own ideals and idiosyncrasies. As a medium of remembrance, writers' houses not only recall the poets and novelists who dwelt in them, but also the ideologies of those who turned them into memorial sites.

The first impulse to this crucial transformation, though, is still soundly rooted in the nature of the writer's house itself. Its prospective orientation, in fact, necessitates it to be driven from the author's private sphere into the public domain. Having established and fixed in matter one's self-representation, the result needs to be communicated and possibly perpetuated in collective memory. This may be done at the initiative of the authors themselves, interested in erecting monuments to their own creativity, or even inclined to fuse the creative process and the building of monuments to oneself, as we can see in the cases of Walter Scott's Abbotsford and Gabriele D'Annunzio's Vittoriale.[25] But also other agents may interfere, from heirs and personal friends to admirers or public bodies at a local or national level. What makes them want to remember, and what they want to remember exactly, directs the specific character of the literary cults that may rise around such houses and determines the meanings those places may convey. As monuments and museums, writers' houses thus reflect several and sometimes even contrasting kinds of memories, forged as they are by the interpretations and appropriations both of those that initiated this specific kind of literary memory making and of the later generations who continued and perpetuated its existence.

As has been asserted in the many recent works focusing on the change from individual to collective memory and on the functions of *lieux de mémoire*,[26] processes like these show a dynamism largely dependant on distance in time and on shifts in ideology. When individual memory starts to fade, the need to fix in matter what is considered valuable grows.[27] This is even more so the case when collective memory is yielding.[28] But in order to determine what is valuable, interpretation and selection is called for. Here literary but also political ideology becomes a crucial factor. In this process, writers' houses can assume a double function. Since memory tends to preferably stick to places, as the *ars memoriae* has shown, the existence of a house facilitates the rise of a cult and favors its subsistence. Just as—the other way around—the existence of a cult tends to invent and construct places, if they are not yet at hand, as the example of Shakespeare's Stratford, or Dante's house in Florence notoriously demonstrate.[29] Such mechanisms, however, occur only if the interpretation of what the house expresses agrees with dominant opinions on what their dwellers and their literary works stand for. And since interpretations of literary works vary in time, the attention to writers' houses does accordingly. So writers' houses, on the one hand, stimulate their masters being canonized. On the other hand, though, they also depend on this very process of canonization, and especially on the directions it takes in course of time. This may call for changes in the way houses are being presented, for manipulations and even for complete reconstructions. It may also make them obsolete.

As a medium of remembrance, writers' houses however do not depend on the literary dynamics of changing interpretations and canonizations alone. Their significance and success is dictated likewise by elements we can find at the very basis of so many other *lieux de mémoire*: the admiration for "illustrious men" that as of early modern times was integrated in a discourse of first local and later national pride;[30] the romantic interest in personality, especially in genius, and the desire to identify with such extraordinary persons;[31] the need to get in touch with history directly and physically, in the places where history was made or ideas were conceived.[32] In various combinations and intensities, these elements operate both on the part of the people responsible for founding and taking care of museums in writers' houses, as on the part of their visitors, in the past as well as in the present. The fierce polemics between Americans and Cubans on who should be in charge of Ernest Hemingway's house in Havana illustrates the topicality of the matter just as well as the steady flow of publications in which contemporary journalists and writers relate their literary pilgrimages to the houses of the authors they particularly feel close to.[33] The places also have meaning for the general public, as visiting numbers suggest. Yet empirical research on the motivations of present-day visitors done by scholars working in the field of Tourism Studies has established that this meaning is not exclusively or even primarily of a literary or an ideological kind.[34] It is the more general idea of authenticity, of getting in touch with the world of the past and of the imagination, that turns out to be the greatest attraction of the visit to places like writers' houses,[35] and their curators wisely have taken this into account when rearranging their museum's display.[36]

Whether the remarkable present-day concern for memorial places like writers' houses, both on the part of local and national authorities or with the general public, is due to the yielding of memory at large and to its substitution by experience and consumption, as some critics argue,[37] is not a question this book intends to answer or even address. While exploring the writer's house as a medium of expression and of remembrance, the book's focus is instead on the house's literary and historical significance. Therefore, it offers in its first section an overview of the long history of the European writers' house and of its particular attraction as a remembrance site. It shows that the origins of this phenomenon go back as far as early modernity. From the sixteenth century onwards a new attention for the author's biography as suggested by his work stimulated people to perceive of his house as of a place full of meaning, and through his house people felt able to establish a kind of contact with the author and the imaginative world he had created. As the cases of Petrarch and Shakespeare amply attest, this awareness caused visitors to concentrate on specific items— chairs, mulberry trees, mummified cats, desks—that could act as mediators in this contact. But also the visit itself as of the 1530s became a ritual that, while immediately integrated in newly established tourist practices like the Grand Tour and later railway tourism, tended to expand its performance-like character into grand theatrical occasions—the Shakespeare Jubilee in 1767—where life and work of poets and novelists were re-enacted by huge crowds of visitors.

From the outset, however, these practices were not uncontested. They provoked skepticism particularly regarding the authenticity of the places and the objects they contained. Although a recurrent feature until the present day, such criticism yet never was able to diminish the appeal of writers' houses, as the history of the three homes in Frankfurt, Rome and Weimar dedicated to the memory of Goethe shows. Since their foundations were largely dictated by ideological and political motives and thus by the appropriation of the poet's memory by civil society, these houses lived the ups and downs of modern German history, regardless of their being authentic or not.[38] The meaning of such houses clearly goes beyond their material appearance, as the case of Scott's Abbotsford illustrates particularly well. Being constructed as an autobiography, like Goethe's Weimar residence, this "romance of a house I am making" was conceived by Scott as an assemblage of objects full of associations and meaning. In the end it became not only a monument to Scott's historical imagination but also an iconic object that itself could easily become appropriated by others and be moved all over the world.

As the Brontë Parsonage persuasively shows, this process of becoming a mobile icon full of symbolical meaning can have serious consequences for the way the writers and their works are being perceived. In fact, to a large extent it conditions this perception and thus precludes an open-minded and critical approach to the authors whose memory is linked to the house. And incorrectly so, since this particular case reminds us that the Parsonage should not confirm the stereotypical view of the Brontë sisters as leading a secluded and sad life, but suggests, on the contrary, that at the basis of their authorship we can detect a joyful existence particularly fit to stimulate the sisters' imagination. Writers' houses clearly depend on the image readers have constructed of their inhabitants, not only in the way they are perceived and function as sites in the ever-growing heritage industry, but also with regard to their very existence: this is what the very foundation of the Keats-Shelley Memorial House in the first years of the twentieth century and the circumstances surrounding it make clear.

The second section of the book shows that writers' houses, besides being the focus of remembrance practices, can also mirror and express their authors' private and artistic ambitions and dreams. Again, this becomes evident in early modernity when people like the artist and historiographer Vasari start to use their house in order to confirm their status and to construct an artistic persona. From the outset this implies taking the house to be some kind of mnemonic device and taking the opportunity of such a privileged "theatre of memory" to integrate personal history and artistic ambition. But, moreover, the medium in which such ambitions materialize, architecture and interior decoration, offers the opportunity to experiment with new ways of expression, and to realize an artistic identity based on the ambition of versatility and on the dream of the *Gesamtkunstwerk*. This fusion of autobiography full of personal recollections and the pursuit of a new kind of art where the intellectual and the material meet is at the basis of the houses of the Rossettis and of William Morris. These buildings tend to change from private dwellings into sometimes provocative artistic and even political statements. Since they materialize ideals that the authors actively propagated, they even are projected as attractions for profane pilgrims, like the ones we meet in Morris's utopian novel *News from Nowhere*, in which his Kelmscott Manor figures as destination in what is a modern version of a pilgrimage.

The self-awareness expressed in such details becomes most pronounced in authors like Pierre Loti and Henry Rider Haggard. They use their houses not only to express their identity as they have construed this on the basis of real or imagined travels and adventures. They conceive their houses foremost as an ideal framework to perform that identity, exploiting to this end not just the endless opportunities that interior decoration in the age of orientalism and bric-à-brac offers, but also and especially the qualitative leap that the new medium of photography can guarantee. Both Haggard and Loti have been photographed with their houses and invite reporters to portray them as part of the spectacular arrangements in their self-designed dwellings. But especially Loti seems to totally fuse with the imagined world of his exotic house, sending around autographed postcards of its rooms and posing for the camera as its only living soul. These houses clearly serve as theatres, not just as "theatres of memory," but also as real theatres where life is only lived when performed.

Interestingly, in these same years the parallel concept of the writers' house as a "theatre of memory" finds its most monumental expression in the house of the Goncourt brothers and the book *La Maison d'un artiste* (*The House of an Artist*) Edmond de Goncourt later dedicates to this dwelling. As in the case of Loti, life and imagination as expressed in a house get confused. Here again, as with the Rossetti's and Morris, interior decoration becomes an instrument in an artistic struggle against current aesthetics. But this battle in the end seems no more than a pretense or a good occasion. Building and decorating a house for the Goncourts, ultimately, is their life, not just shaping it. Writing a book on this house doubtlessly coincides with writing an autobiography. And thus it is for Mario Praz, who is perhaps the most telling example of this tradition that beyond the Goncourts finds its origins in works like Joseph de Maistre's *Voyage autour de ma chambre* (*Journey Around my Room*, 1795). Still today, Praz's Roman apartment, together with his *La Casa della vita* (*The House of Life*), imposes itself as a living record, as an eminent theatre of memory. But it is the stage of a depersonalised memory not inclined to show its author but, on the contrary, eager to hide his personal life, as shown by the revealing detail of Praz's erasing every reference to his ex-wife and to the text by De Goncourt that might direct the reader's attention to this fact.

And, finally, there is Proust. While De Goncourt and Praz fill their rooms with carefully arranged objects charged with associations and meaning, thus transferring and appropriating their symbolical value and creating a house where matter can take over life, Proust makes himself a mental room. Isolating himself from the outer world and avoiding an interior decoration that might impose unwelcome associations, he creates the perfect tool for his authorship: a house, a room, a bed that may erase itself and give way to an unrestrained flow of involuntary memory and imagination.

NOTES

1. Zankl, 1972.
2. 'Fédération des maisons d'écrivain et des patrimoines littéraires'; its website is at http://www.litterature-lieux.com. Spain has an analogous organisation covering some fifty houses: 'ACAMFE-Asociacion de Casas-Museo y Fundaciones de Escritores' (http://www.acamfe.org). The Italian 'Progetto Nazionale Case della Memoria' was established in 1998 (http://www.casedellamemoria.it). For the United Kingdom, see: www.lithouses.org. On an international level, literary museums collaborate in the 'International Committee of Literary Museums' (ICLM), a separate unit of the Unesco 'International Council of Museums' (ICOM). In the late 1990s, there have been initiatives to establish a European network of literary museums, 'Castalia. Coopération entre lieux de mémoire d'écrivains,' but without being institutionalized.
3. For a recent yet incomplete inventory, see Coletto, 2002.
4. See the national website (http://www.parchiletterari.it). Initiated by the private Fondazione Nievo, the project was sustained by European Union funding and accompanied by a series of publications: Nievo, 1990; Nievo, 1991; Nievo, 1998; Nievo, 2000; Barilaro, 2004.
5. Allegri, 1999; Bloch-Dano, 2005; Braun, 2003; Cabanis and Herscher, 1998; Camus, 1995; Chambouleyron Lanzmann, 1998; Eagle and Carnell, 1977; Ehrlich and Carruth, 1982; Fiorani, 1996; Fiorani, 2002; Hardwick, 1968; Hardwick, 1973; Igoe, 1994; Ignasiak, 1996; Kaufelt, 1986; Klein, 2005; Lees-Milne, 1985; Levine, 1984; Listri, 1996; McClatchy, 2004; K. Marsh, 1993; Maurer and Maurer, 1988; Naldini and Roiter, 1999; Nestmeyer, 2005; Poisson, 1982; Poisson, 1997; Premoli-Droulers, 1994; Rochette, 2004; Schauffelen, 1981; Selmin, 2004; Semsek, 2000; Wißkirchen, 2002.
6. Bann, 1984, especially Chapter 5 "The historical composition of place: Byron and Scott" (93–111).
7. Terraroli, 2001.
8. Fuss, 2004.
9. In chronological order: Hoh-Slodczyk, 1977; Leopold, 1981; Schwarz, 1981; Hoh-Slodczyk, 1985; Hüttinger, 1985; *Case d'artista*, 1988; Schwarz, 1989; Schwarz, 1990; Settis, 1992. On the houses of architects, artists and composers, see in addition to these scholarly works also: Winkler, 1955; Gefen, 1997; Jor and Turner, 1999; Lemaire, 2004.
10. On the origins of this iconography, see Liebenwein, 1977; Bialostocki, 1988; Thornton, 1998.
11. On Walpole see Guillery and Snoding, 1995, and Iddon, 1996. On Dumas see Schopp, 2000, and Cazenave, 2002.
12. On the Vittoriale see Mazza, 1988, and Terraroli, 2001.
13. Though initially designed by the architect Adalberto Libera following Malaparte's indications, controversies between the author and Libera caused the villa's final outline (1943) to be largely dictated by Malaparte. On the building history and Malaparte's frequent references to the autobiographical nature of his villa, see Attanasio, 1990; Talamone, 1990; Pettena, 1999.
14. Bachelard, 1957, 19. See also Agamben, 1977; Berry, 1983; Heidegger, 1971; Lefebvre, 1991; Levinas, 1961; Marc, 1972; Rybczynski, 1986; Tindall, 1991.

15. Cesaretti, 2003; Chandler, 1991; Gill, 1972; Goebel, 1971; Innocenti, 1995; Kelsall, 1993; Manguel and Guadalupi, 1999; Marcus, 1999; Nissim, 1980; Papasogli, 1988; Rubino and Pagetti, 1988; Ruzicka, 1987; Tristram, 1989; Watson, 1999.
16. Frank, 1979; Genette, 1969; Lutwack, 1984.
17. On Ibsen's Oslo apartment, see Edvarsen, 1998.
18. On Kafka's various houses in Prague, see Salfellner, 2002.
19. Deledda, 1930; E. de Goncourt, 1881; James, 1902; Praz, 1958.
20. See note 15.
21. Fuss, 2004.
22. Yates, 1966.
23. Praz, 1958. On this book see the chapter by Paola Colaiacomo in this volume, and, moreover, Cattaneo, 2003; on the apartment, see Rosazza Ferraris, 1996.
24. On the significance of his apartments for Proust's work, see the essay by Jon Kear in this volume, and moreover Praz, 1952; Poulet, 1963; Frank, 1979, 113–65; Fuss, 2004, 151–212.
25. On Scott's Abbotsford see the essay by Ann Rigney in this volume, and moreover: Bann, 1984, 93–111, and Bann, 1995, 99–101, 152–53. On D'Annunzio's Vittoriale, see above, Note 12.
26. On cultural memory, see: Assmann, 1999; Erll, 2005; Halbwachs, 1950; Lowenthal, 1985; Samuel, 1994. On *lieux de mémoire* consult the various series edited in France, Italy, Germany and The Netherlands: Nora, 1984–92; Isnenghi, 1996–97; François and Schulze, 2001; Wesseling, 2005–07. On monuments, see also Le Goff, 1978, and Tobia, 1991.
27. Assmann, 1992.
28. See especially Lowenthal, 1985.
29. On Shakespeare's house in Stratford see the chapter by Michael Rosenthal in this volume, and, moreover, Holderness, 1988. Dante's house in Florence was constructed by the town administration in 1911, on the spot where he and his family supposedly had lived, but without any specific evidence as to its original location or appearance.
30. On Italian *uomini illustri* (illustrious men) and their integration in local and national discourse, see Irace, 2003.
31. Arthaud, 1967; Bénichou, 1973; Bonnet, 1998; Colton, 1976; Raabe, 1970. On the habit of visiting writers in person, see Nora, 1986.
32. Ankersmit, 2005; Greenblatt, 2000; Pieters, 2005.
33. The debate on Hemingway's *Finca Vigía* was unleashed when on 2 June 2005 the American National Trust for Historic Preservation named the writer's Havana home to its '2005 list of America's 11 most endangered historic places'. On contemporary literary pilgrimages, see Amerongen and Rothuizen, 1984; Bottiglieri, 2004; Curtis, 2005; Fens, 1998; Petrignani, 2002.
34. Herbert, 2001. For more historically oriented research on literary tourism, see Adler, 1989; Lemon, 1996; Santesso, 2004; Stagl, 1995.
35. Fawcett and Cormack, 2001; Pocock, 1987; Wang, 1999.
36. Barthel, 1996; Busch and Beermeister, 1999; Leoncini and Simonetti, 1998; Wehnert, 2000; see also the various articles dedicated to museum display in the *Bulletin d'informations* of the French 'Fédération des maison d'écrivain et des patrimoines littéraires,' as well as the extensive bibliographie by Florence Lignac, both available on their website (see Note 2).
37. See Lowenthal, 1985; Urry, 1990; Urry, 1995; Rojek and Urry, 1997; Kirshenblatt Gimblett, 1998.
38. On the relevance of authenticity with regard to the houses of Goethe, see my discussion in Hendrix, 2007.

Part I
Cultural Memory

2 The Early Modern Invention of Literary Tourism

Petrarch's Houses in France and Italy

Harald Hendrix

In the early 1340s, when his reputation as an intellectual and poet started to gain him ever wider acclaim all over Europe, Francis Petrarch engaged in an ambitious project to actively reinvent several of the traditions aimed at honouring and remembering literary men, both the living and the dead ones, rituals he had read about in the works of his cherished Roman pre-decessors. When on a diplomatic mission to Naples at the end of 1343, together with two friends he undertook an excursion to those sites on the northern part of the cities bay—to Baia, the lakes of Averno and Lucrino, to Cuma and Pozzuoli—that stimulated memories of Virgil and his works, relating this experience of a literary pilgrimage in a letter to his close friend Giovanni Colonna.[1] This unusual initiative to visit places associated with poets he admired was a follow-up to the events of some two years earlier, when on Easter Sunday 1341 Petrarch himself had been crowned a poet laureate, after having been cross-examined for three days by the king of Naples, Robert of Anjou. Actively engaged as he was in the re-invention and re-enactment of this ancient ritual and in publicizing it through his extensive network of correspondents, Petrarch succeeded in both reanimating literary memorial practices long neglected and in inscribing himself into this newly polished tradition to publicly honour literary accomplishments.

While thus projecting strategies of self-fashioning into ancient memorial practices, Petrarch was well aware of the symbolical and emotional impact the element of space could add to such rituals. Not only was his coronation re-enacted on a highly symbolical site, Capitol Hill in Rome, in his accep-tance speech the poet laureate explicitly recalled the association of place and memory by quoting his favourite author Cicero:

> Our emotions are somehow stirred in those places in which the feet of those whom we love and admire have trodden. Wherefore even Athens delights us not so much through its magnificent buildings and its exquisite works of ancient art as through the memory of its great men: 'twas here they dwelt, 'twas here they sat, 'twas here they engaged in their philosophical discussions. And with reverence I contemplate their tombs.[2]

The awareness of a meaningful link between space and memory, and the desire to remember favourite poets in places where they had lived or were buried, soon was applied to Petrarch himself, who after his coronation indeed attracted even greater attention and acclaim. Some nine years later, in the Holy Year 1350, on his way back from a visit to Rome he made a short stop in Arezzo, the town where he was born in 1304 but where he had never lived, not even as a child, and that he himself did not consider his home town—that was Florence. Nonetheless he was received with great honours. To his great surprise, at the end of the visit he was taken to the house where he had been born. This house, his hosts informed him, was put under a special kind of protection, since a few years before the municipal government had denied its owner the permission to make alterations, in order to guarantee it to remain exactly as it was when Petrarch was born there. When twenty years later in one of his letters he recalls this episode, Petrarch reacts with a mix of pride and embarrassment, interpreting it both as a welcome expression of esteem and as a hardly appropriate attempt to use his fame in order to promote the interests of the city of Arezzo.[3]

And this is of course the case, then as it is now. In fact, the building that we nowadays can visit in Arezzo as 'Casa del Petrarca', besides the location has little to do with the house Petrarch was born in: it is a post-war reconstruction of a sixteenth-century palazzo which was completely destroyed in 1943 and that only as of 1931 was used as the official seat of the local academy called Accademia Petrarca di Lettere, Arti e Scienze; so it offers a fine example of the appropriation by local interest groups of the posthumous fame of a poet, a practice which—by the way—in the twentieth century became one of the main agents in the memorial culture of poets' houses in Italy.

Petrarch's reaction however, besides being discerningly sharp, also reflects an attitude to memorial culture that in the early modern period is highly present and indeed seems to distinguish this era from both the preceding and the subsequent ones. The mix of pride and embarrassment we read in his letter reflects an ambiguous attitude, where the awareness that places and objects can significantly contribute to the expression of respect for esteemed poets and their works is paralleled and sometimes undermined by scepticism and outright opposition to such cult of places. This is at least what the history of the two main sites linked to the memory of Petrarch himself suggest, his house in Fontaine-de-Vaucluse near Avignon, where he lived during much of his most productive years, and the house in Arquà close to Padova, where he died. Not only are the cults that have developed around these places the most ancient ones in the Western world, they also allow us, precisely because they have such a *longue durée*, to document the shifts in the practices of what came to be called literary pilgrimages.

During his lifetime, Petrarch was an exceptionally famous man. After his death, however, this rapidly changed. Petrarch died in his house in Arquà on 19 July 1374 and was buried five days later in the local parish church.

His family then decided to erect a monumental tomb, right in front of the church (see Figure 2.1), and in the year 1380 his body was reburied here. During the first decades after his passing away, in the nearby Padova several commemorative portraits were produced, the humanist Pier Paolo Vergerio was asked to deliver a public eulogy on the poet, and some of Petrarch's friends like Giovanni Dondi wrote poems to honour his memory.[4] But from the start of the fifteenth century this memorial practice seems to fade away, even at a local level, and little is left of the cult status Petrarch enjoyed while alive. Doubtless this is related to the fact that the generation of those who had known him personally passed away. In the process that leads to the formation of cultural memory this is, of course, a crucial moment, when only some of the elements out of the rich and varied, but short and thus weak individual memory are selected and stabilised in the less diverse but more continuous and therefore stronger collective memory.

The earliest history of Fontaine-de-Vaucluse and Arquà can illustrate the effects of this process. In the late fourteenth and fifteenth centuries,

Figure 2.1 Petrarch's tomb at Arquà (© Harald Hendrix).

Petrarch's presence in the French site is completely forgotten, even at the local level, to such point that as yet there is no conclusive evidence that the house which in 1926 was opened as the Musée Pétrarque actually was the place where Petrarch had lived. Arquà, however, all over this period keeps being linked to the memory of Petrarch, but only because of the presence of his monumental tomb, not of his house, which was sold by his heirs at the end of the fourteenth century. This memory is moreover of a certain kind: it is the poet's Florentine background and his Latin work as a humanist that attract the attention, as we can deduct from the few pieces of evidence that inform us on what meanings people attributed some hundred years after the poet's death to this place. First there is the report of the humanist Ambrogio Traversari, significantly from Florence, who visited the site in the year 1443 while making an inspection tour of various convents in the region:

> While on my way, it pleased my to make a short detour, in order to see for myself in the village of Arquà the tomb of Francis Petrarch. For he was a man renowned in our age whose dedication to letters began the awakening of the 'studia humanitatis'. Thus I was easily induced to wish to see his mausoleum. Having paid my respects, and uttered prayers for his repose, I went on to the monastery.[5]

Like Petrarch himself had suggested in the address at his Roman coronation, Traversari wants to pay his respect to the tomb of the man he considers his model, because of their common dedication to humanism and probably also because of their shared Florentine background. This becomes clear when we consider the other piece of actually rather unusual evidence. Some ten years later, in the early 1450s, the Florentine merchant Palla di Nofri Strozzi, who was exiled from his home town and who in his library had several volumes of Petrarch's works, bought a house fifty yards away from the poet's tomb in Arquà, and at an exceptionally high price. This most probably indicates that for Strozzi this place had a highly symbolical meaning: the vicinity of his compatriot's tomb could compensate for the loss of a direct connection to his Florentine roots. Stripped of his patrimony, Palla acquired the next best thing, a site associated with a cultural ancestor to whom he felt intellectually and spiritually bound.[6]

Together these few pieces of evidence suggest that during the fifteenth century the memory of Petrarch's legacy was restricted to only a few elements: his Florentine identity and his work as a humanist and an intellectual. The only spatial expression that the cult of the poet could take was a visit to his tomb, an only rarely performed ritual taken over from classical culture and as such an expression of pre-modern attitudes towards the function and significance of literary places.

All this changed radically in the first decades of the sixteenth century, as a result of a major shift in the attention for Petrarch's work. This turnover was largely dictated by the strong movement for the emancipation of the modern languages that in Italian culture found its final expression in Bembo's *Prose della volgar lingua* (*Proses in the Vernacular*) of 1525, where Petrarch's work was hailed as the supreme model for modern poetry in the vernacular. In this process instead of his erudite and philosophical Latin works, Petrarch's lyrical poetry in Italian came to be the focus of attention, and as a result of this in the perception of the early sixteenth century Petrarch changed from being an intellectual and a Florentine into something like the universal lover, the man whose passion for his Laura would inspire generations of poets to come, all over Europe. This immediately triggered massive interest in Petrarch's biography, and especially, of course, in the details of his supposedly passionate relation to Laura.[7] But since there was no documentation besides the poetry itself, enquiries were started to make up for this lack, and those enquiries—being conducted in the places where this alleged love affair had taken place—soon gave rise to a practice that can be best defined as the early modern variety of literary tourism.

Of pivotal importance in this development is the work of Alessandro Vellutello, who in 1525 produced a hugely successful and influential edition and comment on Petrarch's poetry, significantly called *Il Petrarca*. In this work Vellutello includes a short biography of Petrarch in which he focuses on the poet's passion for Laura, and tries to reconstruct this love affair on the basis of extensive research he had been doing in France in the year 1520. As tangible proof he reproduces a map (see Figure 2.2), where all the locations near Avignon that in some way might be linked to this love affair are highlighted. So in the year 1525 we not only have Bembo's *Prose della volgar lingua*, where Petrarch's lyrical production is canonised as the supreme model of vernacular poetry, but also Vellutello's comment that not only offers a predominantly biographical interpretation of Petrarch's poetry but moreover invites its readers to link this biography to a certain number of places.

Such invitation was widely accepted. A few years later, another editor of Petrarch's work, Fausto da Longiano, gives in his 1532 edition a minute description of the trip he made to Avignon and Fontaine-de-Vaucluse, and of his elaborate enquiries regarding the figure of Laura. Other contemporary editors, like Giovanni Andrea Gesualdo in 1533, do the same. But not only Italian admirers of Petrarch engage in this rush. Their French counterparts do as well, and they even do it better, since their motivation is stronger. They in fact are driven by the desire to give a historical identity to Laura, and thus to underline the central importance of French and especially Provençal culture in the work of the poet who rapidly was growing into the model figure of modern European literature.

This explains the curious episode of the discovery of Laura's grave in Avignon, which occurred in the year 1533. After extensive research in a large number of churches in Avignon and its surroundings, the poet Maurice

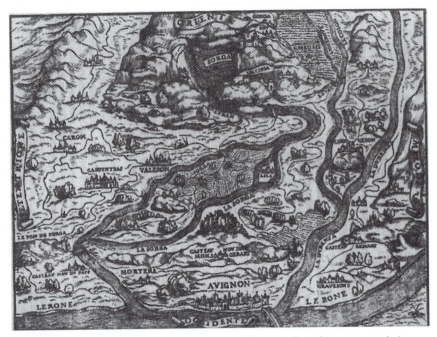

Figure 2.2 Map of the locations associated with Petrarch and Laura near Avignon, from *Il Petrarca con l'espositione d'Alessandro Vellutello [...]*, 2nd ed. Venice: Giolito, 1547, 9.

Scève identified in the church of Saint Francis a grave that he concluded to be the one where Laura was buried, since it contained a coffin-like box with the inscription M.L.M.I, that according to Scève meant "Madonna Laura Morta Iace" (here lies the dead lady Laura).[8] This finding caused great excitement, to such an extent that the king of France, François I, who happened to be on his way to Marseille, visited the grave in Avignon, allegedly composed an epigram in memory of Laura, and gave orders to erect a monument on the spot of the grave. Although we can doubt the exact details of this episode, because the monument sponsored by the king was never completed, this does not mean that the episode itself did not occur. Royal interest in the discovery of Laura's grave is in fact documented in a number of laudatory texts by contemporary poets like Clément Marot, and thus attests to the great impact of the newly construed link between literature, memory and place.

This impact however was such that to some contemporaries it seemed excessive and ridiculous. In 1539 Nicolò Franco, an author who specialised in polemical controversies, published *Il Petrarchista (The Petrarchist)*, an obvious though ironical reference to Vellutello's *Il Petrarca*.[9] In this pamphlet-like book, Franco fiercely attacks the practice of the literary pilgrimage to the places in Southern France linked to the memory of Petrarch and Laura's alleged love affair, by offering a detailed account of such a pilgrimage. This obviously turns out to be an outright parody, based as it is on the ironical rewriting of elements taken from recent editions of Petrarch's poetry, especially the one by Fausto da Longiano published seven years before. In fact, Franco does have no personal knowledge of the places he describes and is therefore still unaware of Maurice Scève's discovery of the alleged grave of Laura. He relies on the information found in his Italian sources and turns this into a comical and highly polemical portrait of what he sees as uncritical fans and scholars of Petrarch's poetry. But beyond its polemical nature, Franco's parody offers us a clear and detailed compendium of how a literary pilgrimage in the 1530s looked like. It included the visit to a small house in Fontaine-de-Vaucluse that matched the descriptions offered by Petrarch himself in his poetry; but it strongly focused on the tour of the various places in Avignon and other nearby towns that could be linked to Laura's birth, life and death.

Franco's book, moreover, gives us information on what motivated Italians to travel to the Provence. They were driven on the one hand by a scholarly desire to better understand Petrarch's poetry, in order to be able to fill what they themselves considered to be gaps in their knowledge, especially with regard to the figure of Laura and the nature of Petrarch's love for her. Doing research on the spot would therefore allow them to make sharper observations in their comments on Petrarch's poetry, a project all of them were engaged in. On the other hand, however, they considered the trip to the Provence a significant ritual, a profane pilgrimage which would earn them some kind of indulgence, exactly as it was the case in religious pilgrimages. This "guadagnare l'indulgenzia" (earn an indulgence) is what Franco especially makes fun of, when at the end of his book he describes the house of a certain Roberto in Avignon, which the owner had turned into a real museum dedicated to Petrarch and Laura. This Roberto allegedly had collected all kinds of objects linked to the couple, from the poet's pens to Laura's toothbrush and even parts of her chamber pot. Here we enter in the domain of anti-petrarchism, of which Franco is one of the main supporters, and which operates mainly by degrading the language and metaphors used by Petrarch and his followers. On the other hand, however, this part of Franco's pamphlet illustrates that the practice of the literary pilgrimage was not undisputed and attracted as soon as it was established criticism, precisely because it conferred a semi-religious meaning to places and objects, even the most banal ones.

Yet Franco's attack did not in any way affect the success of the new fashion of the literary pilgrimage. An excursion to Fontaine-de-Vaucluse and the trip along the various places in town linked to the famous couple of lovers in fact became as of the 1540s a standard ingredient for those visiting Avignon.[10] Especially the many Italians coming for business—Avignon was still under papal rule—were offered a kind of tourist package by their countrymen working for the local government. Some of these civil servants even specialised in this tour, as is the case with Gianfranco

Leoni, who in the 1550s worked for Cardinal Alessandro Farnese, the papal representative.

As I have argued earlier on, the bi-polarity that we can see in the rise of this literary pilgrimage on the one hand, and Franco's reaction to it on the other, is typical of early modern attitudes towards literary memorial culture. Petrarch's reaction towards Arezzo's initiative to turn his house into a kind of monument shows a similar combination of enthusiasm and doubt. And we can detect such ambiguity also in the cult surrounding Petrarch's house in Arquà. But whereas in the case of the French memorial sites enthusiasm and doubt seem to live parallel lives—on the one hand you have Vellutello and the other Petrarch fans, on the other there is Franco—the history of the visit to Arquà shows that here these two elements tend to merge into one, intrinsically ambiguous attitude that combines the cult and the anti-cult, and thus turns into a practice that perhaps can be best characterised as camp.

In Arquà Petrarch's memory had been cultivated ever since his death, but on a limited scale and mostly in relation to his tomb, not his house. In the earliest geographical descriptions of the village we find texts like this one from Leandro Alberti's *Descrittione di tutta Italia* (*Complete Description of Italy*), which was based on an exploration of the territory made in 1528:

> Along these hills there are many beautiful hamlets and villages, amongst which we find Arquà, very well known because of the memory of Francis Petrarch, where he lived for a long time and passed away. And here he was buried with great honours in a tomb made of marble, on four red columns, with the epitaph written by him.[11]

However, when this text was published in 1550, the situation had already drastically changed. In the 1540s literary pilgrims to Arquà started to focus on the poet's house instead of on his tomb, and this new habit rapidly evolved into a cultural practice similar to what had developed in the Provence during the previous decade. As was the case there, it was the grounding of the new image of Petrarch as a universal lover that directly motivated this shift, although not without being severely contested. In fact, as late as 1536, Girolamo Malipiero tried to counter the cult of what he considered a sensuous and thus sinful Petrarch by rewriting his complete poetry in a spiritual manner.[12] At the start of his *Petrarca spirituale* (*The Spiritual Petrarch*) Malipiero relates, as a kind of apology for his radical endeavour, how during a fictitious pilgrimage to Petrarch's grave he met the poet's ghost, who could not find rest since he was denied access to heaven because of the amorous nature of his poetry.

Yet Malipiero's project to restore a more philosophical reading of Petrarch, supported by a cult of his grave and not of his house, was destined to fail, as the material history of Petrarch's house in Arquà can testify.

Not only had this in the early 1540s become a place of attraction to visitors from far away, as the curious graffiti carved by a group of German students above the fireplace in the poet's alleged bedroom, dated 1544 and still present today, attest.[13] No doubt because of this great public interest a few years later the house was turned into a site which, precisely by focusing on Petrarch's love for his Laura, integrated the qualities of a tourist attraction and a museum. In the year 1546 it was sold by the Venetian convent of San Giorgio, which had owned the house for over a century. The new owner, a nobleman from nearby Padova named Paolo Valdezocco, immediately started to radically renovate the place, decorating most walls for example with fresco's that include portraits of Petrarch and Laura and a whole series illustrating the episodes from the poet's *Trionfi (Triumphs)*.[14] Valdezocco consciously turned the house into a commemorative place of worship, making it into the oldest still existing museum dedicated to a poet we know of in Western culture (see Figure 2.3).

Because of Valdezocco's initiative, the house in Arquà immediately became something of a tourist attraction, and continued to attract especially foreigners, as we can deduct from a remarkable document written by a well known scholar from Padova, Sperone Speroni, in the year 1550, the "Sommario in difesa della casa del Petrarca" (Discourse in defence of Petrarch's house). Although this speech was written as a plea for the conservation of another house of Petrarch's, the one in the city of Padova which was at risk because of urbanistic changes and was actually demolished a few years later,[15] Speroni also makes some remarks on the house in Arquà:

> In Arquà Petrarch's tomb is so very honoured, as well as the house where he lived, that from great distances and very remote countries people come to visit the village; and especially revered there is his room. Now that it is in the hands of one of our compatriots, who has decorated it, I like to say something negative about this, stating that one should have conserved it in its ancient state, not only the room as such, but also the mortar and the dust should have been conserved, had that been possible.[16]

This striking plea for authenticity and conservation makes clear that within the tourist attraction the house was turned into by 1550, the poet's study was the *sanctum sanctorum*. Those who visited it were Italian admirers of Petrarch's, like Giovanni Battista Cardogna, who in the summer of 1551 visited the place three times and has left a rather detailed description of its museological disposition after Valdezocco's alterations.[17] But the house especially attracted foreigners, which of course illustrates that Petrarch had become an international cult figure, who had lost the connotation of being a Florentine that had inspired visitors to Arquà in the fifteenth century. It also shows that this place of literary memory was integrated in the new

Figure 2.3 Petrarch's House in Arquà Petrarca, from Iac. Philippi Tomasini, *Petrarcha redivivus*, 2nd ed. Padova: Frambotti, 1650, 123.

phenomenon of the Grand Tour as of its earliest days, and that as such it was linked to what nowadays we would call an experience of authenticity.

In fact, when in the year 1600 the first guidebook specifically made for Grand Tourists by Francis Schott was published in Antwerp, it contained detailed information on the places linked to Petrarch in Arquà.[18] But we have even older evidence, since in the journals Grand Tourists started to write down and sometimes publish as of the 1580s we find reports on visits to Arquà, like this one by English traveller Fynes Moryson, who in the year 1595 at the end of a stay in Padova together with some Dutch friends undertook an excursion to this place of special interest:

And while I prepared all things necessary for my iourney, and expected
a fit season of the yeere, it came in my minde to see the Monument not
farre distant of the famous Poet Francis Petrarch, and being willing
to giue my horse rest, I went on foot with certaine Dutch gentlemen
thirteene miles to Arqua. ... Petrarch dwelt at Arqua, and here in the
same house wherein they say he dwelt, the historie of Petrarches life
is painted, where the owner of the house shewed vs some household
stuffe belonging to him, and the very skinne of a Cat he loved, which
they haue dried, and still keepe. Here I did see his Studie, (a pleasant
roome, especially for the sweet prospect) and likewise a faire picture of
Lucretia ready to die.[19]

Moryson and his friends are taken on a tour of the house by the private
owners, at that moment a lady from Padova, Lucrezia Gabrielli, and her
Venetian husband Francesco Zen. They show them the fresco's installed
by Valdezocco, the room where Petrarch used to work, and some specific
objects and pieces of furniture like the poet's chair (see Figure 2.4). What
captures the visitors' attention most, however, is the mummy of a cat,
allegedly Petrarch's cat, a curious object that today still can be seen in the
house and that during centuries has been one of the main attractions of this
memorial site.

Like the picture of Lucretia also recorded by Moryson, this mummy (see
Figure 2.5) most probably was installed in the house between 1591 and
1595, by the already mentioned owners Lucrezia Gabrielli and Francesco
Zen, who actively engaged in turning their house into a tourist attraction.
The result, however, was not a pure temple of memory, a museum intended
to become the focus of a semi-religious practice of literary pilgrimage. Precisely because of the presence of this cat, the house in Arquà became a place
where the ambiguity typical of early modern attitudes to memorial culture
was turned into a tourist site that could satisfy both literary pilgrims and
those critical of the phenomenon itself. In fact, as was the case with the
places linked to the memory of Petrarch and Laura in the Provence, also
this house in Arquà attracted quite some criticism, especially because of the
presence of objects like the cat's mummy.

Again we find such comments in the works of fierce anti-petrarchists
like Ercole Giovannini, who gives us a parody of a literary pilgrimage
to the house in Arquà, exactly as Franco had done for the places in the
Provence.[20] Best known however became the sharp and amusing remarks
included by Alessandro Tassoni in his comical epic *La secchia rapita* (*The
Stolen Bucket*):

Petrarch's study is very well protected,
By a dry cat who keeps away the mice.

Figure 2.4 Petrarch's chair, from Iac. Philippi Tomasini, *Petrarcha redivivus*, 2nd ed. Padova: Frambotti, 1650, 128.

But as he himself testifies, Tassoni is not the only one, nor the first, to ironically praise Petrarch's cat, since at this point—the poem was written around 1616—apparently the mummy had become itself the object of a cult, as the many poems dedicated to the cat could prove:

> This cat was highly honoured by Apollo
> To make sure that it would always stay intact,
> And that her fame would ever be conserved,
> So a thousand poems on her were made;
> That's why the mausoleums of famous kings
> Are far surpassed in glory by the tomb of a cat.[21]

These ironical comments by Tassoni and the other poets to whom he refers stress the comical dimension of the cat's presence; they lack the fierce

Figure 2.5 Petrarch's cat, from Iac. Philippi Tomasini, *Petrarcha redivivus*, Padova: Pasquati & Bortoli, 1635, 144.

polemical undertone we have witnessed in Franco's attack on Petrarch's cult in the Provence. This is precisely because in the house in Arquà a certain amount of irony had been integrated in the memorial cult itself. The mummy of the cat was surrounded by a number of poems, as Tassoni recalls, that explicitly made fun of this curious object and its function within the commemorative practice focused on Petrarch. These poems, and today we can still see the Latin ones made by Antonio Querenghi as they are sculpted in the marble decoration surrounding the mummy,[22] by their ironical and burlesque nature stimulated the visitors to reflect on the memorial practice they were actually engaged in, and even to question it.

It is this ambiguous attitude which seems to me at the basis of early modern reactions towards literary memorial culture. While we see a clear tendency to increase semi-religious commemorative practices, this is immediately disputed because it entails a cult of objects and places that is considered inappropriate. This attitude gives rise to controversies, but also to an ironical approach to memorial culture. As such, it represents a critical and dynamic state of mind very close to the one represented and promoted by Petrarch himself.

NOTES

1. *Familiares*, V.4.
2. The quotation is from Cicero's *De legibus*, II.2.4. English translation in Wilkins, 1955, 300–13, quotation at p. 305.
3. *Seniles*, XIII.3; see Wilkins, 1987, 129.
4. Pietro Paolo Vergerio, *Sermo de vita moribus et doctrina illustris et laureati poete Francisci Petrarce*, in Tomasini, 1650. See Floriani, 1993, 111–54. Already in the 1380s, Petrarch's friend Giovanni Dondi dall'Orologio (1318–1389) wrote a sonnet 'Cum visitasset sepulcrum domini Francisci Petrarche in Arquade', now in Dondi, 1990, 31.
5. "Placuit medio ex itinere, veluti ex curriculo, deflectere paulisper, ut Francisci Petrarchae tumulum in villa Arqua cerneremus. Vir enim nobilis erat aetate nostra, et literis deditus a quo ferme sunt excitata studia humanitatis, ut Mausoleum suum visere cuperem, facile de me obtinuerat"; Ambrogio Traversari, *Hodoeporicon*, in Dini-Traversari, 1912, 71–72. See also Stinger, 1977, 27 [quotation], 237.
6. Lillie, 2000.
7. See Duperray, 1997, esp. 155–77.
8. The episode is recorded by Maurice Scève himself, whose report is quoted in the dedication to him of *Il Petrarca* by Jean de Tournes from 1545; for a detailed reconstruction see Saulnier, 1948–49,I:38–48, II:27–31 and Duperray, 1997, 160–65.
9. Franco, 1539. See Bruni, 1980, and Sabbatino, 2003.
10. See Duperray, 1997, 165–69.
11. "Sono lungo questi colli molte belle contrade, & ville, tra le quali evvi quella vaga d'Arquato detto Montanare, a differenza d'un'altra, ch'è nel Poleseno di Rovigo, molto nominata per la memoria di Francesco Petrarca, ove lungo tempo soggiornò, & etiandio passò all'altra vita. Et qui fu molto honorevolmente sepolto in un sepolcro di marmo, sostenuto da quattro colonne rosse, & ivi è iscritto il suo epitafio fatto da esso." Alberti, 1557, 425v. (translation HH). In an earlier description of the Venetian countryside, done c. 1474 by the chronicler Marin Sanudo (*Itinerario per la terraferma veneziana*), while describing Arquà he mentions both Petrarch's tomb and his house: "Arquà è mia [miglia] 12 luntan di Padoa ... et è sopra uno monte, loco ameno et soave; è l'arca di Francesco Petrarca Florentino poeta su quattro colonne, et arca marmorea, et qui scripse molto; ... et stagheva in una caxa ch'è adesso de Batista de Bigolino doctor et cavalier, et ivi componeva, et fin ora dura il suo desiato lauro, et mai da quel in qua fin non è morto." See Magliani, 2003, 89.
12. Malipiero, 1536.
13. Magliani, 2003, 63.
14. See Callegari, 1941, Bellinati and Fontana, 1988, Floriani, 1993, Blason, 1995, Montobbio, 1998, Magliani, 2003.
15. On this episode see Bellinati, 1979, and Floriani, 1993, 130–36.
16. "Di lui se tanto è onorata la sepoltura in Arquà, e la casa, ove lui' stava, che di lontanissimi e remotissimi paesi vengono persone a visitar quella villa; ed in

tanto è riverita quella sua stanza, che adesso, che ella è in mano di un nostro cittadino, il quale l'ha adornata e dipinta, intendo dirne alcun male, dicendo che si dovea conservare in quella antichità, quasi non pur la stanza in se, ma la calcina e la polvere del suo tempo, se possibile fosse, si doveano conservare: che biasimo sarebbe ora rovinar la sua di Padova? Se 'l mutar la sua stanza dal suo essere con ornamenti è cosa biasimevole, che saria il roinarla?" Sperone Speroni, "Sommario in difesa della Casa del Petrarca", in Speroni, 1989, 5:559–64, quotation at p. 599, translation HH.

17. Giovanni Battista Cardogna, *Racconto della guerra fatta da Carlo V contro i ribelli della Germania*, ms Biblioteca Civica di Padova, BP 6314, 47f.; see Magliani, 2003, 90.
18. Schott, 1625, 65–66.
19. Moryson, 1617, 174.
20. Giovannini, 1623. Giovannini died in 1591, but his parody was published in a severely edited manner only in 1623.
21. "E 'l bel colle d'Arquà poco in disparte, / Che quinci il monte e quindi il pian vagheggia; / Dove giace colui, ne le cui carte / L'alma fronda del sol lieta verdeggia. / E dove la sua gatta in secca spoglia / Guarda dai topi ancor la dotta soglia. // A questa Apollo già fe' privilegi / Che rimanesse incontro al tempo intatta, / E che la fama sua con vari fregi / Eterna fosse in mille carmi fatta: / Onde i sepolcri de' superbi regi / Vince di gloria un'insepolta gatta." Tassoni, 1962, 139–40 (canto VIII, ottava 32–34; translation HH).
22. "Etruscus gemino vates exarsit amore: / Maximus ignis ego, Laura secundus erat. / Quid rides? Divinae illa si gratia formae, / Me dignum tanto fecit amante fides; / Si numeros geniumque sacris dedit illa libellis, / causa ego, ne saevis muribus esca forent"; "Arcebam sacro vivens a limine mures, / Ne domini exitio scripta diserta darent. / Incutio trepidis eadem defuncta favorem / Et viget exanimi in pectore prisca fides." See Floriani, 1993, 115–18.

3   Shakespeare's Birthplace at Stratford
Bardolatry Reconsidered

Michael Rosenthal

Many years ago, I was struck by how, at Flatford Mill, associated, of course, not with William Shakespeare, but with the nineteenth-century British—though he would have called himself English—landscape painter, John Constable, tourists would congregate around the souvenir shops and tea houses, quietly milling around, in a politely bewildered kind of way, seldom troubling to seek out any of the scenes that Constable had represented, particularly those which involved a walk. I was subsequently intrigued to discover tourists behaving in much the same kind of way at Stratford-upon-Avon, although, of course, on the larger scale, for there were many more shops to interest them. Stratford lies about twenty kilometres from where I live, and I know it well. It is not *that* prepossessing—there are plenty of far prettier country towns nearby—and apart from the association with Shakespeare, and the presence of the Royal Shakespeare Company, it can be difficult for local people to understand why anyone would wish to visit it: a sight of the entrance to the town makes this point. This chapter, therefore, partly constitutes an attempt, first, to sort out for myself why it is that thousands of tourists congregate in Stratford-upon-Avon (after all, McDonaldses are everywhere), and, second, to assess what the experience of the town itself offers. I acknowledge from the outset, that I am following in the footsteps of many other writers who have been interested by the same kinds of things.

The Shakespeare whose spirit, just, still presides over Stratford was an invention of the eighteenth century, and the Shakespeare industry owes its existence to the efforts of the great actor David Garrick.[1] Rowe's 1709 edition of Shakespeare was followed by others; including Alexander Pope's of 1725, or Dr. Johnson's of 1765. The six-volume quarto published by Thomas Hanmer came out between 1743 and 1744 and was copiously illustrated with fine plates designed and engraved by top-end artists, Francis Hayman and Hubert Gravelot; Hayman later developing his inventions in paintings for Vauxhall Gardens.[2] By then, of course, Garrick had stunned London society with that portrayal of the character of Richard III so memorably commemorated by William Hogarth (Walker Art Gallery, Liverpool), and the Scheemakers statue of Shakespeare, posed as elegantly as any English country gentleman, had been placed in Westminster Abbey. Without enquiring too deeply into the relationships between supply and demand, it's clear that there was a rage for Shakespeare and the plays that he and others had written, though these themselves were forming the bases for scripts freely improvised from the originals.

It was, of course, Garrick who inspired the great Shakespeare Jubilee of 1767 which attracted a large portion of the polite world to the quiet, and, let it be said, already unexciting British Midlands town of Stratford-upon-Avon, where they enjoyed, despite the characteristic August rain, three days of spectacular entertainments. These ranged from the firing of thirty cannon, arranged along the banks of the Avon, to fireworks, to a masquerade—Boswell went dressed as a Corsican—a grand procession, and a horse race. The procession took place, despite the rain, on the second day, and, among other things, presented 170 people dressed as characters from Shakespeare's plays, and the passage of a 'Triumphal Car' drawn by six satyrs and in which were people representing Melpomene, Thalia and the Graces, and a great deal else besides.[3] Something of this lives on, just, in the Shakespeare Birthday celebrations when local schoolchildren, academics, diplomats and other dignitaries process through the streets of Stratford, and appropriate speeches are delivered by politicians and other actors at venues in the town.[4] The original jubilee had operated at a higher level—the town's corporation had commissioned from Gainsborough his fine portrait of Garrick with his arm slung round a bust of Shakespeare (sadly, it perished in a fire in 1946)—for the Shakespearian repertoire was integral to contemporary culture (see Figure 3.1).[5] There would have been little point in having 170 people dressed as Shakespearian characters unless you could expect everyone to recognise them.

Besides inaugurating the Shakespeare industry with a bang, Garrick was also responsible for developing the mythology that, to this day, is attached to the Shakespeare birthplace. This house, known to have been in the possession of Shakespeare's father, had been quietly decaying. By the middle of the eighteenth century, the half-timbered front had been neatly faced with brick, and one half had become an inn, The Swan and Maidenhead, "whose refreshments" as Ian Ousby writes, "were never recommended to the genteel traveller"; the other, a butcher's shop. Ousby points out that:

> Garrick was apparently the first to spot its possibilities. By an act of faith rather than scholarship, he had declared the front bedroom over the butcher's shop to be the very birthroom itself and draped its window with an illuminated transparency bearing the legend: "Thus dying clouds contend with growing light."[6]

The 'birthroom' itself has proven to be an adaptable space, as representations from the late nineteenth and late twentieth centuries demonstrate.

Figure 3.1 Valentine Green, *David Garrick*, mezzotint after the lost painting by Thomas Gainsborough, 1769 (© Gainsborough's House, Sudbury, Suffolk).

Garrick had nurtured what was already developing. Shakespeare had actually lived in New Place, which exists today only as a few foundations. In 1753 the Reverend Francis Gastrell had purchased the house for a summer retreat. Its garden was notable for a mulberry tree which the playwright himself was supposed to have planted, and which was already attracting a steady stream of pilgrims. Irritated by these, Gastrell felled the tree and sold the timber to a Thomas Sharp. Then, in 1759, the clergyman demolished the house and, wisely, left Stratford forever. The mulberry tree lived on, and, it turns out, on and on. Sharp began turning out what Ousby aptly describes as "an apparently inexhaustible stream of mulberry trinkets in the form of toothpicks, snuffboxes, spectacle cases, goblets and even pieces of furniture": indeed, in 1769 David Garrick was presented with a box made of its wood, and carved with reliefs of, among other things, himself in the character of Lear. The mulberry tree had rapidly attained the status of a genuine English rival to the true cross.[7]

By the close of the eighteenth century, the butcher's shop beneath the birthplace was occupied by a Mr Hart, whose wife acted as custodian of a shrine whose chief relic was a chair, reputed to have been sat on by Shakespeare, and which also displayed a miraculous ability to regenerate itself. Sold to a Polish princess in 1790, it had re-materialised in 1815 when Washington Irving was among the very many who would sit down on it. This he recorded in *The Adventures of Geoffrey Crayon*. Here, as Christopher Mulvey points out, he wrote a best-selling piece, important for having become the fashionable thing to read in London "ensured its being read throughout America", and because it set out ways in which a visitor might be expected to respond to Stratford.[8] Irving, enchanted by the half-timbered town and surrounding countryside reported, none the less, with his eyes wide open. He, too, noted the degree to which Shakespeare's mulberry tree was so extraordinarily bountiful, and he too likened its capacity to supply a never-ending stream of relics to that of the true cross (see Figure 3. 2). But he balanced his wry commentary with a proper reverence for Shakespeare: "I went to bed, and dreamt all night of Shakespeare, the jubilee, and David Garrick."[9]

An Elizabethan desk from Stratford Grammar School at which the young William Shakespeare may have sat

SHAKESPEARE'S
SCHOOL DESK

STRATFORD-UPON-AVON

Figure 3.2 'Shakespeare's school desk', Visitors' Centre, Stratford-upon-Avon (© Shakespeare Birthplace Trust).

By now the birthplace was rented by a Mrs Hornby ("a garrulous old lady" according to Irving), who was in turn, in 1820, evicted by Mrs Court, landlady of the adjoining Swan and Maidenhead, and who installed herself as custodian, with Mrs Hornby now operating with her collection of relics from across the street. When Mrs Court died, the property was put on the market as, according to the estate agent, a "truly heart-stirring relic of a most glorious period, and of England's immortal bard ... the most honoured monument of the greatest genius who ever lived."

The American, P.T. Barnum, famous, appropriately, as a circus magnate, attempted to buy the birthplace, with a view to dismantling it and shipping it stateside, but was thwarted by a campaign spearhead by Charles Dickens and the actor, Macready, to keep it in England.[10] This battle for the ownership of a British cultural icon is interesting in and of itself. If Nathaniel Hawthorne considered a visit to Stratford as "one of the things that an American proposes to himself as necessary and chiefly to be done on coming to England" this was because, as Christopher Mulvey points out, it was essential "to establish ... for the world that Shakespeare belonged to America, that Shakespeare was America's national bard, as much as he was England's."[11] Language articulated the cultural maturity of a nation, so that, for Henry James, "our consecrated English speech" was also "the medium of Shakespeare and Milton, of Hawthorne and Emerson".[12] That he being fought over by a circus impresario on the one hand, and by a novelist and actor on the other, beautifully demonstrates the extent to which the dramatist's international appeal had already attained the character it has arguably maintained.

This emerges, too, from statistics. By 1853–54 Shakespeare's birthplace was receiving some 3,000 visitors, of whom 500 were American, each year. The age of the railway and of mass tourism was dawning. By 1900 the total figure had risen to 30,000 and it was being administered by the Birthplace Trust that had also assumed responsibility for the other 'Shakespeare properties'; Anne Hathaway's Cottage, Mary Arden's House, the New Place estate, and Hall's Croft.[13] All the ingredients of Shakespeare's Stratford were now firmly in place.

By now there were two other developments to notice. Firstly, while most accepted that the birthplace had been owned by Shakespeare's father, there was no evidence whatever that the writer had been born there. Indeed, on visiting the house today, we read on one of the many informative wall labels that: "There is clear evidence that the house now known as 'Shakespeare's Birthplace' was the family home", which sounds a note of caution. Ian Ousby quotes a report of the auction of the house being interrupted when a heckler called upon the auctioneer "to prove" that this was "the identical" house "in which the poet was born". The auctioneer, began by saying that the association was vindicated by tradition, that, because his father had lived in it, "there could be no doubt that the great Poet was born in the house and lived the greater part of his life in it"—which inspired cheers amongst the crowds—and that he "wished that those who were sceptical on the point would stay away, instead of starting doubts which had no foundation to rest upon," or, as we might say, "move on.[14] The other development was that a building which had been successively altered over time, and which was in uncertain structural condition, was restored to the half-timbered solidity that we still see today. Which means, of course, that the place we visit is an imaginative reconstruction of an historical building in which William Shakespeare may not have been born.

By the end of the nineteenth century 'Shakespeare's Stratford', as it is still announced on the road sign that you meet when approaching the town from the direction of Warwick, had established itself as it remains today. Washington Irving announced he "had come to Stratford on a poetical pilgrimage" and, as we noted, wrote of such items as the mulberry tree or Shakespeare's chair as relics, for this is indeed the role that they played. Donald Horne has subsequently observed that the "social significance of tourism can be clarified if one imagines the modern sightseer as a 'pilgrim', and what is looked at as a 'relic'," and Shakespeare's Birthplace came to be charged with a significance comparable to that of La Verna, where St Francis received his stigmata, and where to this day you can inspect his robe or staff: or what pass for his robe and staff.[15] Indeed, Shakespeare, the birthplace, and the town of Stratford itself had become immune to such charges of in-authenticity as those levelled by Joseph Skipsey when he resigned as custodian of the birthplace in 1891: "not a single one of the many so-called relics on exhibition could be proved to be Shakespeare's— nay … the Birthplace itself is a matter of grave doubt."[16] It simply did not matter. Far more pressing was the need to satisfy the "nostalgic sense of dignity and meaning" which, as Donald Horne has written, was widely understood to be the best antidote for an "uneasiness with the present" that was Europe-wide.[17]

Some notion of the status that had accrued to the secular shrine of Stratford-upon-Avon can be had from the opening paragraphs of *Shakespeare's Town and Times*, published by H. Snowden Ward and Catharine Weed Ward, Fellows of the Royal Photographic Society and Editors of the Photogram, in 1896. Imagining that the visitor has just arrived in Stratford, they write:

> Let us start, then, from the Great Western Station, but not before mentioning that the Great Western Railway has done much for the comfort of the pilgrim to Shakespeare's shrine. Surely few Londoners realise that the quick and convenient trains from Paddington have made it quite possible to see Stratford as a weekend trip, or we should not so often hear them confessing to their American friends that they have never seen the Shakespeare birthplace, or the tomb.[18]

It appears that it was tantamount to a patriotic duty so to have done. The book itself was embellished with numerous atmospheric photographs of the town in all its half-timbered glory, with shots of parts since demolished indicating that some of Stratford's attraction lay in its remaining a threatened species of Merry England such as one might associate with the figure of Sir John Falstaff, and which represented a desirable alternative to the chaos of the modern metropolis. From which, of course, one escaped by the thoroughly modern mode of the railway train.

Comparable books were proliferating.[19] W. Hallsworth Waite's *Shakespeare's Stratford* of 1895 was styled "a pictorial pilgrimage" illustrated after line drawings by an author, proud to be (like Shakespeare) "a Warwickshire man". He covered most of the ground, from the stylish high street to the "Quaint Corners" of the town to the views of the Avon, and by implication, the rest of the attractive countryside in which Stratford nestled. It appears from the rich crop of them gathered at the back of the book, that Waite had been obliged to fund his publishing enterprise through advertisements from such establishments as The Egyptian Hall Billiard Saloons in Birmingham, or the Acme Tone Engraving Company of New Bushey, Herts. In 1928 Edgar I. Fripp, a "Life Trustee of Shakespeare's Birthplace" published *Shakespeare's Stratford*, in which he attempted to recreate the places and people, sights and sounds of the town in which the poet had grown up, displaying an encyclopaedic knowledge of Shakespeare's plays in the liberal illustration of his observations with appropriate, and appropriately footnoted quotations. The following year he followed this up with *Shakespeare's Haunts*.

By 1939 Ivor Brown and George Fearon were subtitling their *Amazing Monument*, "A short history of the Shakespeare Industry" and using a photograph of G.B. Shaw, hands clasped as in prayer, eyes raised to heaven and captioned "Bardolater—Shaw at Stratford" as their frontispiece (see Figure 3.3). This mute reverence, perhaps, signifies the very opposite of the lively Shakespearean conversation in which Stephen Daedalus and various other characters had engaged in *Ulysses*. Fearon and Brown were writing with satirical intent, and we still recognise what they described. The hordes of campers who appear in the warmer months were probably not "all worshippers" yet "Stratford has drawn them. It is a place to know, a sight to have seen, and so they have come." Then, as now, the "first thing you will notice on entering Stratford on a summer day, especially at the weekend, is the enormous number of people who are driving in, driving round, driving out, or just standing and staring." Then, as now, the theatre "is constantly packed, although the level of some of the performances has been severely criticised, and the standard, as some maintain, is not so high as to give the company the international reputation to which Stratford might aspire."[20] *The Shakespeare Anniversary Book* which Dr Levi Fox, then Director of the Shakespeare Birthplace Trust edited for the four-hundredth birthday celebrations in 1964 suggests that nothing had changed.[21] If Shakespeare is the object of pilgrimage, then it is appropriate that, once the forms of a cult are established, that is it.

Figure 3.3 Bernard Shaw as Bardolater at Stratford, photograph by J.H. Bird, reproduced in Ivor Brown & George Fearon, *Amazing Monument. A Short History of the Shakespeare Industry*, 1939.

At first glance this stasis persists. The iconography remains fixed. In the early twenty-first century, postcards show the same half-timbered buildings as have always been shown. The birthplace appears to have assumed its final form. The only addition is, architecturally, a stark contrast: the modernist Shakespeare Centre and Library through which, rather oddly, the visitor now enters the birthplace. Otherwise, the town retains a fair amount of what we would tend to term its 'character'. A visit to the birthplace allows both for anticipation, and for anti-climax. As I have mentioned, you enter through the Shakespeare Centre, to be met by a compact, and well laid-out exhibition, which sets Shakespeare's historical scene. There are maps of Stratford and London in the late sixteenth and early seventeenth centuries, one or two appropriate prints, a nineteenth-century plaster model of the Shakespeare monument in Holy Trinity Church. There are even books: a 1576 edition of the Geneva Bible, William Lily's *Short Introduction of Grammar,* Arthur Golding's 1605 translation of the *Metamorphoses,* and a copy of the 1623 *Folio.* There is a mock figure of Shakespeare himself in his study, which *tableau* has also permitted the organisers of the show to demonstrate how his plays exploited many and various sources. The whole thing —despite the intrusive soundtracks contemporary museology uses to authenticate historical displays—is effective. It usefully sets the scene for the uninformed and informed alike.

The birthplace itself does not. Although the agreeable garden is laid out with plants the playwright himself mentioned, the interior of the house is arranged in a rather more *ad hoc* manner. There are beds and bits of furniture, a mock-up of Shakespeare's father's glove-making workshop, and, over all, an attempt is made to give a sense of how cramped and uncomfortable domestic living in the late sixteenth and early seventeenth centuries would have been. That is, what we have, in the end, is simply a reconstruction of an historic house. I have already quoted one of the relatively informative wall panels that are affixed throughout. Besides casting doubt upon whether Shakespeare was born in the house at all, they are equally honest when it comes to the manufacturing of the Shakespeare myth from the eighteenth century onwards. There is even one of the old inn signs for The Swan and Maidenhead. We exit through a shop where we might purchase tasteful postcards, or Shakespeare baseball caps, candles, teaspoons, and ballpoint pens. I am reminded of the merchandising at such places of pilgrimage, as Monte Berico, near Vicenza, although confused as to the nature of the religion the Stratford pilgrimage inspires. Perhaps, as Horne says, it is simply to do with temporarily relieving a deep unhappiness with the present.

The Shakespeare birthplace, then, is a restored, half-timbered house in which William Shakespeare may well not have been born. Nobody knows: in 2000, local historian, Dr Nat Alcock, proved that the Mary Arden's House, presented as the childhood house of Shakespeare's mother, was standing next door to the genuine article, and there may be more such discoveries to be made.[22] But, for the purposes of this, as for most sites of pilgrimage, this does not matter. Nor does the issue of who wrote Shakespeare's plays. As the display of postcards of, among other places, London, in a nearby souvenir shop hints, Shakespeare and his *oeuvre* are not actually the point of a visit to Stratford.

I shall try to elaborate on this remark focusing on three sculptural groups which feature both William Shakespeare and, in two cases, some of the best-known characters from his plays; two from Stratford-upon-Avon, the other from Sydney, Australia. At Stratford, the memorial carved by

Figure 3.4 Ronald Leverson Gower, Shakespeare Monument, Stratford-upon Avon, 1888 (© Michael Rosenthal).

Ronald Leverson Gower and unveiled in 1888 stands in public gardens, close to the Bridge Foot road (see Figure 3.4). It was, an inscription informs us, "removed from the memorial theatre gardens to this site in 1933." From this, I assume that, once within reasonable proximity of the theatre, it no longer is. Trees screen it from the road, and it stands mainly against a back-drop of gardens or a basin for canal-boats, while the Royal Shakespeare Theatre looms obscurely in the distance. The sculpture, you could say, is isolated, de-contextualised. Likewise, Thomas Banks's 1789 relief of the *Shakespeare between the dramatic Muse and the Genius of Painting, who is pointing him out as the proper subject for her pencil* is now, poignantly, abutting a wall in the far corner of a pleasant public garden, frequented mainly by schoolboy smokers, near the foundations of New Place, themselves given over to horticulture. It is up to chance whether or not visitors will happen upon it; and I have so far found no mention of the sculpture in the standard tourist literature. I write *poignantly* because the relief was designed to mark the impressive entrance to Boydell's Shakespeare Gallery in Pall Mall, in which paintings of Shakespearian subjects by the most significant living artists had, until the Gallery itself failed economically, drawn a wide public during the later eighteenth century. So from once being central to metropolitan public culture, the relief is now relegated to effective provincial obscurity.

Bertram Mackannel's Shakespeare Memorial in Sydney, built in 1929, is set between the State Library of New South Wales and the botanical gardens where, one of the first things you see as you enter is the memorial to the first Governor, General Arthur Phillip (see Figure 3.5).

Figure 3.5 Bertram Mackannel, Shakespeare Memorial Group, Sidney, 1929 (© Michael Rosenthal).

Sight lines are set up from the Library portico, past the Shakespeare memorial to the Phillip monument in the gardens, and, from there, back again. Therefore, the spectator, can, if so minded, be provoked into entertaining varieties of ideas ranging from the contemporary consequences of the British invasion of Australia and the role of culture within all this, to the public necessity to maintain enlightened ideals, as, indeed, the Mitchell Library which is housed in this particular building continues to allow, and the centrality of what tends to get labelled the *universality* of Shakespeare's writings for those aspiring to maintain such values. The contrast with the Gower Memorial at Stratford is rather striking. It may, in a vaguely general way, remind the visitor of some of Shakespeare's plays, but can do little more, for the surroundings permit it only to present Shakespeare himself as some kind of self-contained entity. And, of course, the Banks relief is, to all intents and purposes, hidden; much as it is questionable whether those who do accidentally come across it would recognise or understand the import of its allegory. It seems to have reached the point where the original cult has become peripheral to the shrine. If you're after Shakespeare's *achievement*, the plays, his writing in general, you go to the Royal Shakespeare Theatre, or the University of Birmingham's Shakespeare Institute, each of which plays no part in the classical tourist circuit.

In part this is because the Shakespeare economy in Stratford is principally about making money—the shields, decorated with the emblems of many different countries, which, during the birthday celebrations of April 2005 were attached put the lampposts down Bridge Street were not, I suspected, meant to celebrate anything cultural, but rather to flatter tourists of all nationalities. Akira Kurosawa might have shown what could be done with Shakespeare in such films as *Theatre of Blood* (Macbeth) or *Ran* (Lear), but this was irrelevant to the revenues brought in by Japanese tourists.[23] This is not to be wondered at. Tourism is practically the only economy of Stratford-upon-Avon. Very little traditional industry remains—the Flowers Brewery, a large employer, and a prominent sponsor of precisely such events as the Shakespeare Birthday celebration was closed as long ago as 1968—there any longer.

Since Margaret Thatcher and the imposition of the market as the only means by which British society can be seen to be organised, we have all become *customers*: and in this light it is hardly surprising that the Shakespeare that matters is irrelevant to the Stratford tourist economy, for he could dangerously undermine its very rationale. Here, taking the liberty to ignore the post-modern pyres of dead authors in order to pay attention to their living words I venture, unexceptionably, to suggest that Shakespeare remains central to our cultural consciousness for very straightforward reasons: the power or beauty of the writing, the treatment of large, essentially abstract issues—treachery, bravery, success, failure, morality, immorality, love and death—which are still central to both private and public experience. Otherwise his plays would not get translated from English into other languages; would, indeed, have been forgotten. On one level these plays reveal that language can do far more than simply express fiscal relations between people, on another they offer an engaged and critical understanding of fundamental issues, issues still germane to contemporary politics; or they do unless this potentiality is neutralised. To see a performance at the Royal Shakespeare Theatre costs any school pupil whose interest hasn't been killed by their teachers, and who can achieve the improbable feat of getting to Stratford and the theatre box office on the day of performance £5, *if* tickets remain, but otherwise £10 and rising. The Shakespeare Institute is, very properly, a postgraduate institution; yet its Web site both posts no information on the content of its biennial conference, and reveals that attendance at that conference is limited to invitees. Shakespeare and *hoi polloi* are kept apart.

In this light it is fascinating that journalists reviewing the apparently stupendous Nicholas Hytner production of the two parts of *Henry IV* mounted at the National Theatre in London in 2005 concentrated, despite the centrality of such characters as the Welsh Glendower or Scottish Douglas, on these as *English* plays, which is as stupidly limiting as calling *Julius Caesar* a *Roman* play.[24] Ambition, treachery, *hubris* do not have national boundaries. But this narrowness of focus fits with the presentation of Shakespeare in Stratford-upon-Avon.

It is noteworthy that Shakespeare's birthplace does not even risk offering Shakespeare as *heritage*, as something historically valuable and, therefore, necessarily preserved; which is worth being surprised by, for heritage is the selling point of most other English tourist attractions, from Stonehenge to the royal family. Perhaps in Shakespeare's case it is thought too dangerous to risk people reacting against that representation, which is eloquent on the condition of the national culture. Robert Hewison has remarked that "the culture of an individual, group or nation is not merely an expression of personal, collective or national identity, it *is* that identity," and adds that "the dominant group, culture ... will be an expression of political authority."[25] Our debased culture—where vacuous *celebrity* is valorised and Shakespeare's writing must be reserved only to those who can afford exposure to it, tells much of the nature of that political authority.

NOTES

1. Stockholm, 1964.
2. Taylor, 1990, 70–84 and *passim*. For Francis Hayman see Allen, 1987, 11–23, 62–70.
3. Stockholm, 1964, 17–31; Ousby, 1990, 42–44.
4. Ousby, 1990, 46.
5. For a reproduction of Valentine Green's mezzotint after Gainsborough's painting, see Rosenthal, 1998, 48, plate 52.
6. Ousby, 1990, 46.

7. Ousby, 1990, 39–42.
8. Mulvey, 1983, 77–78.
9. Irving, 1819–20.
10. Taylor, 1990, 216–17.
11. Mulvey, 1983, 74–75.
12. Mulvey, 1983, 76.
13. Ousby, 1990, 51–52.
14. Ibid., 49.
15. Horne, 1984, 9. For this more generally, see White, 1985; Hewison, 1987; and particularly Samuel, 1994.
16. Ousby, 1990, 55–56.
17. Horne, 1984, 22.
18. Ward and Weed Ward, 1896, 9.
19. Building on the precedent of Wheeler, 1863, these included Reed, 1907; Shelley, 1913; and Fripp, 1928a/b.
20. Brown and Fearon, 1939, 12–13.
21. Fox, 1964, is illustrated with photographs which conform to the norms established in postcards and associated imagery.
22. See http://www.bbc.co.uk/coventry/webcams/stories/2003/07/mary-arden-s-house.shtml.
23. Taylor, 1990, 313.
24. For example Billington, 2005.
25. Hewison, 1997, xiv.

4 Remembrance and Revision

Goethe's Houses in Weimar and Frankfurt

Bodo Plachta[1]

Why are you standing in front of it?
Is there no gate, is there no door?
If you came in, just confident,
You would be very well received.[2]

In 1828, when Goethe wrote these verses as a caption for a copperplate of his house in Weimar, engraved by Ludwig Schütze after a drawing by Otto Wagner in 1827, he had become not only a literary, but also a tourist celebrity (see Figure 4.1). For an increasing number of visitors Goethe's house at the Frauenplan was an obligatory part of their sightseeing tours. One could even say that some people went on a pilgrimage to Weimar.[3] If people could not meet the great poet in person, let alone talk to him, they at least wanted to have a look at his domain. To this day, no visitor to Weimar can evade the influence of the *genius loci*, the spirit of the place.[4]

Up to the present day, Goethe's residential building in Weimar belongs to the most important places of commemoration regarding literature in Germany.[5] Yet this importance entails many questions, because not only the writer's house and Weimar but also Goethe himself were "unwieldy places of commemoration".[6] In view of the concentration camp of Buchenwald, which is only eight kilometres away from the town of the classics, Anna Seghers stated that Weimar was "both the worst and the best" place in German history.[7] Neither can Goethe's birthplace in Frankfurt be seen independently of German history. Thus, an examination of Goethe's houses is inextricably linked with Goethe's becoming a classic and embedded in a complex network of processes in the areas of history, politics, and the history of education and mentality.[8]

Despite his numerous tendencies to treat his life and work like museum pieces, Goethe did not want to be an object merely to be looked at. His work, his life and his domain were by no means meant to be a dead museum. Instead, Goethe was interested in people emulating the thoughts and ways of life he embodied. His autobiographical writings give the impression that his life and work formed an integrated whole and should even be regarded as a work of art. Consequently, his house is only the "physical cover"[9] of

Figure 4.1 Otto Wagner and Ludwig Schütze, *Goethe's House in Weimar*, with autograph verses by Goethe, 1828 (© Klassik Stiftung Weimar)

something which today we are used to label the *classical* Weimar. The house and its former owner are not infrequently seen as synonyms of culture as such. One can hardly find another epoch in literary history that is named after one single author, as is "the age of Goethe". But this is a difficult heritage passed on to us because there does not seem to be another place apart from Weimar which is such an exemplary embodiment of the paradoxical combination of cosmopolitanism and provincialism, a combination which is quite problematic within the context of German history. To this day Weimar has remained a provincial small town, a fact which inevitably brings up the question how Weimar could become an intellectual centre for some decades that united the "Weimar giants" Wieland, Herder, Goethe and Schiller, all important writers and philosophers, in one town.[10] But after the end of this "golden" age—Heine talks about the end of the "period of art"—Weimar was by no means condemned to insignificance. Names like Wagner, Liszt, Nietzsche, Harry Graf Kessler, Henry van de Velde and institutions like the Bauhaus testify the continuous cultural importance of the town up to the twentieth century.

"Where else ... do you find so many good things on such a narrow spot! ... Stay with us, ... do make Weimar your domicile. From there gates and roads lead to all ends of the world."[11] With these words Goethe tried to recommend Weimar to Johann Peter Eckermann in September 1823. His efforts were successful and after his moving to Weimar Eckermann became one of the most important chroniclers among the people closest to Goethe. On 10 June 1823 Eckermann entered the house at the Frauenplan for the first time. As early as September 1821 Eckermann, like so many other visitors to Weimar, had been standing in front of Goethe's door during a short stay in Weimar, but he had not seen the house-owner, who at that time had not been in Weimar. Yet when he was received by Goethe in June 1823, the impression the poet made on him was all the more lasting and Eckermann numbered this day "among the happiest of his entire life". He writes in retrospect:

> The interior of the house made a very pleasant impression on me; everything was extremely noble and simple without being brilliant; moreover, various casts of antique statues standing at the staircase gave hints of Goethe's special liking for the fine arts and for the ancient Greeks ....
>
> On having a short look around I went upstairs to the first floor with a very talkative servant. He opened a room in front of whose threshold the word SALVE could be read as a sign of friendly welcome. He led me through this room and opened a second, slightly more spacious one, where he asked me to wait while he went away to announce me to his master. The air in there was very cool and refreshing, on the ground there was a carpet, and furthermore, the room was most serenely furnished with a red sofa and with equally coloured chairs; right by my side there was a piano, and on the walls one could see drawings and paintings of different kinds and sizes.
>
> Through an open door opposite me one could look into a more distant room which was also decorated with paintings. It was this room the servant had crossed to announce me.
>
> It did not take long until Goethe came, dressed in a blue overcoat and wearing shoes; a sublime figure![12]

The description of this entry, which to this day is similarly felt by many visitors of the Goethe house, has become a literary topos. The staircase and the reception room are part of the way in which Goethe was stage-managing himself. Even in his lifetime Goethe regarded himself as a cultural institution that "had the cultural nation participate in its progressing activities."[13]

Goethe had been looking for a representative domicile in Weimar for quite a long time. When he accepted the invitation of Duke Carl August and came to Weimar in November 1775, he at first lived in various provisional lodgings[14] that hardly corresponded to his position as a high-ranking public servant and member of the *Geheimes Consilium* (Secret Council).

The Duke himself tried to remedy the matter and in April 1776 he gave Goethe the summerhouse on the River Ilm as a present to tie him permanently to Weimar. Until 1782 the summerhouse was Goethe's main domicile. After that he used it as a refuge for concentrated work, but also as a place where he could temporarily escape from his official and representative duties connected with the house at the Frauenplan. After his return from Italy, Goethe was again looking for a home. In 1782 he took lodgings in the house at the Frauenplan. For a certain period of time he lived, together with Christiane Vulpius and their son August, born in 1789, in the so-called *Jägerhaus* (hunter's house), which does not exist anymore today, on the outskirts of Weimar. In 1792, however, he returned to the house at the Frauenplan, which the Duke gave him as a present in 1794. After moving there Goethe had the house rebuilt to be able to live in it according to his own ideas.

The house had been built in baroque style in 1709 and was one of the few large town houses in Weimar. The inscription on the triangular pediment above the entrance says that this house is meant to decorate the town of Weimar and to praise God who may protect it. Its builder was the craftsman, entrepreneur and ducal official Johann Kaspar Helmershausen.[15] Strictly speaking, the house consists of two houses "which are combined by connecting constructions."[16] On the one hand, Goethe's renovation of the house aimed at connecting the two parts of the house more closely. On the other hand, it emphasized the division of the house into a representative and a private section. The private Goethe lived and worked in the back house, whereas the official one did so in the front building. The garden, which Goethe frequently called his cloister garden, was also restricted to the sphere of private life; the garden's layout corresponded to Goethe's scientific studies of the morphology of plants.

The house also served the purpose of keeping Goethe's extensive art collections, which at the time of his death comprised more than 26,000 objects.[17] These works of art underline the insights gained during the Italian journey according to which the history of art has to be studied with the help of its artistic products. In this way, the laws of man's aesthetic acquisition of the world can be recognized. Goethe's encyclopaedic thinking also made use of the scientific collections which contain about 18,000 pieces of minerals and around 5,000 objects from various fields of science ranging from botany and anatomy to physics. Yet the house also served as literary archives whose most various records were an important prerequisite for Goethe's literary and scientific work. Certainly, even today every visitor will be surprised at the simple furnishings of Goethe's private rooms in the back house where the study, the library comprising about 6,500 books and the bedroom can be found.

The renovation of the house initiated by Goethe mainly concerned the front building. The poet had representative rooms built on the first floor of this building that were meant to create a serene atmosphere and to offer

space for the presentation of selected works of art. The concept of the renovation becomes clear especially with regard to the rebuilding of the staircase.[18] Goethe had the former narrow staircase removed and designed a
new broad staircase modelled on Italian renaissance flights of stairs (see
Figure 4.2 and Figure 4.3). The design of this staircase was inspired by
Palladio, whom Goethe greatly revered. The steps, which had deliberately
been laid out low, prevented a person from going hastily. Goethe firmly
said to Eckermann that the idea of the 'beautiful staircases' also had an

Figure 4.2 Staircase in the Goethe House in Weimar (© Klassik Stiftung
Weimar).

Figure 4.3 Staircase in the Goethe House in Weimar, drawing by Goethe, 1792 (©
Klassik Stiftung Weimar).

educational effect because it taught a person to control him- or herself.[19]
When going slowly upstairs visitors could already watch the works of art
placed on the half landings. The selection and presentation of these works
of art, which were all copies of famous antique sculptures, were programmatic and pointed to the important role antique art played in Goethe's
understanding of art. In the lower part of the staircase the *Praying Boy* and
The Satyr Carrying a He-Goat were put up. On the following half landings visitors could look at the heads of the *Apollo Belvedere* and the *Ares
Borghese* and at the *Group of Youths of Ildefonso.* Quite clearly, it was
Goethe's wish to create already on the stairs a "miniature museum showing
works of classical antiquity."[20]

The threshold leading to the living rooms, which was decorated with the word *Salve* (Welcome), also prepared visitors for a house devoted to the art and culture of classical antiquity. This programme is continued in the rooms of representation. These rooms are impressive not because they contain valuable furniture, but again because they show certain works of art. Casts of antique sculptures and both original and copied Renaissance paintings, but also contemporary paintings dominate these rooms. In 1830 Goethe said to Chancellor von Müller that the collections also served his "own on-going education", and in *Dichtung und Wahrheit (Poetry and Truth)* he writes:

> To counteract this, I trained myself first of all to enjoy remembering how I came into possession of all the things I own and from whom I received them, whether as gifts, by exchange, purchase, of some other way. When displaying my collections I have made it a custom to keep in mind the persons who were instrumental in procuring the individual items for me, and even to take into account the occasion, the coincidence, the remotest prompting and assistance that led to my acquisition of things dear and valuable to me. By this means, our surroundings come alive, we see things in their spiritual, loving, genetic relationships, our present existence is enhanced and enriched by recollections of past conditions, and the authors of the gifts emerge again and again before the imagination, combined with pleasant memories.[21]

This great educational programme is completed by references to classical mythology and culture which, for example, dominate the ceiling frescos and overdoors created by Johann Heinrich Meyer, a friend of Goethe's since the latter's stay in Italy. Furthermore, the colouring of the walls was important to Goethe.[22] The coloration not only follows the main aspects of his own theory of colour, but it also takes up decorative elements Goethe had seen in Pompeii.[23] The reception rooms are done in a cool blue-green and thus convey the impression of distance. Shades of green characterize the rooms containing the collections because in Goethe's opinion this colour gives real satisfaction. The dining room is done in serene yellow and the rooms painted in red-yellow or red are meant to convey the impression of warmth, grace and loveliness.

Goethe has repeatedly been described as an author who does not work according to an inner plan, but rather reacts to external forces. In this way, the author becomes a medium of outer impulses of the most different kinds. Goethe saw himself as a "collective being". The immediate view of things and persons is just as important to him as any kind of communication. Goethe was an author who, as far as his thinking and working was concerned, depended on talking to other people and exchanging his ideas with them. His friendship, or rather his alliance, with Schiller became a model for this. Many elements of his personality as a writer can be found in his house. Therefore, it is a poet's house in the highest degree, which was used not only for representation, but also as a basis to combine life and art in manifold ways.

After Goethe's death in 1832 the house, which in Goethe's lifetime had been frequently visited, was virtually closed to the public. When preparing his last will Goethe explicitly said to Chancellor von Müller on 19 November 1830:

> What matters most to me is that my estate should be treated liberally and in accordance with my own ideas. It should not be dealt with pedantically and carelessly. The surviving and active people should try to continue me, as it were, and to preserve my legacy in every respect.[24]

In his will he recommended preserving his collections of art and natural objects as a whole and selling them, if possible, to the state of Weimar. After Goethe's death his grandchildren anxiously shielded his estate from curious people, but also from academics. They also reacted sceptically to various proposals to transfer Goethe's heritage to a national foundation as well as to efforts of the ducal family to establish a number of commemorative rooms regarding Goethe, Schiller, Wieland and Herder in the Weimar castle. But then the will of the last surviving grandchild of Goethe's, Walther Wolfgang von Goethe, who died in 1885, brought about a surprising change and clarified matters. Goethe's house, his furniture and his collections were passed to the Dukedom of Saxony-Weimar, while the then Grand Duchess Sophie inherited Goethe's hand-written estate. The reading of the will, which had already been written down two years before, took place at a time when the public was making a hero and a monument of Goethe.

It is uncertain whether in making his provisions Walther Wolfgang von Goethe finally bowed to these expectations of a public which was both middle-class and aristocratic. Historically, the revolution of 1848 is considered the turning-point regarding a new evaluation of Goethe. The failure of this revolution caused the classical author Goethe to be seen as the main authority regarding the reconciliation between nationalism and humanism.[25] This development was accompanied by a rising interest in the life and work of the great Weimar author, whose biography was increasingly built up into a work of art. Finally, the educated classes in Germany were confirmed by the foundation of the Empire in 1871 not only in their national striving, but also in their admiration for Goethe. The metaphors of Goethe being the "prince among poets" and the "Olympian" became standard formulas for the admiration of a poet. This development also found expression in a memorandum of 5 May 1885 in which Grand Duchess Sophie stated that Goethe's Weimar estate should lay the foundation of Weimar "becoming the generally acknowledged intellectual centre of Germany".[26]

In 1886 Goethe's Weimar house was opened as a memorial, one year after the foundation of the Goethe National Museum, which was entrusted with the care of the art objects and the scientific collections of Goethe's estate.[27] In June 1885 the Goethe Society was founded, and in 1896, after Schiller's estate had also passed into public possession, the Goethe and Schiller Archives were established. This completed the strong institutional basis for the launch of a "rebirth" of Goethe, which was initiated in Weimar under the patronage of the aristocracy. At the same time, the Goethe memorials became the centres of a commemorative culture whose visual presence underlined Weimar's status of being a classical "Athens on the River Ilm".[28]

At first the Goethe house in Frankfurt, where the poet had been born and had lived with his parents, was standing in the shadow of its Weimar counterpart. While in 1778 Christoph Martin Wieland called Goethe's parental home still ironically a *Casa santa* (holy house), in 1932 Thomas Mann described it as a "place of relics" and Gerhart Hauptmann talked about a "national shrine".[29] But when the first part of Goethe's autobiography *Dichtung und Wahrheit* (*Poetry and Truth*), which deals with his younger days in Frankfurt, appeared in 1811, the educated middle class of Frankfurt began to remember its famous son. The people in Frankfurt particularly remembered the famous works from Goethe's early days as a poet, which he had written in his parental home in Frankfurt, namely *Götz von Berlichingen* (*Götz of Berlichingen*) (1773), *Die Leiden des jungen Werthers* (*The Sorrows of Young Werther*) (1774), *Clavigo* (1774), *Stella* (1775) and the *Urfaust* (Original Version of the Faust). Goethe's parental home gradually became a "praiseworthy sight".[30] In the *Journal des Luxus und der Moden* (*Journal of Luxury and Fashion*), for example, an engraving of Goethe's birthplace was printed in 1824 (no 9, plate 2, p. 70; see Figure 4.4). On this engraving visitors and a guide explaining the house to them can be seen. Added to the illustration was a sonnet by Stephan Schütze, which was dedicated to "the house where Göthe was born." Yet the most important stimulus to the public interest in Goethe's parental home came from Bettina von Arnim's book *Goethes Briefwechsel mit einem Kinde* (*Goethe's Correspondence with a Child*), which appeared in 1835 and which was to a large degree devoted to Goethe's youth.[31]

In 1773 Goethe's grandmother, Cornelia, bought this house as her widow's residence. It had been built at the Großer Hirschgraben about 1618 and originally consisted of two half-timbered houses.[32] In the years 1755 and 1756 Goethe's father had both half-timbered houses rebuilt into a spacious building with a representative front. In this way, he demonstrated that his family had acquired property and a good reputation in the free city of Frankfurt. The poet was born in the house at the Großer Hirschgraben in 1749 and spent his childhood and youth in it. In 1765 he left Frankfurt to study law in Leipzig and Straßburg. In 1774 Goethe returned to his parental home and worked as a lawyer in Frankfurt until he was summoned to Weimar in 1775. In 1795 Goethe's mother sold the house and most of the

Figure 4.4 Front view of the Goethe House in Frankfurt, drawing by Friedrich Wilhelm Delkeskamp, before 1823 (© Klassik Stiftung Weimar).

furniture, household goods and collections to live more modestly after her husband had died and her children had moved away. Thus, the Goethe house in Frankfurt represents the young Goethe, his education, studies and the lifestyle of the wealthy and educated middle class at that time.

When having the house renovated Goethe's father attached less importance to the outward appearance of the house than to the interior furnishings. It was important to him to have an impressive library, a picture gallery containing works of contemporary artists and to have ample space for the exhibition of souvenirs and works of art he had brought home from his journeys, for example to Italy. But he also set great store by the noble layout of the stairwell. This stairwell was modelled on the famous imperial staircase in the Frankfurt Römer (the town hall of Frankfurt am Main), which the German emperors used to climb when walking into the coronation hall. To the present day, the Frankfurt Goethe house has kept the memory of this phase in Goethe's life and the context surrounding it. Thus, it visualizes in a certain way the childhood and youth described in *Dichtung und Wahrheit* (*Poetry and Truth*).

After Goethe's mother had sold the house in 1795, it changed hands several times. In 1863 the "Freie Deutsche Hochstift" (Free German Foundation) bought it and opened it to the public. Strictly speaking, it was the commemoration of Schiller's 100th birthday in 1859 which occasioned the foundation of the "Freie Deutsche Hochstift für Wissenschaften, Künste und allgemeine Bildung" (Free German Foundation for the Sciences, the Arts and General Education).[33] Prompted by citizens from Frankfurt and by artists and intellectuals from all German-speaking areas this institution was intended to preserve the political ideals of the failed revolution of 1848, ideals which, however, had been turned into spiritual and cultural ones. The Freie Deutsche Hochstift was an organization which was open to everybody and which dedicated itself to the promotion of the public education system and disapproved of any patronizing by the authorities and the church. The organization aimed at keeping alive the idea of German unity in view of a common cultural identity.

The "Hochstift" wanted to be an intellectual centre for the entire German nation. Yet after buying Goethe's parental home the organization was confronted by a new challenge. Now it had to do justice to the historical significance of the house where Goethe had been born.[34] Step by step, the state of the house during Goethe's younger days was reconstructed. From the beginning, much attention was paid to the documentation of the historical context. This concept of documenting not Goethe's life but his epoch has been characteristic of the Goethe house and the Goethe museum in Frankfurt to this day. Various generous donations were the financial prerequisite for buying paintings, original manuscripts and books. These acquisitions, particularly the collection of paintings, are to this day indicative of the importance and function of the "Hochstift" as "a memorial, a cultural institution and a place of research".[35]

In 1897 the "Frankfurter Goethe Museum" (Frankfurt Goethe Museum) was built right beside the Goethe house. It not only took up the collections, which had become quite extensive in the meantime, but also developed concepts to make these collections accessible by own research. The layout of the museum rooms, which are typical Rococo reconstructions from the early days of the Prussian Empire, once again mirrors the intention of concentrating on the Frankfurt phase of the young Goethe with a main emphasis on the fine arts. The former director of the Goethe Museum, Ernst Beutler, who firmly supported this concept, talked about an "authentication of literature with the help of the fine arts".[36] On 22 March 1944 the Frankfurt Goethe house and the Goethe Museum were hit by bombs and completely destroyed. Yet the inventory and collections had been taken out in time and could be preserved. Furthermore, drawings had been made and photos had been taken of all parts of the Goethe house by means of which the house could be reconstructed between 1947 and 1951. In 1954 the Goethe Museum could also be reopened. Between 1992 and 1997 it was thoroughly renovated and rebuilt into a modern research institute.

Apart from its function as a museum, the "Freie Deutsche Hochstift" at present devotes itself not only to the research into Goethe and his time, but also to the literature and culture of the Romantic period. In the "Hochstift" the critical editions of the works and letters of Clemens Brentano and Hugo von Hofmannsthal are being prepared, which are two outstanding projects in German scholarly editing. The research programme is completed by exhibitions, series of lectures, readings by various authors and concerts.

In 2001 Dieter Borchmeyer stated that Goethe today is no longer a "living memorial of the Germans".[37] According to him, the occupation with Goethe's life and the interpretation of his works "has to a large degree been transferred to philology" and his works have been disappearing more and more from the stages and "the horizons of the average reader".[38] Borchmeyer's diagnosis seems to be contradicted by the thousands of people visiting Goethe's houses in Frankfurt and Weimar every year. While the Frankfurt house, like so many other parental homes, derives its significance mainly from the biographical context, the Weimar house is part of a more comprehensive and unique "aestheticized topography".

By using a concept like "aestheticized topography", Georg Bollenbeck tried to capture the ambivalence resulting on the one hand from the real topography *within* Weimar including its memorials and on the other hand from "a spirit *of* Weimar independent of its geographical place".[39] In this way, memory is provided with visual fixed points and can attribute meaning to concrete things. The starting point of this aestheticized topography is the personalization of Goethe's house that is being presented "like a shrine", as the Russian writer Alexander Turgenjew put it. Even though this personalization is counterbalanced today by accompanying exhibitions using polished teaching methods to explain the context surrounding the poet, it is mainly owing to the person of Goethe that visitors regard Goethe houses as tourist attractions with museum shops and cafeterias. It is only in the second place that Goethe houses are seen as symbols of Germany being the nation of poets and philosophers.

It is amazing that after German reunification Weimar was not re-established as the cultural centre of Germany with a corresponding unifying potential. The year 1999, when Weimar was appointed European City of Culture, the celebrations on the occasion of Goethe's 250th anniversary were characterized by emphatic detachment which could even be noticed in the speeches of the politicians. The "spirit of Weimar" alongside the "spirit of the great philosophers and poets", which at the opening of the German National Assembly in Weimar on 6 February 1919 German President Friedrich Ebert had conjured up as an alternative plan to the militaristic and imperialistic spirit of the Wilhelmian period, is only important to Germans today from a historical point of view, namely when they talk about Goethe and the Weimar classical period. This is certainly in part owing to the fact that Hitler deliberately claimed the "spirit of Potsdam" as a motto of his dictatorship after seizing power in 1933. Although Goethe was still held up as the role model of a "great German" during National Socialist dictatorship, he could, unlike Schiller, hardly be ideologized apart from that. To the National Socialists Weimar was important for different reasons: In Weimar the second party conference of the NSDAP was held in 1926, and in Thuringia the National Socialists participated in the government even before 1933 and thus already tried out power seizure.

Despite these historical facts, both German states regarded Weimar as "the treasure chamber of German culture" after 1945.[40] Thus, they explicitly conjured up the "other" Germany which had definitely known humanist traditions. Thomas Mann's visits both to Frankfurt and to Weimar in the Goethe year of 1949 had this as a motto. In the first decade after the Second World War, Goethe and the Weimar classical period were seen by both German states as combining elements creating a unified national culture, but after the final separation of the two German states they were increasingly used to dissociate them from each other. Each of the two German states wanted to distinguish itself as the real administrator of the classical heritage. In 1954 the German Democratic Republic founded the "Nationalen Forschungs- und Gedenkstätten der klassischen deutschen Literatur" (National Institute of Research and Commemoration Concerning Classical German Literature) in Weimar, a large institution which was not only in charge of the care of the monuments in and around Weimar, but which also felt obliged to archive, document and edit important material and texts and to take bibliographical details. But even this large-scale concept did not succeed in consistently taking up the traditions of classical Weimar. In the Federal Republic of Germany there had been early warnings against using Goethe and Weimar without thinking as an alibi for an undamaged cultural tradition. Finally, the academic debates of the 1960s and 1970s completely did away with the "legend of the classics".

Today the self-evident quality of the classical heritage seems to be lost and thus people once again try to combine the "legacy and topicality" of Weimar and to define the places of the classics as "places of integrated education" in "times when roots are lacking".[41] Nevertheless, the Weimar classical period and the Goethe memorials carry on being difficult territory that should still be approached critically and not with blind admiration. In the Goethe year 1949 the German scholar Richard Alewyn, who two years earlier had returned to Germany from his American exile, made the following admonishing remark: "Between us and Weimar there is Buchenwald".[42] This admonition always has to be kept in mind when in Goethe's house at the Frauenplan in Weimar we are greeted by the serene *Salve*.

NOTES

1. Translated from the German by Dieter Neiteler.
2. "Warum stehen sie davor? / Ist nicht Thüre da und Thor? / Kämen sie getrost herein / Würden wohl empfangen seyn."
3. Nutz, 1994, 604, and Barth, 1971.
4. Raabe, 1996, 11.
5. Borchmeyer, 2001, 187, states that it is probably "the most important institution in German cultural and educational policy."
6. Bollenbeck, 2001b, 224. See also Bollenbeck, 2001a.
7. Quoted from *Weimar in Urteil der Welt*, 1975, 434, 436.
8. Lämmert, 1971, and Raabe, 1970.
9. Seifert, 1994, 27.
10. Borchmeyer, 1994, 45.
11. "Wo finden Sie ... auf einem so engen Fleck noch so viel Gutes! ... bleiben Sie bey uns, ... wählen Sie Weimar zu Ihrem Wohnort. Es gehen von dort die Thore und Straßen nach allen Enden der Welt." Eckermann, 1939, 36.
12. "Das Innere des Hauses machte auf mich einen sehr angenehmen Eindruck; ohne glänzend zu seyn war alles höchst edel und einfach; auch deuteten verschiedene an der Treppe stehende Abgüsse antiker Statuen auf Goethe's besondere Neigung zur bildenden Kunst und dem griechischen Alterthum .... Nachdem ich mich ein wenig umgesehen, ging ich sodann mit dem sehr gesprächigen Bedienten die Treppe hinauf zur ersten Etage. Er öffnete ein Zimmer, vor dessen Schwelle man die Zeichen SALVE als gute Vorbedeutung eines freundlichen Willkommenseyns überschritt. Er führte mich durch dieses Zimmer hindurch und öffnete ein zweytes, etwas geräumigeres, wo er mich zu verweilen bat, indem er ging mich seinem Herrn zu melden. Hier war die kühlste erquicklichste Luft, auf dem Boden lag ein Teppich gebreitet, auch war es durch ein rothes Kanapee und Stühle von gleicher Farbe überaus heiter meublirt; gleich zur Seite stand ein Flügel, und an den Wänden sah man Handzeichnungen und Gemälde verschiedener Art und Größe. Durch eine offene Thür gegenüber blickte man sodann in ein ferneres Zimmer, gleichfalls mit Gemälden verziert, durch welches der Bediente gegangen war mich zu melden. Es währte nicht lange so kam Goethe, in einem blauen Oberrock und in Schuhen; eine erhabene Gestalt!" Eckermann, 1939, 29f.
13. Nutz, 1994, 614.
14. Biedrzynski, 1993, 169f.
15. Concerning the history of the house see Maul and Oppel, 2000, 6–18, and Biedrzynski, 1993, 182–89.
16. Trunz, 1980, 48.
17. The collection included 11,691 prints and drawings, 13,697 carved stones, medals and coins, 348 small sculptures, 293 majolicas and ceramics.
18. See Pielmann, 1998.
19. Eckermann, 1939, 322.
20. Schulze, 1994, 602.

21. "Diesem zu begegnen, gewöhnte ich mich zuvörderst, bei allem, was ich besitze, mich gern zu erinnern, wie ich dazu gelangt, von wem ich es erhalten, es sei durch Geschenk, Tausch oder Kauf, oder auf irgend eine andre Art. Ich habe mich gewöhnt, beim Vorzeigen meiner Sammlungen der Personen zu gedenken, durch deren Vermittelung ich das einzelne erhielt, ja der Gelegenheit, dem Zufall, der entferntesten Veranlassung und Mitwirkung, wodurch mir Dinge geworden, die mir lieb und wert sind, Gerechtigkeit widerfahren zu lassen. Das, was uns umgibt, erhält dadurch ein Leben, wir sehen es in geistiger, liebevoller, genetischer Verknüpfung, und durch das Vergegenwärtigen vergangener Zustände wird das augenblickliche Dasein erhöht und bereichert, die Urheber der Gaben steigen wiederholt vor der Einbildungskraft hervor, man verknüpft mit ihrem Bilde eine angenehme Erinnerung ...." Translation cited from Goethe, 1987, 305–06.
22. Schulze, 1994, 602.
23. Trunz, 1980, 66.
24. "Es kommt mir vor allem darauf an, daß meine Verlassenschaft liberal in meinem eignen Sinne behandelt werde, daß man nicht pedantisch und lieblos damit verfahre, sondern daß die Überlebenden, Schaltenden und Waltenden mich gleichsam fortzusetzen, allenthalben konservatorisch zu verfahren suchen." Müller, 1956, 177f.
25. Golz, 1996, 14.
26. "Denn mein Bestreben, soviel an mir liegt, geht dahin, Weimar den Vorzug zu sichern, der Mittelpunkt aller Bestrebungen zu sein, welche den großen Name [sic!] Goethe betreffen. Mit seiner Geschichte, seinen Erinnerungen und seinen Sammlungen bildet Weimar das allgemein anerkannte geistige Zentrum Deutschlands." —"As far as I am concerned, I endeavour to secure Weimar the advantage of being the centre of all efforts concerning the great name of Goethe. His personal history, his memories and his collections make Weimar the generally acknowledged intellectual centre of Germany." Cited from Schmid, 1992, 101.
27. In the foundation charter, dated 8 August 1885, Grand Duke Carl Alexander described the National Museum's task as "preserving Goethe's house together with its equipment in a respectful way worthy of Goethe's memory, of keeping Goethe's collections and other objects both having belonged to Goethe and being connected to him and his activities and of presenting a supportive and solemn place to the research into Goethe and the admiration for the poet."—"das Goethe-Haus nebst dessen Zubehörungen in einer dem Andenken Goethes würdigen, pietätvollen Weise zu erhalten, die Goetheschen Sammlungen sowie andere von Goethe herrührende oder zu ihm und seinem Wirken in Beziehung stehende Gegenstände zu bewahren und der Goethe-Forschung wie der Verehrung für den Dichter eine fördernde und weihevolle Stätte darzubieten". Cited from Schmid, 1992, 102.
28. Bollenbeck, 2001b, 214.
29. Maisak, 1997, 50, notes 1 and 2.
30. Schuster and Gille, 1999, 1:169.
31. Perels, 1999, 121f.
32. Maisak, 1999, 21f.
33. Concerning this aspect see Seng (n.d.).
34. See Beutler, 1962.
35. Perels, 1997.
36. Maisak, 1997, 29.
37. Borchmeyer, 2001, 206.
38. Ibid.

39. Bollenbeck, 2001, 213.
40. Piana, 1955, 14.
41. See Müller, 2004.
42. Alewyn, 1948–49, 686.

5 Goethe's Home in the "First City of the World"

The Making of the Casa di Goethe in Rome

Dorothee Hock

When thinking about the houses of Goethe, our mind obviously goes to those buildings inhabited by Germany's First Poet that have been transformed into places of commemoration. Apart from some inns and restaurants which claim to have given shelter to the poet on occasion of his numerous journeys in Germany, it's the homes of Goethe in Frankfurt and Weimar that spring to our minds. And since May 1997 also the Casa di Goethe, the House of Goethe in Rome. This chapter focuses on the long, complex, and sometimes adventurous history of this memorial place, which is not only Germany's first and only museum on foreign soil but also a *Goethe Haus* that in several ways is untypical and different from the other buildings associated with the poet. In fact, what the numerous visitors to the Casa di Goethe actually find when they first set foot in the rooms that once hosted Goethe's Roman apartment is not what an average literary tourist might expect to find.

Philipp Möller is the cover-name used by Johann Wolfgang von Goethe during his journey to Italy.[1] The pseudonym is intended to protect from public curiosity the already famous author of *Die Leiden des jungen Werthers* (*The Sufferings of Young Werther*) and other dramas, but it also fits well his ideas of a playful and light-hearted approach to his Italian experience.[2] In the early hours of 3 September 1786 he secretly leaves the Bohemian spa Carlsbad, not saying a word about his final destination to his employer and friend, the Duke Carl August. Goethe, a long-year member of the Privy Council and of several other administrative bodies in the small duchy of Saxe-Weimar-Eisenach, is exhausted and painfully aware of the yet unfinished state of his various literary projects. Many years later he will tell his confident, Eckermann, that "in the first ten years of my Weimar ministerial and court life, I accomplished virtually nothing."[3] The thirty-seven-year-old is in the throes of what we would call today a deep existential or mid-life crisis, and the frustrating affair with Charlotte von Stein, a married lady-in-waiting, does the rest to convince the poet that only a complete break with his routine existence will help him to overcome his crisis and be reborn. Moreover, the journey represents the fulfilment of his life-long dream to visit "classical soil" and to look for new experiences and knowledge. Twenty-two months later Goethe will return to Germany with a greater understanding of himself, his art, and his role in life. Rome, the "First city of the world" is the final destination of this journey of self-recovery.[4]

On 30 October 1786, after only one night in the Roman guest house Locanda dell'Orso,[5] Möller alias Goethe moves to a flat in Via del Corso 18, property of the Roman Moscatelli family where his pen friend, German painter Johann Heinrich Wilhelm Tischbein (1751-1829) invites him to stay with him and two other German artists, Friedrich Bury and Georg Schütz (see Figure 5.1). Goethe writes the same night: "I've moved in with Tischbein and now have relief from all the life of inns and travel."[6] The rooms where Goethe will stay during his Roman sojourn are those of a simple pension, managed by the Roman coachmen family Collina: Sante Serafino and his wife Piera Giovanna di Rossi. (Before moving to Via del Corso in 1786, the Collinas had been hosting Tischbein and other artists in the nearby Via del Babuino.) Goethe gets a "small and modest room"[7] close to Tischbein's studio and apparently does not miss the luxury of his official Weimar dwelling.[8] He obviously appreciates the easy going lifestyle of this temporary home, and in these simple rooms on the Corso he will find inspiration to complete the works that as yet only existed as fragments—*Tasso*, *Egmont* and *Iphigenie*—and to start new projects. The apartment's strategic location on the Corso, at that time scene of the Roman carnival races, may have been decisive for the writing of *Römische Karneval* (The Roman Carnival) published in 1789 and later integrated in his *Italian Journey*. The German speaking community in Rome —among them writer Carl Philipp Moritz, Winckelmann's pupil Johann Friedrich Reiffenstein and painter

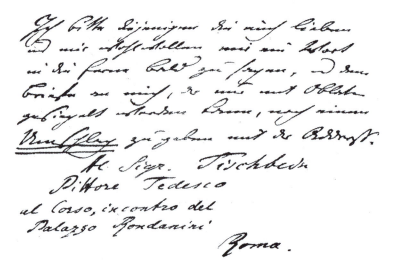

Figure 5.1 Johann Wolfgang von Goethe, Undated letter-card (but c. 1786) stating his Roman address (© Casa di Goethe, Rome).

Angelica Kauffman—adopts him as a friend and will often join him in his domicile.

In this pleasant domestic setting Goethe starts to draw and study, guided and instructed by this intimate circle of artist friends, he dedicates himself to literature again, and thus engages in a completely different life. He is aware of the central location in the city and underlines the positive atmosphere on several occasions. On 1 November 1786 he writes to his Weimar friends:

> It is a piece of luck for me that Tischbein has pleasant quarters, where he lives with several other painters. I am staying with him and have entered into their settled household, and this way I am enjoying peace and domestic harmony in a foreign country. The landlord and landlady are an honest old couple who do everything themselves and look after us as if we were children. Yesterday they were inconsolable when I did not eat the onion soup, and straightaway wanted to make another. Only someone who has tried it himself can understand how well this Italian boarding house life suits me. The house is situated in the Corso, not 300 steps from the Porta del Popolo.[9]

Apart from occasional allusions to the refreshing coolness of his studio in the hot Roman summer,[10] there are little descriptions of the lodgings in his letters and in the *Journey to Italy*. Neither does Goethe tell us much about the apartment's size or its interior decoration and furnishings, nor do his friends and co-tenants (see Figure 5.2). It was clear from the beginning that his stay would be limited in time, and busy as he was Goethe obviously did not even consider to leave a personal mark on his temporary home. His frenetic shopping of casts taken from antique Roman statues in the first days of his Roman stay was clearly intended for his personal delight and not for embellishing his small room.

After his return from Sicily in June 1787, Goethe first moved to Tischbein's studio—the painter was still in Naples—and then in March 1788 settled in rooms that had become available on the second floor of the palazzo. The German artist was not the first to establish his studio in Via del Corso 18: the house had been frequently occupied by foreign artists. In 1771 for example, a certain "Lavino Amilton" was registered, most probably Gavin Hamilton, a Scottish painter of classical-mythological scenes and an archaeologist, who belonged to the circle around Anton Raphael Mengs and Johann Joachim Winckelmann and died in Rome in 1798.[11]

Goethe's stay in Rome came to an end in April 1788. He would never visit his most-loved city again. After the dissolving of the Collina hostel some years later, the apartment was let out to other families and the building would change hands many times in the course of the centuries.[12] Inevitably in Rome at this time nobody thought of preserving furnishings and objects of the rooms once occupied by a poet whose most important works

Figure 5.2 Johann Heinrich Wilhelm Tischbein, *Goethe at the window of his Roman apartment*, 1787 (© Freies Deutsches Hochstift / Frankfurter Goethe Museum).

were still to come and who had taken most of his personal belongings and Italian purchases back to Weimar.

How important the Italian journey and especially Rome were for Goethe as a man and for the development of his work is well known. The Italian episode gives his life a new beginning and new meaning. Southern climate and setting and the different lifestyle in an artist community produce an inward transfiguration, and when back in Germany the poet has changed forever, full with new vitality and destined to become one of the central figures in German and indeed European culture. No wonder that sooner or later someone would remember the importance of the house where he had spent so many happy days of his journey.[13]

Standing in front of the building in Via del Corso 18, attentive visitors will note the plaque placed high up on the right-hand on the palazzo's façade: "In questa casa immaginò e scrisse cose immortali Volfango Goethe" (In this house Wolfgang Goethe imagined and wrote immortal words; see Figure 5.3). In 1872 the City of Rome had commissioned the historian Domenico Gnoli to identify homes of famous visitors.[14] As a result of Gnoli's research, that same year the plaque was installed, perhaps to signal the positive disposition towards Germany of the new-born kingdom of Italy and its gratitude for the free publicity the famous poet had given its recently established capital. Gnoli's research was mainly based on Goethe's own words, like the above mentioned "300 steps from the Porta del Popolo," or the poet's frequent remarks on Palazzo Rondanini, situated in front of the artist community (and still in existence). In the beginning of the twentieth century Friedrich Noack, a well-known writer and *Deutschrömer*, continued an enquiry started and published by Carletta[15] and confirmed by Vogel,[16] presenting great part of the sources that prove Goethe's sojourn in the building.[17] At this particular moment in time, Goethe seems to have been very much present in Rome, since in these same years the German emperor Wilhelm II donated to the city a statue of the poet, executed by Gustav

Figure 5.3 Commemorative plate on the façade of Via del Corso 18, Rome, 1872 (© Casa di Goethe, Rome).

Eberlein and erected in the heart of the Villa Borghese where Goethe had conceived the "Witches kitchen" scene of *Faust*.

During the first half of the twentieth century, commemorations of Goethe's stay in the capital continued in various forms: a street and a school were named after the poet, a play inspired by Goethe's Roman sojourn was performed in the Teatro Argentina[18] and a publication of Italy's public railway company in 1930 reconstructed his Italian trip.[19] But it was not before 1972 that the *genius loci* of the house on the Corso was recalled again—this time in Germany. The only basis for this operation was the poet's address—no objects, no relics, no furniture, no detailed images or descriptions to be used in a reconstruction—a challenging starting point for the creation of a memorial site.

In the early 1970s, the "Freies Deutsches Hochstift," a German foundation which owned the Goethe house in Frankfurt, took the initiative to set up a "Goethe Museum Rom" in an apartment of a few rooms (210 square meters) on the second floor of Via del Corso 18 that happened to become available for rent.[20] Since the late 1960s the Hochstift had been considering the possibility of creating a place of commemoration on the Corso. Some basic restoration preceded the opening of this privately sponsored museum on 29 October 1973,[21] but there was no money left to start a historical reconstruction or to elaborate ideas for an appropriate display. It was definitely the location that mattered at this moment. After almost two centuries, Goethe's Roman address in Via del Corso 18 finally was on the agenda once again. But as a consequence of the modest financial resources, the exhibit on Goethe's Italian journey was limited to some basic documentation and staff was limited to just one curator. Moreover, some rooms were put at the disposal of the local Goethe Institute. Ironically, the memorial site was forced to close its doors in the Goethe year 1982, when the 150th anniversary of the poet's death was celebrated. The high running costs could not be met anymore by donations alone and the number of visitors—mostly German tourists—had been stagnating.

But with the Goethe year celebrations approaching, even before it was a fact the closure started to arouse quite some public debate and indignation in (Western) Germany. Moreover, rumours about a serious interest in a takeover on the part of the German Democratic Republic persisted, for obvious reasons.[22] The main part of Goethe's estate (and particularly the part related to his Italian trip) was in fact preserved in the Weimar archives, and in these years the Eastern German authorities had frequently brought those materials to exhibitions in Italy. Thus the house on the Corso slowly became a political issue. The museum had closed in July 1982, but the lease of the Hochstift was for a term of five more years—enough time to try a new start to save this transnational heritage. In 1983 the Administration Committee of the Hochstift asked the support of the West-German Ministry of the Interior to find new patrons and sponsors interested in reopening the museum.

One year later the first step was made in order to entrust the Bonn based "Arbeitskreis Selbständiger Kultur-Institute" (Association of Independent Cultural Institutes, AsKI) with the running of the future museum.[23] AsKI, a consortium of important and independent cultural establishments in the Federal Republic, is financed by the Ministry of the Interior. During a general meeting of its members, the decision was taken to install a special committee for this Roman project. AsKI's managing director was appointed co-ordinator and as members of the committee the directors of the Goethe-Museum Düsseldorf, the Goethe-Haus Frankfurt and the Deutsche Schillergesellschaft (today Schiller-Nationalmuseum und Deutsches Literaturarchiv) were appointed unanimously; Goethe's Weimar domicile would join the AsKI only after Germany's reunification.

In November 1984 the committee travelled to Rome to have a closer look at the abandoned rooms on the Corso. At that moment most of the exhibits had been taken back to Frankfurt, but some of the larger sculpture casts were stored by the local branch of the Mercedes Benz company. Contacts with other German Institutes in Rome were established and there was general agreement that a new and ambitious concept with great potential was called for. Failure was considered politically unacceptable. Due to the limited space available, the future museum—its opening was expected to take place on the occasion of the 200th anniversary of Goethe's arrival in Rome in 1986—was again conceived on a small scale. Yet the minutes and agenda's of the committee meetings start to mention new elements, such as the creation of an apartment for scholars and the distinction between standing and temporary exhibits which could involve other AsKI member institutes. Moreover, the idea to create a special "Goethe room" with furniture of a bourgeois eighteenth-century home persisted. As soon as the German Department of the Interior finally agreed to a long-lasting funding of the museum as of 1986, the committee contacted the Embassy in Rome, local authorities as well as architects and lawyers, in order to handle the lease takeover and other legal matters. At that point, also private sponsors in Germany like the Robert Bosch Foundation started to promise important contributions.

These plans were however completely overturned when the owner of the building, the "Mensa Vescovile di Civita Castellana" (Diocese of Civita Castellana), a local ecclesiastical institution which had inherited the entire palazzo in 1948 from the last heir of the Bracci family, surprisingly announced its intention to sell the apartment instead of prolonging its rent, in order to make up for the financial losses it had to face as a consequence of the 1984 concordat with the Italian state. German authorities reacted quickly to this unexpected development. They immediately considered the possibility of buying the Goethe rooms, and started to negotiate a preliminary contract.

Yet the Roman "Goethe affair" was far from being concluded, since other complications were on their way. It was rumored that an important bank intended to buy the apartment and was willing to double the established prize. Moreover, serious doubts about the legal mandate of the owner's representative made the members of the AsKI committee apprehensive. They decided to turn for advice and help to circles within German diplomacy, thus turning Goethe into an affair of state. The German Embassy to the Holy See was asked to contact cardinal Casaroli, the Vatican Secretary of State, underlining "the political and cultural interest of the Federal Republic of Germany."

In the meantime, also in Germany the affair had started to attract public attention. On the occasion of the 200th anniversary of Goethe's arrival in Rome, the well known playwright and frequent visitor to Rome Rolf Hochhuth (*Der Stellvertreter—The Deputy*) published an open letter to Hans Dietrich Genscher, the minister of Foreign Affairs, complaining about the "shame of the 1982 closure" and pleading for a rapid public intervention and solution.[24] The appeal unleashed an avalanche of reactions, from articles in several national newspapers to letters by outraged readers. AsKI headquarters received offers from people willing to volunteer in the future "Goethe Museum Rom." For many Germans, preserving Goethe's memory in their favorite holiday destination apparently was and still is a matter of the utmost importance. Yet only a few months later, a sharp comment published in one of the most prestigious national weekly papers and a subsequent debate again shed serious doubts on the authenticity of the building, thus questioning the sense of such a substantial German cultural enterprise abroad which to some people seemed quite extravagant and unjustified.[25]

In order to counter these criticisms, in Rome more detailed research had to be done. New evidence was necessary to corroborate the position of the institutions and experts involved. On behalf of the German Embassy, the highly respected Bibliotheca Hertziana for the History of Art tried to find out more. Again, one of the conclusive sources turned out to be—as had been the case with Carletta and Noack—the *Stati delle Anime* deposited at the "Archivio del Vicariato" (Archives of the Roman curacy), an official list of inhabitants' names and addresses of that time. In this list, at the year 1787 the German artists are registered as living on the first floor of the Casa Moscatelli in the Via del Corso 18–20. Goethe is registered under his pseudonym Miller [Möller]. A new investigation in the same Archive showed that later the house passed from the Moscatelli to the Giorgi family, and the register of 1824, preserved in the State archives, proved that the Giorgi home was actually situated in the corner building Via della Fontanella/Via del Corso.

When the results of these detailed inquiries were published, the debate calmed down for a time.[26] But only shortly after a new challenge was to be met: if Goethe had lived most of the time on the first floor, it was clear that these rooms had to be transformed into a museum instead of the second floor apartment where he had sojourned only briefly after his return from the South. This obviously would entail the purchase of a different and indeed much more consistent part of the Roman palazzo. At this stage however, the affair had gained such momentum and visibility that it was considered politically impossible to back out over such details, however costly they were. The German Ministry of the Interior once again reacted very quickly and demonstrated great flexibility by authorizing AsKI to negotiate the acquisition of the much bigger first floor apartment occupied by a small business, with positive results. Already during his visit to Rome in the autumn of 1987, a senior staff member of the Ministry could inform the press that the owner was willing to sell only in case of a takeover of the entire first floor (two apartments of ca. 600 square meters), but that the German Government had agreed to these conditions in order to preserve this "national heritage"; this also explains why it was the Ministry of the Interior and not the Ministry of Foreign Affairs to conduct the case. At the same time, substantial sponsoring by Mercedes Benz (today Daimler Chrysler), which had agreed to cover a quarter of the costs of purchase, was announced.

After all these entanglements, it is no wonder that the signing of the preliminary contracts was greeted with great relief and satisfaction. Subsequently, steps were taken to give AsKI an Italian identity (bank account, tax numbers etc.) but bureaucracy still impeded a quick procedure. For the final sale, various permissions from Italian authorities had to be obtained, and since the buyer was a foreign institution even the Italian President had to give his consent to the sale by issuing a special decree. Italy's consul in Germany and the German Embassy in Rome intervened in order to accelerate the process, but further delay occurred when the owner could not present all the necessary documentation. AsKI used the waiting time (the final contract was signed only in March 1990) to develop a new concept for the Goethe Museum Rom (GMR). With the input of more experts that joined the committee, the idea of a "living memorial" was developed and presented to sponsors and the public.[27]

At the basis of this memorial would be a permanent exhibition, consisting of objects from the museum's own collection related to Goethe's Italian journey: on the many places he visited during this journey, on his various interests—from archeology to science—on his stay in Rome and on the appearance of the city at that moment. Next to this there would be temporary exhibits, cultural events, a specialized library with public access and a scholarship programme. The curators thus envisaged a Goethe Museum Rome which had to become more than just a place of remembrance, another destination of literary pilgrimage in Goethe's footsteps in Italy. They hoped to create in the apartment something different, a center of continuous renewal and cultural encounter, not unlike its function in Goethe's time, when artists and their guests gathered in Tischbein's studio to exchange opinions and share experiences (see Figure 5.4). Thus it was exactly this spirit of creativity, universality and openness characteristic of their community that was taken as key concept for the mission of the new institution.

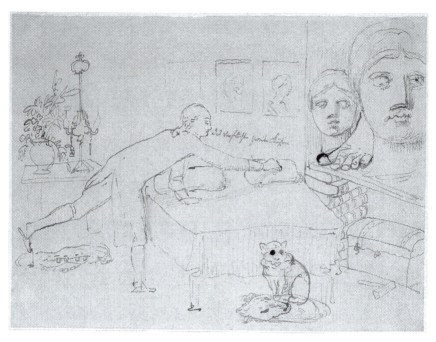

Figure 5.4 Johann Heinrich Wilhelm Tischbein, *Goethe in his Roman apart-ment: The damned second cushion*, 1786-87 (© Klassik Stiftung Weimar, Museen, Weimar).

The curators, however, also wanted the museum to have a collection. That's why AsKI/GMR continued in these years to collect illustrations and drawings, autographs, paintings, sculptures, photographs and instal-lations. A particularly successful period of collecting were the early 1990s, when several important autographs could be acquired at the auction of Herbert Albrecht's Goethe collection in Basel, among them an autograph letter-card with the poet's Roman address (see Figure 5.1). Almost at the same time the Museum managed to acquire the Goethe portrait by Andy Warhol, a contemporary adaptation of the icon image *Goethe in the Cam-pagna romana* painted by Tischbein in his studio on the Corso (see Figure 5.5). By a lucky chance AsKI moreover was able to acquire the outstanding Goethe library collected over a period of sixty years by publisher Richard Dorn.[28]

In the early 1990s public attention for the Goethe museum *in statu nascendi* was intense. In a special edition of the AsKI six-monthly newslet-ter[29] and in a detailed essay on the history of the apartment, published in the prestigious *Goethe-Jahrbuch*,[30] the history of the house and the initiative to turn it into a museum was amply illustrated. An exhibition in the Federal Chancellery in Bonn on the future museum and on the recent important acquisitions clearly underlined the political relevance of the project.[31] Due

Figure 4.5 Andy Warhol, *Johann Wolfgang von Goethe,* 1982 (© Casa di Goethe, Rome).

to the persisting difficulties with Italian authorities, AsKI's lawyer advised against using the term *museum* in the delicate phase of securing necessary permits. Because of this, the new Italian denomination *Casa di Goethe* was chosen, in order to convey an ideal of a happy and homely place, and also a tribute to Italy and to its language so loved by Goethe.[32]

Yet the actual making of the Casa di Goethe still took some more years. A close cooperation between AsKI and a Roman architectural studio accompanied the long restoring and rebuilding process of the run-down apartments, formerly used as offices. Detailed checks of the floors and walls showed that very little was left from the interior architecture of the Goethe age. However, the construction work and the unification of the two apartments brought to light new traces of the building's history. Stone door frames with the inscription of the name 'Jacobus Scala' confirm that the house was built at the end of the sixteenth century.[33] Beautiful painted wood ceilings—originating mostly from Goethe's time—were discovered and carefully restored. Then the apartment was completely restyled. One of the few images that document everyday life in the artists' residence, Tischbein's watercolor *Goethe at the Window,* gave the first inspiration to the project (see Figure 5.2). It took some time to convince all members of the committee that the initial idea of a Goethe room with antique furniture had to be abandoned because it would not harmonize with the rest. The architects did, though, design and recreate four-paneled shutters according to those seen in the Tischbein watercolor and decided to put small format terracotta on the apartment's floor. Instead of the typical wall decorations of the Goethe age they had the walls painted in light tones, in order to better accommodate future exhibits. The museum's functionality and transparency are supposed to recall the former use of the apartment as an artist's studio.

The long process of planning the museum—building permissions, strict conditions imposed by Italian authorities as well as unforeseen architectural and structural problems—was not without problems and repeated delays, and the date of the opening was postponed from year to year. This however gave the AsKI curators time to conceive the Casa di Goethe's first major exhibition on the poet's life and work, his journey to Italy and examples from the history of its reception. Numerous international museums agreed to supply originals for the show and a bilingual publication in two volumes (catalogue and essays) was prepared.[34] During the years of restoration and preparation, more sponsors were found for other acquisitions, for the fittings of the museum and for the scholarship programme (Mercedes Benz/Daimler Chrysler), although the main financing continued to be guaranteed by the Ministry of the Interior.[35] Some of the German-Italian staff was already employed and busy on the spot. Their task was supervising the construction site and the organization of "Goethe's household's" arrival——collection, library, showcases and office furniture made in Germany.

With the opening of Germany's first museum abroad on 30 May 1997 by the Minister of the Interior Manfred Kanther, a dream came true for those who had been following the making of the Casa di Goethe for years. The event attracted huge press coverage in both Germany and Italy, and during the first weekend of free entrance hundreds of curious tourists and of Roman citizens paid a visit to Goethe's new old domicile. The years since then have proved that the idea of a living memorial backed by loyal and constant public and private commitment works out well. The temporary exhibits on the tradition of the journey to Italy and on the critical encounter with this country up to the present day have attracted large numbers of visitors coming from various countries. Also the public access library and the frequent cultural events, based on collaborations with many partners in Italy, in Germany and in other countries, have turned out to be successful. Only time can show if Goethe will stand firm as a long-term Rome resident.

NOTES

1. Goethe, 1891, *Briefe*, 4(7), 253. In this letter of instructions to his servant Philipp Seidel (23 July 1786) Goethe mentions his new pseudonym for the first time: "für Rechnung Herrn Joh. Philipp Möller" (on the account of Sir Joh. Philipp Möller).
2. Zapperi, 1999, 40–41.
3. "... dass ich in den ersten zehn Jahren meines Weimarschen Dienst-und Hoflebens so gut wie gar nichts gemacht, dass die Verzweiflung mich nach Italien getrieben." Goethe to Eckermann (3 May 1827), in Eckermann, 1987, 539, where he states that "despair drove me to Italy"; translation DH.
4. "Now, at last, I have arrived in the First City of the world!" Quoted from Goethe, 1970, 128. For a recent contribution to the vast literature on Goethe's journey to Italy and on its motivations, see Miller, 2002, in particular 39–57.
5. Noack, 1904, 188. Today the Locanda is a piano bar and luxury restaurant. According to its web site, Goethe stayed here several times.
6. "Ich bin zu Tischbein gezogen und habe nun auch Ruhe von allem Wirtsaus und Reiseleben" (translation by T.J. Reed in Goethe, *The flight to Italy. Diary and Selected Letters,* 1999, 111).
7. "Er begehrte von mir ein Klein Stüpgen, wo er in Schlaffen und ungehindert in arbeiten könnte, und ein ganz einfaches Essen, das ich ihm den leicht verschaffen konnte, weil er mit so wenigem begnügt ist." "He wanted of me a small and modest room, where he could sleep and work undisturbed, and very simple food, which I had no trouble providing him with since he is content with so little." Letter by J. H. W. Tischbein to Johann Caspar Lavater on 9 December 1786. Quoted from Christian Beutler. *J.H.W. Tischbein—Goethe in der Campagna.* Stuttgart, 1962, 265; translation by Morwenna Symons in Bongaerts, 2004, 53–54.
8. Noack, 1907, 108–12.
9. "Für mich ist es ein Glück daß Tischbein ein schönes Quartier hat, wo er mit noch einigen Malern lebt. Ich wohne bey ihm und bin in ihre eingerichtete Haushaltung mit eingetreten, wodurch ich Ruh und häuslichen Frieden in einem fremden Lande genieße. Die Hausleute sind ein redliches altes Paar, die alles selbst machen und für uns wie Kinder sorgen. Sie waren gestern untröstlich als ich von der Zwiebel Suppe nicht aß, wollten gleich eine andere machen. Wie wohl mir dies aufs Italiänische Wirthshausleben thut, fühlt nur der der es versucht hat. Das Haus liegt im Corso, keine 300 Schritte von der Porta del Popolo." Goethe, 1891, IV-8: 37 (translation by Morwenna Symons in Bongaerts, *La Casa di Goethe a Roma,* 2004, 50–51).
10. Goethe, 1970, 358, 373.
11. Konrad Schuermann, "Nachspürungen," in Schuermann and Bongaerts-Schomer, 1997, 1:13.
12. For a detailed account of the building's history see Christoph Luitpold Frommel, "Zur Geschichte der Casa di Goethe," in Schuermann and Bongaerts-Schomer, 1997, 1:78–95.
13. Bongaerts, 2004, 33–34.
14. Gnoli, 1872.
15. Carletta, 1899, 7–17.
16. Vogel, 1905, 20–22.
17. Noack, 1904, 190–93.
18. Jandolo, 1914.

19. Gray and De Rosa, 1930, 13–14.
20. On the occasion a small volume was published: Lüders, 1973.
21. See Albert Wuche, "Wo Goethe am glücklichsten war," *Süddeutsche Zeitung*, 31 October/1 November 1973.
22. See Elke Pfaff, "Mittellos am Corso," *Kölner-Stadt-Anzeiger*, 4 March 1982.
23. The remaining part of this essay is based on archival research in the AsKI records 1984–96 concerning the Casa di Goethe in Rome (correspondence, minutes, agendas, etc.).
24. Rolf Hochhuth, "Das Goethe-Museum in Rom," *Frankfurter Allgemeine Zeitung*, 29 October 1986.
25. Hansjakob Stehle, "Rom: das falsche Goethe-Haus?," *Die Zeit*, 20 February 1987.
26. Christoph Luitpold Frommel, "Doch das echte Haus!," *Die Zeit*, 6 March 1987.
27. A small brochure was published: Pflug and Schuermann, 1989.
28. Richard W. Dorn and Michael Drucker, eds., *"In der Ferne gegenwärtig." Katalog der Goethe-Bibliothek Dorn*, Wiesbaden: Harrassowitz, 1986, supplementary volume 1993. Its numerous first editions, press cuttings and illustrated editions also make it an invaluable source of material for permanent and temporary exhibitions.
29. "Goethe Museum Rom," *Kulturberichte AsKI*, 1990, 2.
30. Claussen, 1990.
31. *Casa di Goethe. Eine Ausstellung zum Goethe-Museum Rom im Bundeskanzleramt Bonn. 10. November 1993 bis 28. Januar 1994.* Exhibition catalogue. Bonn: AsKI e.V., 1993.
32. Goethe writes on 11 September 1786: "How happy I am that the beloved language is now going to be the language of everyday use."
33. See Christoph Luitpold Frommel, "Zur Geschichte der Casa di Goethe," in Schuermann and Bongaerts-Schomer, 1997, vol. 1, 85.
34. Schuermann and Bongaerts-Schomer, 1997.
35. For more information on sponsors and persons otherwise involved in this enterprise, see the acknowledgements in Schuermann and Bongaerts-Schomer, 1997, vol. 1, 6–9.

6 Abbotsford
Dislocation and Cultural Remembrance

Ann Rigney

It is generally accepted that collective remembrance converges on communally accessible memory sites, literally "common places" that serve as points of reference for different individuals and groups in figuring the past.[1] While these "sites" are sometimes of a virtual nature, involving cultural icons rather than actual places, they do tend to be linked to specific, material locations which can be visited in the here and now. This much has been recognized, and this insight informs the present collection. As yet, however, we have little insight into how specific locations actually work as media in the ongoing production of collective memory, though some brief comments in Aleida Assmann's work *Erinnerungsräume* (*Spaces of Remembrance*, 1999) offer a good starting point for further elaboration.[2]

In the course of her analysis of the different media of remembrance, Assmann distinguishes between "places that are in themselves carriers of meaning"—because for example, something happened there like a battle, or because someone is actually buried there—and places that have acquired meaning through processes of symbolisation. The latter occurs when a monument is set up in one particular place to commemorate or represent something that happened elsewhere (think, for example, of Nelson's pillar in Trafalgar Square). According to Assmann, the use of symbolisation in order to invest specific locations with meaning increases along with modernisation. The more people move around, the more they are "dislocated" as it were from their original environment, the greater the necessity to invest new places with memory using the artificial means of symbols. Whereas people in traditional societies live close to where their ancestors lived and are buried, those living in modern societies are increasingly mobile and have to look for other means of establishing their connection with their ancestors than that of continuing on in the same place. As Assmann writes, "In the age of modern mobility and innovation the memory of places and the attachment to specific spots of ground becomes obsolete."[3]

In this way, Assmann reformulates from the perspective of spatial practices and modern mobility, Pierre Nora's basic argument about the development of modern memory culture, namely, that the rise of specific sites of memory (his *lieux de mémoire*) is in inverse proportion to the demise of traditional societies in which people's connectedness to the past was so self-evident and unremarkable that it was not an issue. It is only because there are no longer any such traditional "milieux de mémoire" (memory environments) that modern memorial practices came into being, according to Nora, and with them, the practice of locating memory in particular sites that can be visited in the here and now, if only occasionally, for the specific purpose of carrying out acts of remembrance.

In what follows I want to elaborate on the relationship between modern mobility and the symbolic investment of places.[4] Where Assmann limits symbolisation to the setting up of monuments in new locations, however, I propose adding to the discussion other forms of symbolisation that are less material and, accordingly, less tied down to specific places: texts and images. These are mobile media in the sense that, in contrast to material monuments which are always located somewhere, be this on the original site of the things they commemorate or elsewhere, texts and images are not tied down to any single place: they can be reproduced at will, circulate freely between places, and be in many different places at one time. As is well known, the link between specific locations and memorial media has become even more tenuous with the advent of digitalisation and internet, which has made it possible for a memorial to be at once "unlocated" and accessible from multiple locations, both nowhere and everywhere at once.[5]

The case with which I shall illustrate these principles is Abbotsford, the house where Sir Walter Scott (1771–1832) lived with his family from 1812 until his death in 1832. Nowadays, the name of Scott has something of an old-fashioned ring to it, and he is best known as father of swashbuckling, but now rather passé novels in the style of *Ivanhoe* (1819), but in his own lifetime and for at least a generation after his death, he was a cultural figure of immense stature. My argument here is that Abbotsford exemplifies a radically modern form of cultural remembrance, in which attachment to custom-made sites of memory is closely intertwined with human mobility both in the form of migration and of tourism.

The large country house Abbotsford, located south of Edinburgh in the border area of Scotland, is remarkable for its combination of lordly allure (it has something of a small medieval castle) and comfort (the spacious drawing rooms at the back have large windows affording an open view down to the lawns and the river Tweed). It seems, on the one hand, to advertise its link to history through its many neo-medieval features; at the same time, to have been designed as a modern family home (see Figure 6.1). This combination of the old and the modern tallies with the fact that Scott was at once a key figure in the development of Romantic historicism and, at the same time—as Virginia Woolf pointed out—a moderniser who installed gas-lighting and pneumatic bells in the house (the latter suitably moulded in the shape of gargoyles).[6]

Abbotsford is, in the first instance, the place one visits in order to see the exact spot where the famous Waverley novels were written: the book-

Figure 6.1 John Bower, *Image of Abbotsford* (1833) (Reproduced with the permission of Edinburgh University Library, Special Collections Department).

lined study is maintained as a shrine to the site "where it all happened" (present-day postcards are available of "The Study") with pride of place given to the chair upon which Scott sat when working at his desk (this chair is a recurrent topic in the representations of Abbotsford arguably because the place where Scott placed his buttocks is the closest one can get to the physical presence of the man himself in the act of writing). The significance of the building is not limited, however, to the fact of its being the historical backdrop to Scott's novelistic production, as if the house were an empty vessel that he filled with his presence. Instead, the house itself, both its architecture and its furnishings, were purposely designed by Scott himself to make of Abbotsford a site of memory. In other words, the posthumous remembrance of Scott as an individual writer is simply one level of the many levels of remembrance already at work in this place.

In turning the fairly modest farm that he had bought in 1811 into the substantial country house we see today,[7] Scott used his literary fortune and his antiquarian interests to "found" an ancestral home in the border area where his family had originated, engaging in elaborate building works in 1816–19 and again in 1822–24.[8] Whereas someone like Byron had inherited an ancestral home, Scott set out to make one, and he did so by transferring models and objects from elsewhere (Stephen Bann has referred in this regard to a "technique of transference and assemblage").[9] He thus recycled architectural elements from existing medieval buildings, using generic features such as castellation and a round tower, but also specific models which he then copied (the ceiling of the library, for example, reproduces the ornate ceiling of Rosslyn Chapel). He also recycled actual building materials from elsewhere and incorporated these salvaged objects into the very fabric of the new building. Thus original Roman friezes are built into the wall of the garden alongside nineteenth-century reproductions; an original door from the Tolbooth in Edinburgh is built into the side of the house, while other pieces of wood from the same building were recycled in making the shelves which line the library (the Tolbooth prison, that also figures prominently in the novel *The Heart of Midlothian* [1816] had been demolished in 1815).[10] Scott's study also contains objects made from recycled wood with a more indirect historical significance but with some sort of material link to great events. The latter includes a chest made from one of the wrecks of the Spanish Armada and a chair, with no more and no less a historical significance, than that it was made from the wood of a tree which actually stood near the spot where William Wallace was betrayed. In all this recycling of models and materials, the boundaries between original and copy, between the functional and the ornamental, between the historical and aesthetic seem less relevant than the possibility of maximising the symbolic presence of history through a multiplication of its material traces.

In her *Destination Culture* (1998), Barbara Kirshenblatt Gimblett links the phenomenon of display to the framing that occurs when something is re-located: if an ordinary object is taken out of its everyday environment and exhibited in a museum or a special case, it takes on a new aura. No longer a mere functional object, it invites a new type of attention and interpretation. Following Gimblett's argument, then, one could say that Abbotsford not only exists as house, but also as 'display building': architectural features reminiscent of the middle ages are both used and displayed *as* historical remainders by virtue of being de-contextualised and relocated.[11] The house in itself may not be old, but it signals "oldness" in multiple and multifarious ways.

Moreover, the building's display function is of a piece with its furnishings. Particularly in the reception rooms (the entrance hall and library), bits and pieces from the past are exhibited rather higgledy-piggledy in the manner of an old-curiosity shop and of an age when the principles of modern museum design were still a thing of the future.[12] The sheer quantity and eclectic range of these objects reflects Scott's considerable achievement as a collector of antiquities, which was fed by his passionate interest in the material details of the past: polished axes, several suits of armour, lots of small arms from different historical periods, the original key to the Tolbooth, various relics that he had picked up on the battlefield of Waterloo in 1815, a display case with various leftovers of Scottish history including a piece of oatcake found on the body of a Highlander after the battle of

Figure 6.2 George Washington Wilson, *Entrance Hall at Abbotsford* (c. 1880) (© Aberdeen University Library).

Culloden and a purse belonging to Helen McGregor wife of Rob Roy (see Figure 6.2).[13]

As these examples illustrate, the objects on display, which Scott himself had picked up on his travels or that had been sent to him by others, range historically from prehistoric times to recent Scottish and European history, but the frame provided by the house allows for them to co-exist side by side in the a-chronological way typical of collections. Scott's wide-ranging library on Scottish history and popular culture (including many pamphlets which are now proving to be of great interest) forms the bibliophile counterpart to this collection of objects.[14] In short, Abbotsford had all the marks both of a family home and of a public museum and library, with Scott as its curator. In bringing together in one place so many original and copied bits of history, Scott succeeded in turning Abbotsford, like the other more official museums that have emerged as custom-made *lieux de mémoire* since the beginning of the nineteenth century, into a place where disparate memories were made materially present in highly concentrated doses.

"The *Waverley* novels in stone": as a number of commentators have pointed out, Scott's imaginative investment in Abbotsford represents a variation on his other cultural work as historical novelist, poet, historian, antiquarian, public figure.[15] His innovations in the field of historical writing were closely linked to his passion for the material aspects of past life and to his imaginative involvement in the individual experiences of past events (in this sense his keeping an oatcake carried by an anonymous Highlander is a variation on his novelistic descriptions of what historical individuals ate and the clothes they wore).[16] He himself was highly conscious of the parallels between his various activities, moreover, referring repeatedly to Abbotsford as the "romance of a house I am making."[17] That there was an intimate link between his novelistic work and his role as curator at Abbotsford is confirmed by his *Reliquiae Trotcosienses*, a work written at the end of his life in which the persona of the antiquarian John Oldbuck (the protagonist of one of his earlier novels *The Antiquary* [1816]) gives a playful design for an imaginary house which bore many resemblances to the actual Abbotsford.[18] These variant forms of literary production were not only linked thematically, but also in a more material way that is indicative of Scott's place in the transition to a modern, commercial-based literary culture: arguably the huge financial burden in building and maintaining Abbotsford provided an ongoing stimulus to him as novelist to keep producing new works for the market; in other words, that the novels subsidized the house with which he was passionately involved.[19] The financial catastrophe which struck him in 1826 was largely not of his own making, but its impact was aggravated by the heavy financial toll the house was having on him. Not just in terms of the initial outlay, but also in terms of the ongoing expenses incurred by his hospitality and his ongoing performance as "Laird of Abbotsford."

At an age when identity and self-fashioning were not the explicit issues they are today, it is remarkable how many different identities Scott assumed or had attributed to him: from the various personae he invented as narrator of his novels, to the various roles he was known by, often alongside each other—"Sir Walter Scott," the "Wizard of the North," the "Author of Waverley," the "Shirra" (the name he was known by in the locality where he served as sheriff) and, finally, the "Laird of Abbotsford," the way he often styled himself in his letters. Where the actual building can be seen as a form of self-fashioning in which the "author of Waverley" expressed himself in an alternative medium, his lifestyle as "Laird of Abbotsford" involved the acting out of a related role: this involved not only being curator of Scottish memory, but also being the father of his family and protector of his servants, livestock and dogs (he was known for his extraordinary loyalty to canines and was often pictured with them)[20] and showing hospitality on an almost feudal scale to the many friends and guests who regularly filled the house. In contrast to the roles assumed by later artists and writers, Scott was certainly no starving, isolated individual burning the midnight oil in a garret or an isolated aesthete, but a man surrounded by visitors and family, with responsibilities in the public sphere, and a love of being out of doors and telling stories from Scottish folklore and history. Thus Washington Irving, having benefited from Abbotsford's hospitality for several weeks in 1817, expressed his amazement that Scott found any time at all for writing, not to mention the many bestsellers that came from his pen, since he seemed never to be alone (in fact Scott, in order to find some time for himself, had built a hidden entrance to his study that he could reach unnoticed from his bedroom).

"Sites of memory" in the sense of *lieux de mémoire* function as such because they represent—as Pierre Nora put it—a concentration of remembrance in a limited number of signs ("un maximum de sens dans un minimum de signes").[21] It should be apparent from this brief description of Abbotsford that it had all the makings of such an over-determined site. To begin with, as we have seen, the property was designed as a placeholder for all the memories associated with the objects that Scott had collected or incorporated into the building. Secondly, by virtue of its displaying history in such variety and quantity, it also thematizes as it were history and remembering as such. Finally, from 1832 onwards, the place also became the site where Scott himself *had been* and where he had lived out his historicising dreams and his role as writer and Laird of Abbotsford. In a memorial layering typical of memory sites,[22] its role as museum (recalling Scottish history) is overlaid by its role as a monument recalling the life and works of the maker of that museum, Sir Walter Scott. As W.S. Crockett wrote of Abbotsford in 1905, it was even more reminiscent of Scott than the custom-made memorial put up in Edinburgh in 1840: "So far as monuments to Scott go, there is none to equal [Abbotsford], not even the most splendid and costly pile which is one of Edinburgh's proudest ornaments."[23] As Crockett's reference to the human and financial *cost* of Abbotsford indicates, a certain tension exists between the different memorial layers in the case of this particular site: the fact that Scott had to struggle to keep up Abbotsford highlights the "artificial" character of this remembrance site and the fact that it is the result of huge effort rather than a natural accretion of historical objects.

When Scott was travelling back home in 1832 on what was to be his last trip abroad, he happened to visit a bookseller in Frankfurt who, on hearing that there was an English speaker in the shop but not recognizing who it was, hastened to offer this potential customer something that would be sure to interest him: a print of Abbotsford.[24] The anecdote illustrates the extraordinary popularity of Scott's work and the fame of his home, a fame which in the form of a printed image had literally travelled the world in advance of its owner. Nor was the presence of this print in a Frankfurt bookshop an outrageous fluke; even within the lifetime of Scott, Abbotsford had become the subject of many representations, the metonymic mark of "Sir Walter Scott" and everything associated with him. In the form of images and texts, Abbotsford had travelled to those living elsewhere and, as the Frankfurt story shows, had become an internationally recognised cultural icon.

Just as Scott's books circulated widely throughout the British Isles, Europe and North America, so too did his reputation and representations of his home as the material embodiment of the writer's life. It is indicative of the intimate connection between Abbotsford, Scott's life, and Scott's other creative activities, that the many tie-in publications dealing with the "original" sites in Scott's novels and poetry were often supplemented by images or descriptions of Abbotsford as the site where the writing itself took place (thus *The Land of Scott: A Series of Landscape Illustrations, illustrative of real scenes, described in the novels and tales, of the author of Waverley* [1848] included a drawing of the study at Abbotsford alongside images of the various sites which had figured in his historical fiction, as if the writer's home were a natural extension of his writing.)[25]

Images of Abbotsford were disseminated from an early stage in a variety of media and genres, from oil paintings depicting "Sir Walter Scott and his literary friends at Abbotsford" (see Figure 6.3), to the engravings of the house that were reproduced in popular magazines, to the photographs and lantern slides of the interior and exterior of the house that were mass-produced from the 1860s onwards (*Abbotsford: 12 Photos for your Album* [1900], for example), to the souvenirs—miniatures of the writer's chair (see Figure 6.4), key rings with pictures of Abbotsford—that are a feature of the last part of the century and that continue today. Characteristic for this whole process is its increasing self-referentiality: earlier acts of remembrance are recalled along with their original objects. Thus images of Abbotsford and its owner continuously return to the building itself in a self-reflective looping that seems characteristic of the formation of cultural

Figure 6.3 Thomas Faed, *Sir Walter Scott and his Literary Friends at Abbotsford* (1849) (Reproduced with the permission of Edinburgh University Library, Special Collections Department).

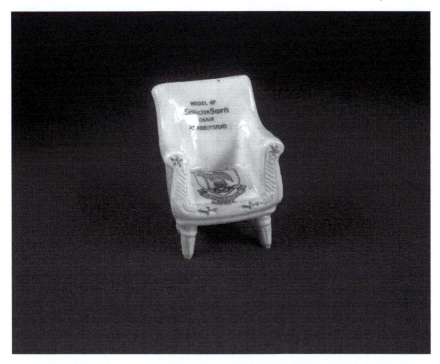

Figure 6.4 Porcelain souvenir of Scott's Chair at Abbotsford, Corson Collection. (Reproduced with the permission of Edinburgh University Library, Special Collections Department).

icons: thus one of the many photographs of Abbotsford made by George Washington Wilson (1823–93) now hangs in the entrance hall, and a miniature of the colossal Scott monument in Edinburgh is kept in the drawing room. The symbolic Abbotsford continues in this way to overlay the actual place as it presents itself to the visitor (the latter comes prepared, moreover, with certain ideas about the house gleaned from the many images of it that have been in circulation). This ongoing "symbolisation" of Abbotsford continues a process that Scott himself had set in place for, as we saw earlier, there never was an original Abbotsford beyond the modest house Scott moved into, but only a site where acts of remembrance are continuously being performed and where they continuously leave their material traces.

While the circulation of images of Abbotsford enabled the famous property on the banks of the Tweed to become virtually present in households across the world, they also helped mobilise people to go and visit Scott or, after his death, the house that he had built and in which he had lived. As was mentioned earlier, scores of visitors found their way to Abbotsford during Scott's lifetime, including many illustrious literati with whom Scott had corresponded, but also more opportunistic travellers wanting to be "in" on the Scott phenomenon and ready to profit from a free lunch. The sheer number of visitors led Scott to complain in his journal in November 1825:

> Abbotsford begins to be haunted by too much company of every kind. But especially foreigners. I do not like them .... I hate the impudence that pays a stranger compliments and harangues about his works in the author's house, which is usually ill breeding. Moreover they are seldom long in making it evident that they know nothing about what they are talking of excepting having seen *The Lady of the Lake* at the opera.[26]

Despite such reservations, Scott's entry for the next day mentions a visit from a Russian youth (whom he praises for being "kind, modest and ingenious") and two Frenchmen ("whom I liked"): apparently his own bonhomie regularly got the better of his desire for peace and quiet. His reputation as a friendly host thus worked together with his literary fame to encourage this continuous stream of visitors.

After Scott's death, Abbotsford became something of a nineteenth-century Graceland, a major pilgrimage destination for book-lovers from far and near. As one writer put it in 1833, it was "the spot to which pilgrims from all parts of the civilised world will bend their footsteps."[27] (The site still attracts about 70,000 visitors a year and remains thus a living memory site, although it is not as popular as other tourist destinations.)[28] It attracted many literary noteworthies, including the Brontë sisters, Charles Dickens, Harriet Beecher Stowe, Nathaniel Hawthorne, Theodor Fontane and Harriet Martineau, to name just a few of the names in the visitors' book kept since 1837.[29] Abbotsford was often also on the itinerary of visits by royalty, though usually the spouses, children or cousins of reigning monarchs rather than the monarchs themselves (a notable exception being Scott-lover Queen Victoria who visited in 1867).[30] From the late 1840s, however, as organised tourism got under way in Scotland and destinations were usually defined in terms of their historical and literary interest, Abbotsford increasingly attracted a broader, genteel public. With the introduction of an entrance fee and the provision of guided tours, the conditions in which these visitors were entertained changed quite radically, being no longer a matter of visitors staying three weeks "on the house," as Washington Irving had done back in 1817, but of receiving "the package" in an hour-long tour of the house.

These later visitors on organised tours often combined a trip to Abbotsford with a visit to the nearby Melrose Abbey, which Scott had invoked in his *Lay of the Last Minstrel* (1805) but which was also historically interesting in its own right.[31] (That a tourist has not just one, but several reasons to go to a particular site or locality seems to be an important condition in the emergence and subsequent development of tourist destinations, and in that sense Abbotsford and locality had, as we saw earlier, quite a bit to offer.) Modern organised tourism in general, and Abbotsford in particular, was enormously facilitated by the introduction of the railway which made it possible to make brief excursions to particular places, but which also played a role in designing destinations by the mere fact of making it relatively easy to get there. In the case of Abbotsford, accessibility was greatly enhanced by the fact that several railway lines passed in the vicinity, including the so-called "Waverley line," that started in 1862, ran from the Waverley Station in Edinburgh (built in 1848), had engines called after characters in Scott's oeuvre, and stopped near Scott's old home on its way to Carlisle. Typical of this interplay between literary heritage, tourism, and the railways, is a publication like *To the Homes and Haunts of Scott and Burns by the Caledonian Railway*, written by George Eyre Todd (c.1911) and published by the railway company itself.[32]

All of this might lead one to follow John Urry (1990) in emphasizing all that is "inauthentic" about this packaging of Scott and Scotland; but it should be realised that the production of a "tourist gaze" on Scotland was not so much a radical new departure from Scott's own principles, but rather a radicalisation of the virtual "packaging" of Scotland and its history that was an essential part of his literary and architectural work, and arguably an intrinsic part of all forms of cultural remembrance. As I have argued at length elsewhere, cultural remembrance is always dependent on someone having "figured" the past in such a way that it becomes concentrated in particular sites that can be shared by different people.[33]

As the visitors' books reveal, a significant portion of the visitors to Abbotsford in the nineteenth century came from North America. These included groups from Philadelphia and Cincinnati, but also noteworthies like the defeated leader of the Confederacy Jefferson Davies, who visited in 1869, followed some years later in 1883, by the victorious Union general Ulysses S. Grant (as if to keep up the tradition, General Omar Bradley turned up in 1947).[34] In the light of what was said earlier about the relationship between mobility and remembrance sites, I would like to close this survey of Abbotsford by examining the ways in which Abbotsford as an actual site and "Abbotsford" as cultural icon functioned specifically within emigrant cultural remembrance.

That a group from Cincinnati should have visited Abbotsford in 1862 was not merely the result of the fact that the railway lines headed that way and that Abbotsford had become a well-known tourist destination. It was linked up with the role that Abbotsford played within the cultural remembrance of North America, among specific migrant groups as well as within the public culture at large. Cincinnati was, among other things, home to the oldest Caledonian Society in North America (founded in 1827) and the local loyalty to Scott had expressed itself among other things in the number of Mississippi paddle steamers registered in Cincinnati bearing "Scott" names (including several "Sir Walter Scotts" whose fictional avatar figures as a wreck in Mark Twain's *Adventures of Huckleberry Finn* [1885]).[35]

The reception of Scott within the English-speaking former-colonies is complex and fascinating, and deserves a full-length study in its own right. Suffice it within the context of the present discussion to point to the "virtual" relocation of Abbotsford in the "New world" landscape, in the names of streets, suburbs, and cities that are dotted across the maps of Canada, the United States, Australia, New Zealand and South Africa; many of these namings seem to date to the 1870s, around the centenary of Scott's birth, but some are later: witness the case of Tallahassee, Florida where a 1950s suburb has "Scott" street names, including an Abbotsford Street (see Figure 6.5).[36] While the specific use of Abbotsford in such names can often be traced back to particular individuals, often with Scottish connections, the use of "old world names" can also be seen as part of a larger-scale "importation of memories" or what I propose calling the *memorial colonisation* of the new world. Significant in this regard is the decision made by the New York authorities in 1872 to put up a statue to Sir Walter Scott in Central Park, alongside Shakespeare and Columbus.[37] As the speech made by the poet and liberal activist William Cullen Bryant on the occasion of the official unveiling revealed, Scott had been symbolically "relocated" in Central Park as a way of recalling Americans' connection with a long literary tradition, but also as a way of "peopling" the hitherto virgin ground of Manhattan with "new memories" and "old traditions." Or, to quote Bryant himself as he waxed forth in blithe Victorian neglect of pre-Columbian America:

> And now as the statue of Scott is set up in this beautiful park, which, a few years since, possessed no human associations, historical or poetic, connected with its shades, its lawns, its rocks, and its waters, *these grounds become peopled with new memories*. Henceforth the silent earth at this spot will be eloquent of old traditions, the airs that stir the branches of the trees will whisper feats of chivalry to the visitor. ... [Scott's characters] will pass in endless procession around the statue of him in whose prolific brain they had their birth, until the language we speak shall perish, and the spot upon which we stand shall be again a woodland wilderness.[38]

As this eulogy to "the author of Waverley" suggests, Scott's role in "peopling" Central Park with memories was over-determined: he was not only a sign of "literature" as such, but specifically, of a literature which was itself a memorial medium. In other words: whoever puts up a statue for Scott, or whoever inscribes or "plants" his name in other ways into the landscape, gets a whole load of history into the bargain. With the name "Scott" or its metonym "Abbotsford" comes a host of historical characters to "people" in Manhattan, Boston, Winnipeg, or wherever you may be. "Scott" and "Abbotsford" did not just travel, then, as icons of a particular writer back in Scotland, they functioned as a ready-made icon of history itself (or at least a Eurocentric version of it). Moreover, these names had

Figure 6.5 Street sign, Tallahassee, Florida, USA (© Ann Rigney).

the added advantage because of its association with a best-selling author that, while having a particular value among Scottish migrants, it was also recognisable and cherished by many different groups for whom Scott had "packaged" an identifiable and consensus-building past.[39]

In 1882 Thomas Mellon (1813–1908), founder of the Mellon Bank and patriarch of the Mellon family in Pittsburgh, retired from business and, together with his son, took what he called in his autobiography a "trip to Europe."[40] In fact, this was a return trip to the British Isles, from whence he had emigrated as a child some sixty-five years earlier. As such, it had something of the character of a pilgrimage. Within the context of the present essay, what is of interest about his trip is the way in which it is mapped around a number of memory sites, on which he expands at some length. In the course of two weeks he made a round trip from the port of Cobh in Southern Ireland via Dublin through Northern Ireland down to London and back to the port of Cobh. The high point of the whole trip was his visit to the original family home in Northern Ireland, which was tied up with his personal memories of the area and the stories he had heard within his family. He followed up his visit to his homestead (as he said, this was really 'all he cared to see of Ireland' [316]) by visiting Scotland. The focus of his time in Scotland, both in terms of the length of his description and the enthusiasm which it expresses, was his visit to the houses of two writers: that of Robert Burns near Glasgow and that of Scott at Abbotsford.

(That Mellon should identify so closely with Scotland can be explained by the fact that his Presbyterian family had descended from Scottish 'planters' who had settled in Northern Ireland in the seventeenth century).

Mellon's account shows that he identified in a deeply felt and highly personal way with the figure and writings of Burns whose humble house he sees as a copy of his own homestead in Northern Ireland (he describes the visit as a personal "pilgrimage" [Ibid.]). Having paid his tribute to Burns, he also expounds at length about his visit to Abbotsford in terms which are generally enthusiastic, but also more impersonal, evincing more of a cultural than of a personal interest. Despite the persistent rain and despite his initial sense that Scott's poetic descriptions of Melrose were in fact much more interesting than the real thing, he found the day excursion by train to Abbotsford and environs to be very much worthwhile on balance. At Abbotsford, he was initially put out by the overly-businesslike character of the reception (as he had been dismayed by the overly tidy and modern appearance of the graveyard where Burns was buried), but he ended up impressed by the sheer range of historical objects on display, which made the excursion "far more than the worth of our money and time and discomfort" (238).[41] This sense of having had cultural value for money and effort ("The labor and discomfort of the afternoon was richly repaid ...." [Ibid.]) was reinforced by his subsequent visit to Scott's grave at nearby Dryburgh Abbey, which really seemed to bring him away for the first from the modern age:

> And here lies buried the remains of Sir Walter. ... those wild ruins in this solitary domain, with nothing of the modern world in sight or hearing to disturb the repose, afford a most appropriate resting place for what is perishable of so renowned a man (330).

Having experienced this momentary encounter with "the past itself," Mellon completed the rest of his journey and, without the least trace of sentimentality headed back to the New World, leaving "bygones as bygones":

> With the prow of our great ship turned westward as the shades of evening came on, the barren lofty coasts of Ireland disappeared, and I bade it farewell forever, with a pleased feeling of satisfaction with my visit, but a consciousness that a repetition or more protracted stay would be undesirable (335).

What Mellon's itinerary suggests is a highly schematised memorial map in which various frames are embedded. His personal and familial memories, which are linked to the homestead in Northern Ireland, are subsequently linked to the broader cultural frame of "Scottishness" as exemplified by the two writers who, throughout the nineteenth century, had often been mentioned side by side.[42] But while Burns provides this migrant with a personalised link between his family traditions and public culture, Abbotsford and Scott seem to be part of a much more impersonal, indeed purely cultural frame which allows Mellon as an individual to partake of "history" as such. That an excursion to Abbotsford should work as a "port key" to history for the returning migrant is evidence of the power that "Scott" had acquired as a cultural symbol, but also of the erosion across time and space of the historical complexities with which he himself dealt in.

Abbotsford as an actual location is caught up with its representations. It is always on the move, as it were, in the virtual sense that its meaning shifts as time passes and it becomes commodified and adapted to new contexts. Having surveyed the ongoing shifts in the meanings of Abbotsford, I finish by arguing for the importance of looking at sites of memory as not just fixed locations, but as crossroads where ongoing exchanges take place between "immobile" places and mobile media of memory, between people who stay put and people who travel. It is in the course of such exchanges that we can see the ongoing production of collective memories alongside its continuous erosion.

NOTES

1. See P. Nora, 1984–92. Halbwachs, 1950, 234, also indicated that collective remembrance gravitates towards particular locations. In a forthcoming essay entitled "The Movements of Memory: Technologies and Transfers" I discuss at greater length the theoretical issues underlying the present case study.
2. Assmann, 1999, 298–399.
3. Assmann, 1999, 326 (translation AR).
4. The link between modern memory culture and "dislocation" has been recently reiterated from another point of view in Fritzsche, 2004; see also Clifford, 1997. The distinction between *milieux de mémoire* and *lieux de mémoire* is made in P. Nora, 1997.
5. The effect of mobility on contemporary funerary practices has been analysed by Hans Geser (1998), who notes that family graves in the neighbourhood of the family home are becoming a thing of the past, giving way to "portable" graves (crematory urns) and virtual gardens of remembrance which family members located in different places can access through internet.
6. Woolf, 1948.
7. In the 1850s Scott's heirs converted to Catholicism and added a chapel and other buildings to the property, but the disposition of the main house and gardens has been otherwise left largely as they were at the time of his death in 1832.
8. On the construction and design of Abbotsford, see John Frew, "Scott, Abbotsford and the Antiquaries" in Brown, 2003, 37–48.
9. The contrast between Byron's Newstead Abbey and Abbotsford was first drawn by Washington Irving (1835); it is the subject too of Stephen Bann's pioneering analysis of the semiotics of both buildings: "Byron and Scott" in Bann, 1984, 93–111.
10. MacVicar, 1833.

11. I use the notion of a "display" building here on a par with the notion of "display" text developed in Pratt, 1977, 132f.
12. On the early development of the rhetoric of museum display, see Bann, 1984, 77–92.
13. A more detailed account of the collection can be found in Hugh Cheape, Trevor Cowie and Colin Wallace, "Sir Walter Scott, The Abbotsford Collection and the National Museums of Scotland," in Brown, 2003, 49–89.
14. For a catalogue of the Library in Abbotsford, see Cochrane, 1838.
15. For an excellent account of the many aspects of the building of Abbotsford, see Iain G. Brown, "Scott, Literature and Abbotsford" in Brown, 2003, 4–36. For the phrase '*Waverley* in stone' see ibid., 5. Crockett, 1905, is more hagiographic, but gives a good overview of the contents of the house.
16. *Waverley* (1814), the bestselling work which marked Scott's breakthrough as a novelist, was conceived in 1805 alongside Scott's other activities as antiquarian and poet; see Rigney, 2001, 168.
17. Letters 14–15 March 1822, 27 March 1822; 14 November 1822; quoted in Brown, 2003, 18.
18. See Scott, 2004. This work, left unfinished at Scott's death, was recently published for the first time, with a scholarly introduction by David Hewitt.
19. The link between the financial burden of Abbotsford and Scott's prodigious literary output has been made by among others Brown, 2003, 16–17.
20. See Jeanne Cannizzo, "'He was a Gentleman even to his Dogs': Portraits of Scott and his Canine Companions" in Brown, 2003, 115–35.
21. P. Nora, 1997, 1:38.
22. See Rigney, 2005, on the way in which memory sites become points of convergence.
23. Crockett, 1905, 44.
24. Johnson, 1970, vol. 2, 1249; also recalled in Brown, 2003, xiii.
25. Visual representations of Scott's home were also supplemented on occasion by dramatic portrayals of "the author of Waverley" c.q. "the laird of Abbotsford"; these included a funerary masque set in Abbotsford called the *Vision of the Bard*, written in 1832 by S. Knowles, and a radio play by W.E. Gunn dealing with his financial difficulties called *Scott's folly* (broadcast 21 September 1935). The name "Abbotsford" was also disseminated through publishing spin-offs like the *Abbotsford series of the Scottish Poets*, edited by J.E. Todd (1891) and the *Abbotsford Song Book: A Collection of Songs for Two Voices* (1901).
26. Scott, 1998, 13, 15.
27. In Durie, 1992, 43. As an example of an early "guide to" Abbotsford, see Lizars and Morton's illustrated *Abbotsford: The Seat of Sir Walter Scott, Bart* (1832).
28. Figures in Durie, 1992. That the power of Abbotsford as a memory site has been eroded became very evident to the present writer on a trip to Edinburgh in January 2005: requests for directions to Abbotsford drew blank looks from the local staff members at an Edinburgh hotel, one of whom surmised, in an effort to be helpful: "Abbotsford, isn't that the new centre for computer research?" *Sic transit gloria mundi.*
29. For the following details of the development of Abbotsford as a tourist site I am indebted to Durie, 1992, and Crockett, 1905.
30. This pattern of visits by "secondary" royalty continued into the twentieth century; the scrapbooks of newspaper cuttings in the Corson collection in Edinburgh University Library reveal a steady flow of such visitors throughout the century; my thanks to Paul Barnaby for permission to consult these scrapbooks.

31. For the general background to the rise of organised tourism in Scotland, see Brendon, 1991, Buzard, 1993, Glendening, 1997.
32. On the "Waverley route" see Siviter, 1988.
33. Rigney, 2005.
34. Durie, 1992, 50–51; the visit by General Bradley is recorded in a newspaper clipping from 9 October 1947 (Corson collection).
35. Mitchell, 1975, includes various ships registered in Cincinnati called "Walter Scott" including one built in 1829 and snagged near New Orleans in 1838.
36. See for example, the City of Abbotsford in Wisconsin (USA), and British Columbia (Canada); the suburbs of Abbotsford in Melbourne (Australia), Dunedin (New Zealand); the Abbotsford streets in Johannesburg (South Africa), Winnipeg (Canada), Larimer County (Colorado, USA), Boston (Massachusetts, USA), Hamilton (New Zealand), Leederville (Western Australia).
37. Shakespeare, Scott, and Columbus were later joined by Robert Burns in 1880 [see note 32] and by the American poet Fitzgreene Halleck (1790–1867), the latter illustrating the principle that monumentalisation is no guarantee of lasting literary fame.
38. Bryant, 1873; italics AR.
39. See Rigney, 2001, 27–38, on the tendency of Scott's narratives to work towards consensus-building, in which past conflicts are recognised and, at the same time, overcome.
40. Mellon, 1994; all further references in the text. I am grateful to Dr. Brian Lambkin, Director of the Centre for Migration Studies at the Ulster-American Folk Park, for drawing my attention to this autobiographical account.
41. Mellon himself makes some businesslike observations in passing on the difference between the American and the European approaches to monuments, noting that Europeans are ready to wait long enough for historical buildings to become so interesting that people will pay to see them, whereas Americans tidy up their ruins and replace them by buildings that will be immediately useful; see Mellon, 1994, 325–26.
42. On the relationship and rivalry between Burns and Scott within the Scottish diaspora, see Brown, 1984.

7   Myth and Memory
Reading the Brontë Parsonage

Christine Alexander

The Brontë Parsonage is probably the best-known literary shrine in Britain, apart from houses associated with Shakespeare and perhaps Jane Austen's house at Chawton. Each year some 100,000 national and international visitors pay homage at the home of the Brontës. What is enshrined here is the myth of three famous writing sisters—symbols of adversity and endurance, isolated in a stone house standing on the edge of the windswept Yorkshire moors. The story of their struggle as Victorian women to become writers, to earn their own living and to express their unconventional views, led to their identification with the heroines of their novels. They were conflated with the unhappy orphan Jane Eyre and the wild Catherine Earnshaw roaming the moors; this is still essentially the image of the writers that tourists bring with them when they visit Haworth parsonage for the first time. Like all myths, that of the Brontës involves a simplified view and is easy to manipulate; the house is always isolated, always on the edge of the windswept moor, always surrounded by death and always seen from the outside.

The first part of this chapter explores the way the writers' house and the cultural practices that have grown up around it have played a central role in this simplified, partial narrative that is the Brontë myth. The second part of the chapter suggests that there is a significant lacuna in the Brontë story that has consciously and unconsciously been suppressed because it does not fit with the meta-narrative of the myth. This disparity is the result of the way the house has been used in the construction of memory and involves the perspective from which the house is viewed. The myth of the Brontës is based on an exterior, simplified view of the house, and this needs to be balanced by a view from inside which requires more complex observation and a more nuanced response to the notion of interiority. For this we need to focus on the early writings of the Brontës and to read more carefully the variety of objects that define the interior life of the parsonage. This alternative memory—fragmentary and partly obscured—is still in the process of being recovered. It indicates, however, that the Brontë Parsonage functioned as a material frame necessary for the production of literature: a space that helped define the inner selves of its writing inhabitants and that became a necessary part of their creative life.

The construction of the house as part of the Brontë myth can be tracked through visual and literary documents of the decade following the death of Charlotte Brontë in 1855, at the age of thirty-eight. There is only one contemporary sketch of the outside of the house and a number of early photographs mostly taken around 1860. Together with illustrations to early editions of the novels they confirm the descriptions in obituaries and visitors' memoirs of the desolate house, exposed not only to the vicissitudes of nature but marooned at the edge of an uncouth, isolated village. Harriet Martineau's obituary of Charlotte Brontë in the *Daily News* (6 April 1855) set the tone, describing the "utter ... seclusion" and "dreary wilds" in which Charlotte lived:

> that forlorn house, planted in the very clay of the churchyard, where the graves of her sisters were before her window; in such a living sepulchre her mind could not but prey upon itself; and how it did suffer, we see in the more painful portions of her last novel—*Villette*.[1]

The Brontë myth perpetuates the bleak aspect of the outside of the house and the predominance of the graveyard. The house stands at the highest point in the village beyond the church, and in 1820 when the Brontës arrived it was on the outskirts of Haworth. Curiously, the impression that still remains uppermost in the minds of visitors today—despite the modern houses and busy car park that now border the parsonage—is this same early view of the "forlorn house" and "dreary wilds". Table 7.1 compiled from a questionnaire made in 1983 (one that has been confirmed by a similar recent survey on 16 November 2006)[2] clearly shows that the Brontë novels and writings about the Brontës still primarily condition memories of literary place. Table 7.2 demonstrates that the most common epithets

Table 7.1 The Importance of Different Sources in Forming the Expectations of Haworth Village and Area before Actual Encounter (N = 37)

	Very important	Important	Quite important	Not much	No importance
Brontës' writings	27	7	2	0	1
Articles about the Brontës	13	12	7	3	2
TV or films on Brontës or their work	9	12	8	4	4
Tourist leaflets/brochures	2	6	9	10	10
Guide or travel books	3	5	5	13	11

Table 7.2 Expectations of Haworth before Initial Encounter (N = 37)

Descriptor (≥2 mentions)	Number of respondents mentioning
Bleak	14
Isolated/remote	14
Windswept/wild	13
Gloomy/sombre	8
Small	6
Desolate	5
Brooding/intense	5
Hilly/rolling	4
Cobbled	4
Unchanged by time	4
Stone-built	2
Quiet	2

denoting expectation are "isolated", "bleak", "windswept" and "wild", characteristics that apply more to such narratives than to the present-day house. TV and films are increasingly important, as were the very first photographs made just after the Brontës' deaths and used in biographies and as early tourist postcards.

An early photograph of the parsonage (see Figure 7.1) taken before 1861 (when the church was rebuilt over the one the Brontës were buried in) is designed to show this desolate scene rather than the thriving community out of frame to the right and hidden behind the church. It was this view that Mrs Gaskell romanticised in her notoriously inaccurate but picturesque sketch for her *Life of Charlotte Brontë*, published in 1857 (see Figure 7.2). In this illustration you can just see the stone wall that separates the small parsonage garden from the graveyard, but this has been rebuilt several times and it is impossible to tell how high it was during the Brontë's lifetime or whether there ever was the legendary "gate of the dead",[3] giving access to the churchyard and through which the Brontë coffins were carried to the vault in the church. Gaskell rearranges the moors into looming hills to reinforce her powerful description of the "monotonous and illimitable barrier"[4] of the surrounding landscape. She emphasises the "square unsheltered house", an isolated dwelling subject to the same wild storms of wind and rain that we find in *Wuthering Heights*. She stresses that the parsonage, like the village itself, is difficult to get to: the flag-stones that pave the steep narrow road up the hill between old stone houses to the church and parsonage at the top have been deliberately placed endways "in order to give a better hold to the horses' feet; and, even with this help, they seem to

Figure 7.1 Early photo of the Brontë Parsonage with original church, before 1861 (Courtesy of the Brontë Society).

be in constant danger of slipping backwards."[5] The visitor must struggle just as the Brontës themselves struggled in life.

However, there is clear evidence that by the time of Charlotte's death Haworth was actually a large and busy manufacturing community important to the wool trade of the district; the church, close to the parsonage, was the social centre of the area, and the priest's family would have been prominent in this society.[6] Haworth was also a place of considerable cultural activity as the Brontës' early writings attest. The children had a rich intellectual life—they took music and drawing lessons, read the latest newspapers and journals, were familiar with writers like Milton, Byron and Scott, and even attended local lectures at the Keighley Mechanics'

Figure 7.2 Elizabeth Gaskell's sketch for *Life of Charlotte Brontë*, 1857.

Institute. Gaskell was astonished to read the thirteen-year-old Charlotte's knowledgeable list of the great Italian and Flemish masters whose works she wished to see.[7] Yet (as I've shown elsewhere)[8] Gaskell purposely avoided the rich imaginative life she glimpsed in Charlotte's "wild weird writing"[9] and with the novelist's licence she constructed instead—both visually and verbally—a setting calculated to enhance the tragedy of her deprived heroine.

Gaskell's three-quarter view of the house from the graveyard became the classic scene, endlessly reproduced by artists and photographers to this day. The engraving by E. M. Wimperis for the first illustrated edition of *The Life and Works of Charlotte Brontë and her Sisters* (1872–73) (see Figure 7.3), illustrates the parsonage at dusk amid gravestones and lit by a half-shrouded moon, again a deliberate romanticisation of the scene. A number of early artists' impressions were based on Wimperis's engraving, and further embellished with the house shrouded in mist and the image of death emphasised by the inclusion of tools ready to dig a new grave.[10] A typical photograph taken about three years after Gaskell's biography reproduces the same scene (Figure 7.4; c. 1860–61),[11] this time populated possibly with early tourists. Until recently the figure in the background was thought to be Charlotte herself. She was the sister who lived to experience her fame, at least for a brief period, and following Gaskell's biography she was the sister who was revered by critics and tourists throughout the late nineteenth and first half of the twentieth centuries. It was also her

Figure 7.3 Engraving by E. M. Wimperis for the first illustrated edition of *The Life and Works of Charlotte Brontë and her Sisters* (1872–73).

Figure 7.4 Unsigned photograph of House and tourists, c. summer 1860–61 (Courtesy of the Brontë Society).

public comments in defence of the perceived uncouthness of her sisters' writings that fed Gaskell's grim view of her subject's childhood. Gaskell met Charlotte only in her last years when her attitude to life was coloured by suffering. Charlotte had told Gaskell that she believed some people were appointed beforehand to sorrow and much disappointment and that it was well for those who had rougher paths to perceive that it was God's will and therefore moderate their expectations, abandon hope and cultivate patience and resignation: she said "she was trying to school herself against ever anticipating any pleasure."[12] Public statements like this about her home and family obliterated any memory of a happy writing childhood and prevented subsequent readers from obtaining a more complex view of her life. Thus Gaskell touches on the Brontë's childhood in the parsonage, but she also devotes many pages to the deprivations and tragic experience of the little Brontës away from home at the Clergy Daughter's School—the model for Lowood in *Jane Eyre*—as more in keeping with the novelist's theme of Christian struggle and endurance. Charlotte as orphan child and resigned woman became the object of hagiography.

Photographs like Figure 7.4 were marketed to early tourists in search of relics of Charlotte. The local stationer John Greenwood also sold notepaper with the same view titled *The Home of Charlotte Brontë*. One enterprising American tourist, Charles Hale, used this paper to proudly record his plunder of "some very good memorials"[13] of glass from Charlotte's bedroom window and some moulded timber from her room with which he intended to frame his Brontë photographs. Charlotte's elderly father had just died, her husband had moved to Ireland, and the new incumbent had not yet taken up residence: we might call this a window of opportunity. Such souveniring is a vivid image of the need to fix and objectify memory. In the letter to his mother, Hale states: "we shall look at [the photographs] through the same medium through which Charlotte Brontë saw the dreary landscape before her window and they will be surrounded with the wood that was about her as she sat there."

One of the images on sale at the time of Hale's visit was an ambrotype (c. 1855–59),[14] taken directly from the front and showing clearly the original building before subsequent additions: a small Georgian structure of grey stone, built about 1778–79 and featuring the typical simplicity and symmetry of the period. The central doorway in the front (embellished with pilasters and pediment) has two long sash windows on each side and five similar windows on the floor above beneath the heavy stone-flagged roof, built to resist the wind. There are four rooms downstairs and five upstairs. Downstairs Mr Brontë's study is situated to the right of the door and, across the hall, the family dining room used also as a sitting room by the Brontë sisters.[15] Behind these were an inner kitchen and a storeroom.[16] On the upper floor there were four bedrooms (including one for the servants)[17] and a tiny room over the passageway in the front, known variously as the children's nursery or children's study. During the Brontës' time, a large back kitchen used for washing jutted out from the rear of the house, and in the backyard was a well, a two-seater privy, and a building used as a peat-store. In 1872, after the Brontës had died, the Revd John Wade added a gable wing to the north of the house, seen in an 1879 photo which also shows the location of a barn that no longer exists (see Figure 7.5). The barn has been replaced by

Figure 7.5 Photograph 1879, showing Wade extension (1872) and barn (Courtesy of the Brontë Society).

the large car park and modern houses now extend beyond the parsonage towards the moors.

In 1928 the house was bought by Sir James Roberts and presented to the Brontë Society for use as a museum. The Wade extension was eventually converted into a library downstairs and an exhibition space upstairs, and further extensions were added later to the rear of the building to accommodate museum administration and a shop. These additions now block any view of the moors previously seen by the Brontës from the back or south side of the house. Views from the front are now dominated by tall trees planted in the graveyard in 1864 to disperse the overcrowded and "pestiferous" corpses.[18] The overwhelming impression is no longer one of isolation and expanse but of enclosure and the dominance of the graveyard, "terribly full of upright tombstones" as Mrs Gaskell had said.[19] Figure 7.6, typical of illustrations reproduced nowadays, depicts the same "popular" image symbolising the tragic lives of the Brontës.

Visitors have always come to Haworth with these "popular" expectations of the house: imagined "memories" derived from the novels and stories of the lives. Even Gaskell, who had visited while Charlotte was alive in September 1853, was gratified to find that the "lead-coloured" day helped to confirm the gloomy impressions she had conceived of the place.[20] When Virginia Woolf visited in 1904, she encountered a snowstorm, but decided that if she waited for fine weather for the sake of comfort she would be "rubbing out half the shadows in the picture" she had imagined.[21] From her

Figure 7.6 Modern picture of Parsonage (© The Brontë Society).

reading of Gaskell she "understood that the sun very seldom shone on the Brontë family." Even those who never made it to Haworth but who wrote of the parsonage and its inhabitants were sure that the sisters' final resting place would replicate the poetic ending of *Wuthering Heights*, where the characters are buried as near as possible to the wild moors. After he had written his poem "Haworth Churchyard", Matthew Arnold was annoyed to find that the sisters were not buried "In the dark fermentation of earth" as he had imagined, but inside the church, "the wrong, uncongenial spot" for writers he had located in the Romantic tradition.[22] Reality did not conform to the Brontë myth.

After the establishment of the Brontë Parsonage Museum by the local Brontë Society, the house became central to the anchoring of Brontë myth, confirming Maurice Halbwachs' assertion that cultural memory tends towards spatialization.[23] The original aim of the Brontë Society was "to acquire literary, artistic and family memorials of the Brontës" and "to place the same at Haworth … for public examination."[24] Thus myth and memory become materialised in a particular location that can be visited in the here and now, as in the case of Abbotsford, home of the Brontës' literary hero Sir Walter Scott (see chapter 6 in this volume). Yet given the emphasis on material relics, it is remarkable how few records there are of the interior of the house. Visitors comment on particular objects but they are usually those that emphasise the tragic myth and that, again, were first evoked and memorialised by Gaskell: the four-poster bed (see Figure 7.7)

Figure 7.7 Mr Brontë's bedroom with reproduction of Branwell's four-poster bed (© The Brontë Society).

Figure 7.8 Sitting room with sofa and dining table (© The Brontë Society).

that represents the agonised death of the brother Branwell, so vividly seen in his own final tortured sketch;[25] the sofa on which Emily Brontë spent her final hours, refusing to take to her bed; and the dining-room table (see Figure 7.8). They are each powerful symbolic objects that reinforce the Brontë myth of tragedy. Gaskell had recorded the habit of the three sisters walking round the table each evening, discussing the progress of their novels, their projects and plans for life. She had heard from Martha, the servant, how "Miss Emily walked as long as she could; and when she died Miss Anne and Miss Brontë took it up—and now my heart aches to hear Miss Brontë walking, walking, on alone."[26] Gaskell poignantly adds: "I am sure I should fancy I heard the steps of the dead following me." Again there is the overwhelming memory of adversity that raises ghosts and that has sunk deep into the collective consciousness of Brontë readers.

But there is a different story to be told about the interior of the house— one that does not fit so neatly with the Brontë myth. The remainder of this chapter will be devoted to resurrecting the memory of the Brontë childhood through a new focus on the interior of the house and what it meant for this family of writers. I argue that the space of particular rooms moulded the interior lives of the young writers who inhabited them, and that the association of this space with the imaginative act of composition can be seen as an example of what Bachelard referred to as a "poetics of space".[27]

My focus is on the most physically insignificant of the parsonage rooms: the children's study (see Figure 7.9). It is here that the young Brontës first played with their famous wooden toy soldiers, several of which were found

Figure 7.9 "The Children's Study": bedroom and nursery, arranged in its later role as Emily Brontë's bedroom (© The Brontë Society).

years later under the floor boards; and it is here that they first made their little hand-sewn books that record the imaginative life that took place in this room. Faint sketches on its walls still bear witness to the characters the children created there, based originally on the twelve toy soldiers belonging to Branwell. The miniature books (see Figure 7.10) produced here record their childhood plays, the elaborate sagas of Glass Town, Gondal and Angria, stories of exploration and settlement, of love and war, of Byronic heroes and heroines, and of an imaginary literary society where the young writers could take control of their lives. Their output was prolific: Charlotte's early writing was greater in quantity than all her novels put together.[28] The secret world of juvenilia recorded in script too small for adult eyes allowed not only an authorial apprenticeship but also an uninhibited development of self. This fixing of a writing identity began in this room before extending to other parts of the house, such as the kitchen and sitting room. Virtually no attention has been paid to this material space of

Figure 7.10 Miniature handsewn books of Brontë juvenilia (© The Brontë Society).

writing, yet—sparsely furnished as it was—it entered the consciousness of its inhabitants to such an extent that for the young Charlotte and Emily in particular it was impossible to write a coherent narrative away from the house.

The small children's study (now only 9ft. × 5 ft.) was the girls' first bedroom and playroom for all the children; later it was Emily's bedroom. It originally had no chest of drawers and probably contained several small beds. In 1850, Charlotte enlarged the main bedroom at the expense of this little room. So visitors nowadays, unaware of this change, marvel at the narrow cupboard-like space where five small children read and wrote newspapers and journals in a hive of activity. The altered size dramatises the early accounts of the children huddling together and speaking softly while their mother was dying. But the room was larger than it is now and occupied a happier central place in the writing life of its inhabitants. Both visually and verbally it is represented in the earliest manuscript stories and poems, in the Brontës' own drawings and paintings, and even in the later novels of this family of writers.

On the first page of the earliest extant Brontë manuscript the ten-year-old Charlotte has drawn a house, ostensibly the birthplace of her youngest sister Anne for whom the story is written; but probably modelled on the parsonage itself.[29] Apart from this, there are no sketches of the outside of the house by the Brontës themselves, yet there are several by Emily recording her writing activities inside the house—an indication of the creative significance of this interior space to her writing life. The diary paper of 26 June 1837, jointly signed by Emily and Anne,[30] is illustrated by a sketch showing the sisters composing the manuscript—books, papers, and the "Tin Box" in which the diary papers are kept, are labelled and placed strategically on the table. There is a strong sense of spatial arrangement here in the act of writing. Emily's diary paper, written almost ten years later (30 July 1845; see Figure 7.11), shows the same visual awareness of her position, seated on the still-extant three-legged stool in her bedroom (formerly the tiny children's study), writing with her portable desk on her lap and surrounded by the dogs Keeper and Flossy, and the cat.

The written text of these autobiographical fragments reveals the way imaginative life is an integral part of everyday physical experience of the home: "papa opened the parlour Door and gave Branwell a Letter saying here Branwell read this and show it to your Aunt and Charlott—The Gondals are discovering the interior of Gaaldine Sally mosley is washing in the back-Kitchen."[31] This quotation is from the earliest diary paper, written in the kitchen, where Charlotte is boasting about her apple puddings and the servant Tabby is urging Anne to "pilloputate" (i.e. "peel a potato" in Yorkshire dialect). There is a lively, happy atmosphere where words jostle with boiled beef, piano lessons and household chores. Amidst the family activity the fictional Gondals are exploring Gaaldine, a tropical island in the south Pacific. In her book *The Sense of an Interior*, Diana Fuss reminds us that "the theatre of composition is not an empty space but a place animated by the artefacts, mementos, books and furniture that frame any

Figure 7.11 Detail from Emily Brontë's diary paper, 30 July 1845.

intellectual labour."[32] For the young Brontës "the theatre of composition" was also a place animated by shared experience and collaborative writing. The physical dimensions of that space, the furniture and artefacts were scant to say the least, but the imaginative horizons that that space released were vast.

The best-known literary representation of Haworth parsonage as repository of a memory of security, friendship and creative energy is Moor House in *Jane Eyre*. Here the heroine Jane finds shelter in a fire-lit kitchen like that of the parsonage. The two sisters of the Rivers' family resemble Emily and Anne Brontë, in both their natures and collaborative intellectual pursuits. They love their secluded home and the surrounding moors, and are unhappy about leaving to become governesses and earn their own living. Jane is at home here with the like-minded nurturing sisters, and it is no coincidence that she eventually discovers they are part of her own family. She at last has a home of her own, not unlike that of her author.

Jane Eyre's search for an identity and home has its prototype in the experience of Elizabeth Hastings, one of Charlotte's early heroines. Elizabeth Hastings longs for her home town of Howard (the fictitious name for Haworth in the juvenilia) and its surrounding hills:

> Sometimes when she was alone in the evenings, walking through her handsome drawing-room by twilight, she would think of home and long for Home till she cried passionately at the conviction that she should see it no more. So wild was her longing that when she looked out on the dusky sky, between the curtains of her bay-window, fancy seemed to trace on the horizon the blue outline of the moors, just as seen from the parlour at Colne-moss. The evening star hung above the brow of Boulshill, the farm-fields stretched away between, and when reality returned—houses, lamps, and streets—she was phrenzied.[33]

Elizabeth Hastings even paces to and fro the length of the parlour, her expression "fixed & dreamy" and her mind excited by "feverish Dreams", just as the Brontë sisters paced up and down the sitting room at home "like restless wild animals",[34] lost in thought or in excited discussion of their latest stories.

The parsonage and the Haworth landscape are transposed into many of the juvenilia stories: they always have the same talismanic effect for her heroines as they had for Charlotte herself. Space and place were essential for her creativity. The memory of the parsonage could unlock her imaginative storehouse and unleash Angrian visions, but without the four walls of the house surrounding her she could write nothing more than fragments. Her Roe Head Journal,[35] six semi-autobiographical manuscripts composed away from home during the two years she was a teacher at Roe Head School (1836–37), records the agony of imaginative dislocation. In moments snatched from her busy routine—what she called "this wretched bondage"—she records her unsuccessful efforts to write. She suffered depression and "weeks of mental and bodily anguish"[36] so that the doctor advised her to return home if she valued her life. These fragmentary manuscripts reveal the vital relationship between memory and imagination, and the workings of the creative process.

> There is a voice,[37] there is an impulse that wakens up that dormant power, which in its torpidity I sometimes think dead. That wind, pouring in impetuous current through the air, sounding wildly, unremittingly from hour to hour, deepening its tone as the night advances, coming not in gusts, but with a rapid gathering stormy swell. That wind I know is heard at this moment far away on the moors at Haworth. Branwell and Emily hear it, and as it sweeps over our house, down the churchyard and round the old church, they think perhaps of me and Anne.[38]

Here Charlotte positively welcomes the wind and storm that Gaskell found so threatening and isolating. The sound of the wind triggers the memory of home and ushers in the imaginary world of Glass Town and Angria.

Away from home, Charlotte tries to maintain her sanity by actively remembering, first her home and then the collaborative writing it nurtures. She cannot write at Roe Head but she can remember, and this in itself is comforting. She records how she deliberately sits down "for the purpose of calling up spirits from the vasty deep and holding half an hour's converse with them."[39] If she is lucky and not interrupted by a pupil—an incident that makes her feel physically sick—she receives "a knock at the gates of thought and Memory ushers in the [Angrian] visitors." The value of remembrance can hardly be overstated for the author:

> How few would believe that from sources purely imaginary such happiness could be derived. Pen cannot pourtray the deep interest of the scenes, of the untimed trains of events, I have witnessed in that little room with the low, narrow bed and bare, white-washed walls, twenty miles away. What a treasure is thought! What a privilege is reverie. ... Remembrance yields up many a fragment of past twilight hours spent in that little, unfurnished room. There have I sat on the low bedstead, my eyes fixed on the window....
>
> Such was the picture that threw its reflection upon my eye, but communicated no impression to my heart. The mind knew but did not feel its existence. It was away. It had launched on a distant voyage. Haply it was nearing the shores of some far and unknown island, under whose cliffs no bark had ever before cast anchor. In other words, a long tale was perhaps then evolving itself in my mind, the history of an ancient and aristocratic family—the legendary records of its origin not preserved in writing, but delivered from the lips of old retainers, floating

in tradition up and down the woods and vales of the earldom or dukedom or barony.

Charlotte begins to develop her vision, to fix on particular characters, but
cannot "make out" her story; in all six fragments of the Roe Head Journal,
her creativity is disrupted and her writing ends abruptly.

At home, the remembering would lead to composition, since for Charlotte her childhood house incorporates those "images of protected inti-
macy"[40] that Bachelard speaks of. It contains those intimate values of inside
space that trigger memory: "We must go beyond the problems of description ... in order to attain to the primary virtues, those that reveal an attachment that is native in some way to the primary function of inhabiting." In
the case of the Brontës, their "little books"—the vast imaginative world of
Glass Town and Angria—hold the key to this "primary function of inhabiting", to the way the writers experienced their home. In other words, the
Brontë juvenilia allow us to begin reading the soul of the writers' house:
that inner space that was instrumental in their creative activity.

The Brontë Parsonage has always been remembered in terms of the adult
writers, the myth of three famous sisters as symbols of adversity and endurance. Its associations are pre-eminently those of isolation, sorrow and
death, reinforced by the crowded tombstones that dominate the graveyard
on two sides of the small parsonage garden. Yet the traces of an alternative happy, industrious and creative childhood lie dormant, attended to by
only a few and waiting to be resurrected. The little books and the early
manuscripts of the Brontë juvenilia indicate the way the children experienced their home not only physically but virtually, by means of thought and
dreams. We have seen how Charlotte—away from her home—recalls it in
flashes of daydream that illuminate the remote region where memory and
imagination are associated. Without this integrative process she cannot
write. If Bachelard is right, it is chiefly "Through [such poetic imagination],
perhaps more than recollections, [that] we touch the ultimate poetic depth
of the space of the house."[41] The Brontë parsonage, far from being the place
of cultural, social and material deprivation projected in the popular myth,
was the richest place on earth to Charlotte, the writer, and to her sisters.

NOTES

1. Allot, 1974, 304.
2. Another survey in D. Pocock, 1987. My recent questionnaire conducted at the
   Brontë Parsonage on 16 November 2006, with the same criteria and similar
   numbers of respondents, confirms these findings.
3. Barker, 1994, 853, n. 36, argues that the gate may never have existed but also
   points out that evidence is inconclusive.
4. Gaskell, 1857, vol. 1, 4.
5. Gaskell, 1857, vol. 2, 297.

6. Alexander and Smith, 2003, 235–37. Even by 1820 when the Brontës arrived in Haworth, there were eighteen small textile mills, and by 1850 over 2,000 people were employed in the spinning and weaving industry.
7. Gaskell, 1857, vol. 1, 91.
8. Alexander, 2004.
9. Gaskell, 1857, vol. 1, 93.
10. Unsigned photograph and prints in the Brontë Parsonage Museum.
11. Unsigned photograph, c. summer 1860–61, in the Brontë Parsonage Museum.
12. Gaskell, 1857, vol. 1, 302–03.
13. Lemon, 1996, 81. The first page of the letter, with the letterhead illustration and date 11 November 1861, appears on p. 80.
14. Illustrated in Alexander and Smith, 2003, 239.
15. This room was enlarged in 1850–51 when substantial alterations were made to the house including moving the interior wall of the sitting room into the hall: Kellett, 1977, 41–44.
16. Altered in 1854 to become a study for Charlotte Brontë's husband, the Revd Arthur Bell Nicholls.
17. When Mrs Brontë died in 1821, the main bedroom at the left front of the house became her sister Elizabeth Branwell's room and Mr Brontë moved to the bedroom above his study. The bedroom behind this is thought to have been used by Branwell as a studio while he was training to be a portrait painter.
18. The adjective is Mrs Gaskell's, used in a letter to a friend: Smith, 1995–2004, vol. 3, 196. Some 44,000 burials are said to have occurred in the Haworth churchyard. Mr Brontë was active in its closure in 1856 and a new graveyard was opened some distance away.
19. Gaskell, 1857, vol. 1, 6.
20. Chapple and Pollard, 1966, 248.
21. Lemon, 1996, 125.
22. Allott, 1974, 306–10. "Haworth Churchyard" was first published in *Fraser's Magazine*, May 1855, 527–30. Arnold did visit Haworth in his role as school inspector but he appears not to have visited the church or churchyard and his reference to "the desolate house" may be simply poetic "memory".
23. Halbwachs, 1992.
24. Lemon, 1993, 4. Haworth Parsonage became the Brontë Museum in 1928; until this time the Brontë Society (founded in 1893) used a small room above the Yorkshire Penny Bank in Haworth as a museum.
25. Alexander and Sellars, 1995, 362–63.
26. Chapple and Pollard, 1966, 247.
27. Bachelard, 1994.
28. See Introductions to Alexander, 1987–2006.
29. Alexander, 1987, vol. 1, 3; the illustration is reproduced in Alexander and Sellars, 1995, 154.
30. Composed by both sisters but written by the eighteen-year-old Emily: discussed and illustrated in Alexander and Sellars, 1995, 377–78.
31. 24 November 1834, the first of the diary papers signed by Emily and Anne: published in Ratchford, 1955, appendix 2. For further information on the Diary Papers see Alexander and Smith, 2003, 163–66.
32. Fuss, 2004, 1.
33. Extract in Ch. Brontë, 2001, 424.
34. Gaskell, 1857, vol. 1, 209.
35. Alexander, 2001, includes the complete text of the Roe Head Journal.

36. Smith, 1995–2004, vol. 1, 178.
37. A Biblical reference: I Kings.19:11–12; here the "still small voice" heralds memory.
38. Roe Head Journal, in Ch. Brontë, 2001, 407. When Charlotte was employed as assistant teacher at Roe Head in July 1835, her wages were in exchange for her sister Emily's schooling. The following October, Anne Brontë replaced Emily, who was extremely homesick and unable to endure even the relatively relaxed routine of Miss Wooler's school.
39. Ibid., 409.
40. Bachelard, 1994, 3.
41. Ibid., 6.

8 Memory Regained
Founding and Funding the Keats-Shelley Memorial House in Rome

Catherine Payling

That John Keats died in 1821 in a Roman lodging house at Piazza di Spagna 26, unrecognised save by a few passionately believing and loyal friends, is well known, if only because of the early age at which he died and his supposed death at the hands of the reviewers of his work.[1] Although a first collected edition of his poems—with those of Coleridge and Shelley—was published as early as 1829 by Galignani in Paris,[2] it was not until the Victorian age, and the publication of Richard Monckton Milnes's first official biography in 1848, that Keats's poetry began to attract serious attention.[3] Tennyson and Browning were great admirers of Keats's work, and the Pre-Raphaelite painters ranked him with Dante, Chaucer and Goethe (also known for his stay in Rome, in a house just a few blocks away from Piazza di Spagna). By the end of the nineteenth century, both Keats and Shelley had become acclaimed literary figures, their writings as popular as those of their great contemporary, Lord Byron, who had died of fever in April 1824, aged thirty-six, while fighting for the cause of the Greeks at Missolonghi.

As the reputations of these romantic poets grew there was a demand for posthumous editions of their works, both in Europe and in the United States. "The many editions already published of Keats's works have sufficiently attested his popularity," claimed a New York edition of 1846, adding that: "His reputation has been continually advancing since the period of his lamented death."[4] Friends were asked to write their memoirs and items associated with them became prized relics. After their deaths, anything that related to Keats, Shelley and Byron was carefully preserved, first by family and friends, and later by fervent admirers: locks of hair, childhood possessions, items of furniture, books, letters, poetic manuscripts. More than just keepsakes, they were held almost as sacred religious objects (see Figure 8.1).

Shelley's charred remains were kept after his cremation and later given away piecemeal to a favoured few. Other Shelley relics, however, were jealously guarded by his family. His surviving son, Sir Percy Florence, and Sir Percy's wife, Lady Jane Shelley, created a Shelley "sanctuary" at their home, Boscombe Manor, near Bournemouth. There Amelia Curran's portrait of Shelley hung above precious relics: a miniature of the poet as a little

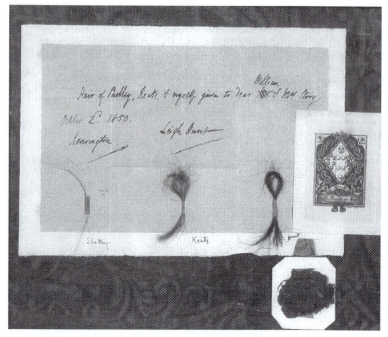

Figure 8.1 Locks of hair of Percy Bysshe Shelley, John Keats and Leigh Hunt (© Keats-Shelley House, Rome).

boy, manuscripts and poems, reliquaries, his rattle, his guitar, and locks of hair. Kept in a silk-lined box was the most sacred object of all: Shelley's heart. The domed ceiling was decorated with stars, and a red lamp burned perpetually.

Keats's manuscripts, including his marvellous letters, were so highly prized that they were sometimes cut into stripes and distributed to friends. Fanny Brawne's son put the majority of Keats's love letters to his mother up for auction in 1888, prompting Oscar Wilde's sonnet "On the Sale by Auction of Keats's Love Letters," written in protest:

> These are the letters which Endymion wrote
> to one he loved in secret, and apart,
> and now the brawlers of the auction mart
> bargain and bid for each poor blotted note,
> Ay! for each separate pulse of passion quote
> the latest price. —I think the love not art
> who break the crystal of a poet's heart
> that small and sickly eyes may glare and gloat.

When in 1877 he came to Rome, Wilde visited Keats's grave in the "Cimitero Acattolico" (Non-Catholic Cemetery) on the same day that he had been granted an audience with Pope Pius IX. Prostrating himself on the grass in front of it for half an hour, he declared it "the holiest place in Rome," and was inspired to write sonnets on the graves of both Keats and Shelley. The sonnet on Shelley beautifully conjures up the atmosphere of the place where his ashes lie:

> Like burnt-out torches by a sick man's bed
> Gaunt cypress-trees stand round the sun-bleached stone;
> Here doth the little night-owl make her throne
> And the slight lizard show his jewelled head.

Thomas Hardy, visiting Keats's grave ten years later, was moved to write a poem on the Pyramid of Cestius and the nearby graves where "two immortal shades abide."

In Rome the Cimitero Acattolico increasingly had become a place of pilgrimage. The American N.P. Willis, visiting it in 1833, could truthfully say: "Every reader knows his history and the cause of his death .... Keats was no doubt a poet of very uncommon promise."[5] From very early on it was American devotion and generosity that ensured the upkeep of the grave. There were also many European pilgrims—in 1838 Auguste Barbier wrote: "The grave which interested me most and held me near it longest was that of the unfortunate John Keats, author of *Endymion*, the English poet who, in modern times ... had the finest and tenderest feeling for the beauty of antiquity."[6] In his *Italian Hours*, published in 1909, Henry James described it as "a mixture of tears and smiles, of stones and flowers, of mourning cypresses and radiant sky, which gives us the impression of looking back at death from the brighter side of the grave."[7] The Aldine British Poets edition of Keats, which first appeared in 1876, was reprinted in 1891 and had gone through six more editions by 1906. Interviews with members of the Hampstead circle became popular reading. Fred Holland Day, an American collector of Keatsiana, sought out Dr Lord, who had been the Brawnes' physician; now white-bearded and blind, he reminisced with great enthusiasm, if questionable accuracy, about events which had taken place over seventy years earlier.[8]

Meanwhile, Piazza di Spagna 26 continued to be a lodging house for foreigners living in Rome (see Figure 8.2). It too became a place of pilgrimage. Admirers of Keats's poetry came to gaze at the building where he had suffered so much. Elizabeth Barrett Browning visited whilst in Rome in the 1840s, recording the details in her journal, and Keats's own sister, Fanny, made the journey in the spring of 1861, meeting Joseph Severn quite by chance in Piazza di Spagna. "For a long time we remained without being able to speak," remembered Severn. "'Twas like a brother and sister who had parted in early life meeting after forty years. How singular that we should meet in the very place where Keats died."[9] Later, at Keats's grave, Fanny planted two bay trees. From 1867 to 1869 the apartment in which

Figure 8.2 Façade of the Keats-Shelley House, Rome, undated photograph (© Keats-Shelley House, Rome).

Keats had died was occupied by the English sculptor George Simonds and the American painter Charles Caryl Coleman. In 1883, after being decorated by the King of Italy for his work in Naples during a devastating cholera epidemic, the Swedish writer and physician Axel Munthe moved into these rooms. Here he stayed until 1902, treating the fashionable and wealthy, but also the poor and disadvantaged, in a clinic he established in Lunghezza, in the Roman *campagna*. He would drive back and forth in a two-wheeled gig drawn by a small—but very fast—Arab horse. Delighted to be living in the rooms once occupied by Keats, he wrote that one of his greatest pleasures was watching the goings-on in the piazza; he often declared that he had the best view in Rome.

It was on a dark autumn night that Munthe met and befriended the great Italian actress Eleanora Duse. She knocked at his door—in evening dress, with no coat—pleading for his protection after escaping from a violent argument with her lover, the poet and novelist Gabriele d'Annunzio, who had been threatening to kill her. Quickly deciding that it would be improper for her to stay in his apartment, Munthe harnessed his horse and took her in the gig along the dark cobbled road to his nursing home, where an old peasant couple who looked after the patients made her comfortable. She remained there for several days before feeling able to face the world—and her lover—again. Many years later, after the First World War, she sent Munthe a beautiful stained glass window representing the Virgin and Child for the nursing home's chapel; later still, she revisited Piazza di Spagna 26 and planted a creeper on the terrace. In his acclaimed memoir *The Story of San Michele* (the villa he built on the island of Capri and where he spent some of the happiest days of his life) Munthe vividly described a Roman summer:

> The last foreigners were vanishing from the stuffy streets. The marble goddesses in the empty museums were enjoying their holidays, cool and comfortable in their fig-leaves. St Peter was taking his siesta in the shade of the Vatican gardens. The Forum and the Coliseum were sinking back into their haunted dreams .... dogs were panting, the monkeys under the Trinità dei Monti steps were yelling for change of air and scenery.[10]

Soon after Munthe's final departure from Rome, the *Casina Rossa* (small red house), which had become almost derelict, was threatened with conversion into a large hotel.[11] During the previous decades, the surrounding area had suffered various vicissitudes. Now the urge for change and renewal even threatened the removal of the Bernini fountain in the piazza. The Cimitero Acattolico had also suffered alarms and upheavals: attempts made by the Roman authorities to remove the remains of Keats and Shelley had frequently been fended off by the British Embassy and on one occasion were prevented only by the intervention of Queen Victoria herself. There had also been moves to create an unnecessary road through the part of the Cemetery lying between Keats's and Shelley's graves.

At the same time, there was a growing interest in buildings associated with writers and artists on both sides of the Atlantic. The first plaque (1867) to be fixed to a building by the Royal Society of Arts commemorated Byron's house in Holles Street (the plaques erected at this time in London were brown, later to be replaced by the famous blue plaques). The Wordsworth Trust, founded in 1891, sought to protect and preserve the building inhabited by William Wordsworth in the English Lake District. Stopford Brooke, founding chairman of the Wordsworth Trust, expressed sentiments directly comparable to those of the founders of the later Keats-Shelley House:

> There is no place ... which has so many thoughts and memories as
> this belonging to our poetry; none at least in which they are so closely
> bound up with the poet and the poems .... In every part of this little
> place [the poet] has walked with his sister and wife or talked with
> Coleridge. And it is almost untouched. Why should we not try and
> secure it, as Shakespeare's birthplace is secured, for the eternal posses-
> sion of those who love English poetry all over the world?[12]

On the anniversary of Keats's death, 23 February 1903, a group consisting of one English diplomat and eight American writers at the time in Rome met to discuss a project for purchasing the whole house by popular subscription and creating a permanent memorial to Keats, Shelley and other English Romantic writers associated with the city. This memorial was to take the form of a library and museum containing printed editions of the poets' works, manuscripts and other relics. The trustees were also to have perpetual guardianship over the graves of Keats, Shelley, Joseph Severn and Shelley's friend Edward Trelawny, who had snatched some of the poet's ashes—and, he claimed, his miraculously preserved heart—from the funeral pyre on the beach at Viareggio.[13]

The group was led by the American poet and journalist (later to become the American Ambassador to Rome) Robert Underwood Johnson (see Figure 8.3). While walking down the Scalinata, he had noticed the extreme contrast in the condition of the narrow twin houses flanking them at the piazza level. The one to his right was in an excellent state of repair, while No. 26, to his left, was—as he later wrote—"shabby and dilapidated and had taken on at the rear a tenement-like appearance." He was "at once struck with the idea that a house so dear by its associations to all lovers of poetry should be saved as a shrine." Living in Keats's former rooms—now in a very poor state—were a pair of American ladies, both writers and originally from New York: Mrs James Walcott Haslehurst and her mother. They were generous in allowing interested visitors to see the rooms, and Mrs Haslehurst would have liked to buy and restore the whole house had she possessed sufficient funds. The house's owner, a Mrs Chadwick, was regarded as a 'difficult' woman.[14]

Johnson (1853–1937) came from a family of liberal Quakers and a world in which literature was preferred to business as a topic of conversation. His great-grandmother was a Spencer and there was a family tradition that she was descended from the author of *The Faerie Queene*. It was also said that they were of the family of James Hogg, "the Ettrick Shepherd." As Johnson says in his memoir *Remembered Yesterdays* (1923): "I should be glad to know that I had the blood of either of these poets."[15] Robert Burns was frequently read at home and Johnson's native Indiana produced many

Figure 8.3 Robert Underwood Johnson, c. 1923 (© Keats-Shelley House, Rome).

writers, a fact he attributed to the early establishment of a system of township libraries in every county. Whilst in Chicago he heard Emerson give an address of inspiring optimism, a sentiment that attended him in all the many projects he initiated.

Johnson made his first trip to Europe in late 1885. During his visit to England, he made the acquaintance of Robert Browning and dined with Whistler. On every visit to Rome Johnson saw much of Elihu Vedder, describing him in the last years of his life as looking "with his skull-cap and long white beard, like a cross between Titian and the prophet Jeremiah."[16] He also went several times to the studio of Moses Ezekiel, in the ruins of the baths of Diocletian—a large unfloored room, dim and mysterious. As a young man Johnson had started work at the *Century Magazine*, a journal he was to edit between 1909 and 1919. Many of the individuals involved in the founding of the museum, and the early years of its life, were old friends of Jonhson's through the magazine, for example wood engraver Timothy Cole, printer Theodore De Vinne, and the author Mark Twain. When the well-known American illustrator Howard Pyle was chosen to make the Keats Shelley Memorial Library bookplate, it was engraved by Cole and printed by De Vinne.

Johnson demonstrated throughout his life a commitment to good causes. In addition to his efforts to preserve the Keats House he campaigned for the establishment of international copyright (for which he received the decoration of the "Cavaliere della Corona d'Italia"), forest conservation (through which he became acquainted with Theodore Roosevelt), the abolition of the tariff on art, and the granting of charters to the American Academy and Institute of Arts and Letters. Later, in 1917, he organised a committee of poets to provide ambulances for the Italian army. Throughout 1918 he raised hundreds of thousands of dollars for war relief in Italy, sending a special message of hope from Helen Keller to Italian soldiers blinded by action.

The group's meeting place was the banking house of Sebasti e Reali, nearby in the piazza. The English Poet Laureate, Alfred Austin, then staying nearby at Frascati, had been invited to join, but declined, explaining in a letter that he considered that "quite enough has been done, as far as England at any rate is concerned, to recall Keats and Shelley to the remembrance of readers." To emphasise, however, his "due regard" for the two poets "long before Keats and Shelley worship set in," he revealed that forty years earlier, on his first trip to Rome, he had paid for Shelley's grave to be cleaned and replanted with primroses, violets and roses. Johnson later commented wryly that the "support of every other author of note in England" more than compensated for the loss of Austin's co-operation.[17]

A hugely important and enthusiastic participant was Rennell Rodd (see Figure 8.4), then Chargé d'Affaires at the British Embassy and afterwards—as Sir Rennell Rodd— British Ambassador to Italy, and the diplomat given the lion's share of credit in ending Italy's neutrality in the First World War. A second cousin of William Makepeace Thackeray, he was a poet and scholar as well as a diplomat. As an undergraduate at Oxford he had travelled with Oscar Wilde, although "when he returned [from America] dressed in a fantastic suit of red plush, assuming a sort of Olympian attitude as of one who could do no wrong, we parted in anger and did not meet again."[18] He was also a former friend of Lady Jane Shelley (the wife of Shelley's son Percy) and had in 1888 been closely involved in the prevention of the proposed road which, Johnson was convinced, would have brought about "the violation of the Protestant Cemetery."[19]

The American members were Martha Gilbert Dickinson (Emily Dickinson's niece and herself a poet); Agnes Repplier (a Philadelphia author and memoirist, known for her gracefully witty and scholarly essays); the poet James Herbert Morse and his wife; the distinguished magazine editor and biographer Norman Hapgood; the genial, Harvard-educated Harry Nel-

Figure 8.4 Lord Rennell of Rodd, c. 1923 (© Keats-Shelley House, Rome).

son Gay (a prolific writer on Italian history, with a famously well-stocked library); and Johnson's wife Katharine. Edith Wharton was unable to attend but gave the scheme her blessing. Invited to preside over the project, Rodd gave it his full support and was authorised to select a British Committee, whose first Chairman was the Marquis of Crewe. Rodd became the ex-officio Chairman of the Rome Committee, with Nelson Gay as Secretary. The American Committee included the writers present at the first meeting, with Edmund Clarence Stedman—poet, essayist, literary critic and highly successful Wall Street broker—as Chairman and Johnson himself as Secretary and Treasurer.

In Johnson's memoir, *Remembered Yesterdays*, he wrote that their first task was to raise funds for the purchase of the house and obtain an option on it, explaining that "the utmost secrecy" had to be observed "lest the price should be increased before the money was raised." The owner remained completely unaware of the people she was dealing with, since they were represented by their banker. Even so, the price was raised from fifteen thousand to twenty-one thousand dollars—although this, Johnson explained, was "merely the natural increase of property in that desirable section of the city during the years occupied in collecting the funds."[20] The American philanthropist Andrew Carnegie, who contributed two thousand dollars to the appeal, was unwilling to advance the total sum required: "It is very easy to lend you the eighteen thousand dollars to buy the Keats House, but you would not get a dollar from subscribers if you did so. People would smile, and very rightly smile, at the idea of subscribing for what the multi-millionaire has made secure." He was also sceptical of the committee's ability to complete the transaction, declaring that "Those Italians will outwit you literary fellows."[21]

They were fortunate, however, in Stedman's business experience and Gay's financial acumen, wide knowledge, tact and judgement. Johnson's task was chiefly "to pass the hat," which he did with great persistence and panache. Two thousand dollars were raised by staging an entertainment at the Waldorf Hotel in New York, at which Mark Twain read Shelley's "To a Skylark" and Browning's "And did you once see Shelley plain?" There were also readings of Keats's sonnet "On Fame," his lyric "In drear-nighted December" and his "Ode on a Grecian Urn." More money came from fund-raising efforts nationwide; prominent amongst the donors were the members of the New York Stock Exchange, who, after the death of Stedman in 1908, gave two thousand dollars in his honour to furnish the largest room in the Museum. Johnson commented that "There was hardly a poet or other author in America who had not a share in the beautiful work."[22] Similar events in support of the fund were organised by the British Committee, and even the Prime Minister, Arthur Balfour, contributed five pounds.[23]

Gay remained in Rome to handle the negotiations for the purchase of the house, and communication by letter and telegram with the American and British fundraisers. Gay (1870–1932), from Massachusetts, had moved to Italy in the first decade of the twentieth century to teach as a history professor in the University of Rome (see Figure 8.5). Faced with the scarsity of American volumes, Gay decided to create his own library, where he collected all the publications of American interest that he could find. Also a great Byron enthusiast and scholar, he donated the entirety of this part of his collection to the Museum.[24]

The purchase was completed in 1906 and the second-floor interiors made ready over the following three years. The library (reminiscent of the panelled libraries found in New York institutions such as the Harvard Club) was in three conjoined rooms, based on a Late Renaissance design by Vincenzo Moraldi, the House's architect until the 1930s. Its tall walnut bookcases were paid for by American sponsors. Many generous donations followed, including a portrait of Keats by Severn from Sir Charles Dilke; a plaster cast of her bust of Keats from the American sculptor Anne Whitney;

Figure 8.5 Harry Nelson Gay, 1923 (© Keats-Shelley House, Rome).

and a collection of letters of Byron relating to Shelley, from Henry W. Cannon. The Keats family in America donated the Severn portraits of George and Tom Keats and the portrait of their sister Fanny by her son Juan Llanos y Keats. Manuscripts, paintings and relics were generously contributed by the Shelley and Leigh Hunt families, the Marquis of Crewe (the son of Lord Houghton, a pioneer among Keats scholars), and the renowned writer and scholar Harry Buxton Forman.

The Memorial was finally opened on 3 April 1909, with support from President Theodore Roosevelt (who made a visit in person in 1910) and King Edward VII, whose Private Secretary, Lord Knollys, sent a telegram to be read aloud to the assembled guests:

> I am commanded by the King to express to you the great interest he feels in the ceremony of today, when the house in which Keats died will be dedicated to the memory both of him and of Shelley. His Majesty directs me to add that he sincerely appreciates the sympathy with which the King of Italy and his people regard this Memorial, the gift of the English-speaking nations.

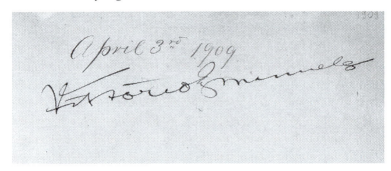

Figure 8.6 Signature of King Vittorio Emanuele III of Italy, from the visitors' book, 3 April 1909 (© Keats-Shelley House, Rome).

The King of Italy himself, Vittorio Emanuele III, was there to hear this tribute (Figure 8.6). On first hearing of the project, three years earlier, he had declared: "The city of Rome will be proud to witness the founding of this civic temple, sacred to the names of two illustrious men, who loved her and within her walls meditated and wrote imperishable poems." Also present were the British Ambassador, the core group of supporters in Rome and a group of interested British, American and Italian writers, including Olivia Rossetti-Agresti, niece of Dante Gabriel Rossetti.

What the guests saw in the apartment formerly occupied by Keats and Severn, Johnson later wrote, was "a delightful library of three rooms lined with dark wood and, overlooking the piazza, the simple, tiny bedroom in which Keats died, the walls and raftered ceiling having been restored to their condition at that time." For him this was "the most sacred shrine in the history of English literature;" its soul was the library, "created by Mr Gay through the happy labours of many years in selecting the books and periodicals." This collection, "devoted to Keats, Shelley, Byron and Leigh Hunt," was generally considered the best "outside the British Museum." Sadly, his duties in New York made it impossible for him to attend the opening ceremony in person, but he sent a letter to be read aloud, in which he declared that "This Memorial has been intended to record the influence of our poets, but it has been intended also to record the influences which they themselves felt, and in a special way Italian influences." He also eloquently pointed out that

> The conservation of the world's resources is little concerned with its resources of beauty: what we have of them is saved by dint of constant struggle. In general the poetic life is looked at askance as that of a drone in the hive. And so it is a matter of rejoicing that hundreds of men and women, out of their love of these two poets, have builded in the heart of Rome an altar for the sacred fire that, by the kindling of torch to torch, may be kept alive interminably.[25]

In a delightful book entitled *The Benedicts Abroad*, published in 1929 by one of the American guests, Clara Woolson Benedict, the author recalls her impressions of this momentous occasion:

> We were most fortunate in being invited, for only twenty ladies could be asked, as the rooms are so very small. Shelley's grandson came from England for the occasion and Severn's son. The addresses were almost overpowering, particularly Mr Severn's simple account of what his father had told him of Keats's last days in the very room where we were sitting .... Afterwards, headed by the King, we all signed our names in the visitors' book. Think how—in the year 2009—people will say, in looking at our names: "But what were the *Benedicts* doing here?" The King sat within touch of us during the addresses, and Kipling *absolutely* within touch, for he bumped against me several times, so I can truthfully say I have had the honour to be "kicked by Kipling!"[26]

Rennell Rodd's *Social and Diplomatic Memoirs* also describe this occasion, with further remembered details:

> Sir Harold Boulton, who had organised the English committee, came to Rome for the occasion with Arthur Severn and Shelley's grandson, Mr Esdaile. By a happy coincidence Rudyard Kipling was also present. Nelson Gay, whose perseverance and devotion to the cause had overcome all obstacles to the purchase of the house, represented the American Committee, and all these, with the exception of Kipling from whom we could not extract a speech, addressed the meeting. Ferdinando Martini, speaking on behalf of Italian men of letters, revealed to us the beauty of his own Tuscan language in the mouth of a master. Severn deposited in the Memorial for perpetual preservation all the relics which he had inherited, recalling his father's friendship with Keats. The American sculptor Ezekiel presented a bust of Shelley and a copy of the first edition of the *Revolt of Islam*. A telegram from King Edward, announcing his interest in the Memorial, was read and the King of Italy then declared it open. The little ceremony was all that the lovers of the two poets would have wished it to be ....[27]

From 3 April 1909 to the present day, the Museum has been continuously open, except for the period 1940–44, when it had to close as a result of the risks the Second World War entailed.[28] Supported by the house rentals, voluntary contributions, admission fees and the membership fees of the Keats-Shelley Memorial Association, the House has been firmly established as a centre of culture in Rome. It received many important donations—of books, manuscripts, paintings, photographs and artefacts of various kinds,[29] held lectures and conferences and attracted a steady stream of English, American and Italian visitors. The number of visitors has grown steadily, and annual numbers now stand at more than 22,000. A glance through the visitors' books for the past fifty years reveals such interesting names as Jean Cocteau (with his adopted son, Edouard Dermit), Julien Green, Sinclair Lewis, Nancy Mitford, Roger Lancelyn Green, Sir Alec Guinness (with the great Shakespearean actor Ernest Milton), Alberto Moravia, Princess Elizabeth (in 1952), Patrick Leigh Fermor, Patricia Highsmith, Lee Strasberg and Seamus Heaney. The regular issues of the *Keats-Shelley Bulletin*, based on unpublished material in the library (now containing 8,000 volumes) were a valuable contribution to scholarship.

Harry Nelson Gay died suddenly in 1932, having attended daily, with little or no remuneration, to the running of the Museum. An important part of his duties had been to care for the graves of Keats and Shelley. In a letter published in the *New York Times* Johnson wrote: "One cannot help wishing that what is mortal of this lovable and high-minded man might lie in the shade of those historic cypresses." Robert Underwood Johnson died, after a series of heart attacks, in 1937; a telegram of condolence was sent to New York by the Keats-Shelley Memorial Association in Rome, deeply regretting the loss of its "beloved founder".

NOTES

1. The myth surrounding Keats's death was fixed in Byron's *Don Juan* (XI.LX): "John Keats, who was killed off by one critique, / just as he really promised something great, / if not intelligible, without Greek / contrived to talk about the gods of late / much as they might have been supposed to speak. / Poor fellow! His was an untoward fate; / 'tis strange the mind, that very fiery particle, / should let itself be snuffed out by an article." On Keats's stay in Italy, see S. Brown, 2005.
2. *The Poetical Works of Coleridge, Shelley and Keats.* Paris: Gallignani, 1829.
3. Richard Monckton Milne, baron Houghton, *Life, Letters and Literary Remains of John Keats.* New York: John Putnam, 1848.
4. *The Poetical Works of John Keats.* New York: Wiley & Putnam, 1846.
5. N.P. Willis, *Pencillings By the Way.* 1835. Ed. L.S. Jast. 1842, 121, quoted in Matthews, 1971, 28.
6. Barbier, 1838, 73.
7. James, 1909, 194.
8. See Richardson, 1952.
9. See Sharp, 1892.
10. Munthe, 1929, 420.
11. The house in which Keats died was not listed for preservation until 1950.
12. Brooke, 1890.
13. The Keats-Shelley Memorial Association now also has guardianship over the graves of the Shelleys' son William, and Joseph Severn's son Arthur.
14. Morris Wrigt, 1981.
15. Johnson, 1924, 14.
16. Ibid., 462.
17. Ibid., 426–27.

18. Rodd, 1922–25, 1:25.
19. Johnson, 1924, 427.
20. Ibid.
21. Quoted from a letter (15 March 1904) from Robert Underwood Johnson to Nelson Gray, in the collection of the Keats Shelley House, Rome.
22. Johnson, 1924, 429.
23. See the list of "Founding Donors of the Keats-Shelley Memorial in Rome, 1903–1906," in Payling, 2005a, 108–13.
24. Incidentally, Gay was also the first Byronist to suggest that Byron had lived at Piazza di Spagna 66 during his own visit to Rome. See Graham-Campbell, 2004.
25. Johnson, 1924, 429–30.
26. Benedict, 1930, Vol. III *The Benedicts Abroad,* 302–03.
27. Rodd, 1922–25, 3: Chapter 5.
28. See Cacciatore, 2005.
29. On the collection, see my "The Museum Collection" in Payling, 2005a, 83–107.

9 The Rooms of Memory
The Praz Museum in Rome

Paola Colaiacomo

Not every writer's house—however important the writer—is preserved as a historical landmark. Of many of them we just lose track, and of many more not even the site is recorded: in the course of time, they simply become other people's homes, merging into the housing history and habits of generations. For a writer's house to be transformed into a museum, it will have to undergo a preliminary process of assessment, at the end of which it shall find itself severed from the housing continuity of the city, or town, or countryside, where it happens to be located. This severance is preliminary to the theatralization of the act of writing of which the museum is to be the setting. A highly personal and private performance, such as writing, will therefore inscribe itself in the visitors' memories by the mediation of the material objects—furniture, books, paintings, bric-à-brac, vistas, the rooms themselves—which accompanied it. What the visitors will be invited to enjoy is the mental *mise en scène* of the writer-at-work. The visible will thus lend enchantment to the invisible.

Considered from this point of view, the Praz Museum in Rome is no exception. Here we have a writer or, more precisely, an essay writer—one working in the great tradition of Charles Lamb, Walter Pater and Virginia Woolf, which he engrafted on the rhythms of the Italian language—who was also a great translator, who was also a prolific critic of literature and the arts, who was also a collector in his own right, who was also a genial interior designer, as witnessed by the fact that the visual documentation by him collected for his book *Conversation Pieces* (1971) inspired Luchino Visconti's film *Gruppo di famiglia in un interno* (1974), whose English title, *Conversation Piece*, and whose character of the old professor living a retired life in his crumbling Roman palazzo, are an explicit homage to the figure of Mario Praz. All this is legend. But let us try to approach our subject somewhat more closely, just to see if any new insights can be gained.

We know that the modern museum, as a public institution, goes back to the early nineteenth century.[1] The word itself, *museum*, coming as it does from *muse*—the nine pagan Muses were the daughters of Mnemosyne, the goddess of Memory—is a reminder of the deep and complex work on memory which this institution engages. There are at least two levels of the museum's mnemonic operation which cannot be overlooked here: that with the "individual" memory embedded in each art or craftwork it keeps in custody, and that with the "collective" memory of its visitors. Since the good health of a modern museum largely depends on the vitality of this link with the public, the second type of memory, diverse and highly changeable as it is, is under a constant process of refocusing and revising by scholars and museum curators.

The link a modern museum succeeds in establishing with its own visitors is nourished in its turn by its relation with the works on show. For the museum to fulfil its vocation as a center for permanent education, the enhancing and animating of this relation is of paramount importance. The abstract "owning" and "exhibiting" of certain works of art—however important—is not enough to interest the general public, but a meaning and an intention must be communicated to them. Many of the initiatives normally undertaken, such as special exhibitions, talks, events for families and children, modernizing of the shops, result in the creation of an image for the place itself, for the very building of the museum, which is then perceived and sought after as a venue in its own right. At that point the very collections it houses would appear in a state of nudity, out of that protective shell. The importance and effectiveness of a museum is thus directly proportional to the capacity it develops to generate the sense of its own site-specificity. The major museums in the world have adopted a long time ago this policy of *cooptati* on of their publics: today no one of the millions of visitors there could imagine Leonardo's Monna Lisa out of the Louvre or the Elgin Marbles out of the British Museum.

Taken at this level, the nature of the museum participates of the nature of the archive. The authority of the archive, as regards the historical documentation it preserves, largely depends on the demonstrable continuity, in time and place, between site and document. The link between these two elements constitutes the "bond" of the archive, which is the prime object of curatorial efforts to preserve in its integrity. Le Goff has introduced the expression "document/monument", to signify that the two terms constitute in fact a conceptual unity.[2] But there is a sense in which all museums aspire to the condition of the document/monument.

If we now apply these ideas to the Praz Museum in Rome, we realize that it has its own peculiar way to situate itself at the crossway with the archive. Roughly speaking, we may say that it produces this effect by a blurring of the partition between the memory contained in the art work and the memory the art work activates in the public. The fact of Praz's having been both a writer and a collector himself—already in his life the author and the historian of his own museum—makes all the difference with other writers' houses: the strains of memory are here too many and too intricate to let themselves unravel so easily.

Let us start with Praz's own memory as materialized in the Museum. We know that of the famous Via Giulia apartment, where he lived for more than thirty years, he went as far as writing the biography, as if to prevent future intrusion by unwanted and unwarranted interpretation. A biography which took the form of an elegantly devious form of autobiography, in that unique book which is *La casa della vita*: a work allusively Victorian, as its title *The House of Life* implies, sprung out of the spirit which dictated Pater's rêverie, *The Child in the House*,[3] and, at the same time, a book which is itself a modernistic monument/document. A masterpiece in the art of self-biography, *La casa della vita* is also a minute record of all the items in the collections, a loving recognition of their histories and characteristics before and after being acquired. In a true spirit of monkish devotion, Praz has registered all the minutest facts relating his cherished possessions, as if to prevent the risk of future infringement of the archival bond. Through writing, the object is made to appear physically linked to the House and, by the mediation of the House, to the very life of the collector. This double bond makes of the stories of successive acquisitions engrossing reading indeed. Suspense is created around the hunting for a specific object on the antiquarian markets of Europe, or the chance finding of it in some obscure Roman or Florentine shop. Not to speak of the pathos which accumulates around the purchasing of it, very often not devoid of material difficulties. The reading of this results even more engrossing at the present distance of time, since we are now in the condition to understand better than when the book first came out, that all this object hunting was in fact the *invention* of a style. This is the reason why he is fascinated by the famous "canonical" name only up to a limited extent: he himself feels in charge of the assessments, the discoveries, the inventions. One has only to think of the pages devoted to a pseudo-Canovian Laura who escapes being authentic only by a hair-breadth, literally—a darker veining in the marble of her cheek, like some hair happening to be stuck there, disturbing the Canovian purity—to understand the extent to which the collector has tied his own life to the marble figure, to the shadow of a different and lost life.[4]

The perfect antithesis to the Museum curator who, as Benjamin notes, aims at the so called "Glanzstücke" (glamourous pieces),[5] the collector has to invent his collection, piecemeal, through patient philanthropic retrieval of things, styles and atmospheres from dusty oblivion. As we now are in the position to judge, the emergence of neoclassic or Empire furniture on the market owes much to Praz's own researches:[6] it is not through film only, that his imaging of interior spaces has entered the cycles of consumption. A chapter in the history of taste, more often of commercial taste, in mid twentieth century, has its archeology in Praz's researches on Neo-classicism. He himself notes how a vaguely Empire taste in interior decoration seems to prevail in expensive, vulgar hotels. And, we may add, that trend is still in full swing, the post-modern love of the fake thus finding one of its earliest expressions in the vulgarisation of a style which, in its turn, was conceived, from its birth, as allusive interpretation and bombastic reproduction of "classic" design.

To the work of the connoisseur and the erudite, there is then to be added that of the interior designer: many are the pages of *La casa della vita* devoted to the narration of how each "piece" came to be located in that precise room, at that precise angle, so that it might receive precisely that slant of light, at that precise hour of the day, varying of course according to the different seasons of the year. And this is where a modernistic type of memory comes unmistakably into play: the quotation from Virginia Woolf's *Diary* on the frontispiece of the book is clear.[7] Between writing and collecting, the House, its furniture, even—memory objectified, that is—acts as a shuttle which weaves the fabric of life itself. This is so true that when, in 1969, Praz had to leave the Via Giulia apartment and relocate his collections in the new one offered him by the Fondazione Primoli—the one upgraded to Museum—not only did he draw meticulous plans for the arrangements of the pieces in the new rooms (these drawings are now part of the Archivio Praz of the Galleria Nazionale d'Arte Moderna, in Rome), but began to project a new edition of his book, which was to see the light ten years after the moving, and twenty after the first edition.[8] As if, in order to make the new situation acceptable, interior designing and writing about it should continue to go hand in hand. Praz was by then seventy-three years old. He had another thirteen to live.

As I hope it will by now be clear, it would be an oversimplification to look at the art objects, furniture and paintings in the Praz Museum as simply the "spoils" of a life spent among beautiful things. There is the very arrangement of the "things"—"always the splendid Things"[9]—to be taken into consideration, when we enter these Rooms of Memory. An arrangement which is in itself an execution, as a piece of music might be, of the things' infinite possibilities. Maybe not the best one, but surely the chosen one, and the more meaningful exactly for that reason. Being used as a special writing, parallel to the alphabetical one, the interior decoration of the rooms becomes the very thing on exhibition here, so that writing and collecting engage the visitors' attention, in the Praz Museum, in their complementarity. To this effect they are exposed whether or not they have read the professor's books: the public's memory is here called into play, in all its diversities of expression. "Simpler" as this "second" memory may be in comparison with the "first" one, of which the House is the monument/document, it is nevertheless in relation to it that the Museum puts its own credibility at stake.

The transit, never a seamless one, between writing and living is staged by highlighting, not so much the "value" of the pieces as authentic works of art, but the role and figure of the collector, comparatively easier to be grasped by the general public. After all each one of us sooner or later enjoys his or her fifteen minutes of feverish bric-à-brac hunting. Had Praz not been a collector, I doubt whether his home would today be a museum. His work as a critic and an essay writer, though immensely important for the student of literature and the critic of culture and of the arts, would not have been sufficient to qualify him as a "writer". On the other hand, to imagine Praz's written *oeuvre* not backed by his activity as a collector would be like imagining the Mona Lisa out of the Louvre: figuratively, then, the Museum contains the writings. There is some good reason in the public's being encouraged to cultivate this sliding from life to work and back. On the other hand, the reading of only a few pages from his most scholarly studies, gives us sufficient evidence that those masterpieces of critical insight, full of learning, erudition, and also of the joy of living, could not have seen the light in absence of that "Leidenschaft" (passion), as Walter Benjamin styles it,[10] which overflows from every single page: without all that travelling, searching, pining, bargaining, suffering, exulting at the sight of an Empire *lit-en-bateau* or a pseudo-Canovian bust, that highly idiosyncratic writing where literary theory, art criticism, rêverie, narration and hobby-horsical erudition live side by side, simply would not have been possible. There are also academic reasons, then, which authorize that sliding.

In the *Introduzione* to his translation of Pater's *Imaginary Portraits* into Italian, Praz neatly defines the faint, typically Paterian characters there portrayed as "corollari psicologici d'una premessa ambientale" (psychological corollaries of an environmental pre-condition).[11] In the conception of his own house, he reverses this critical formula: it is now the House to figure as the environmental corollary of a psychological pre-condition, of an attitude towards the world. It is therefore in a double sense—objective and subjective—that the House can be styled as "The House of Life". The House *is* the life of its occupier and *has* a life of its own. So that, when they are in the Museum, it is this life, mediated and re-mediated between writing, reading, collecting, travelling, teaching and what not, that is supposed to penetrate the visitors' memories.

It was Praz himself to raise the issue of the fate of those pieces of furniture which, after the death of their owners, happen to be turned into museum pieces. A widespread prejudice, he writes in *La filosofia dell'arredamento*, connects museums with the idea of coldness: listed in catalogues, protected by cords, the things exhibited lose their charm and flavour. The logical and chronological orders work jointly to obliterate the magic of things. Yet, he adds, among the crowd of indifferent, distracted, or uncouth visitors, there may always be a sensitive soul, susceptible to the warmth that once animated the fine furnishings. As for himself, he remarks ironically, "io ... per le case ho un debole" (I have a penchant for houses), adding that whenever he happens to be in a new city, his first concern is to visit as many famous furnished houses as are to be found there.[12]

Perhaps, he was already thinking of the fate of his own furniture. But at that time—immediately after World War II—he was still living in the rented apartment on the Via Giulia, and the bond of solidarity between things and walls, as seen both from the inside and the outside of the building, must have appeared to him absolutely unchallenged. Self-reflexively, he foresees the potential of his own house to participate in the creation of a transnational cultural memory, performing that evolutionary leap along a line of sensitivity which links the soul of today's visitors to the objects collected in a more or less remote past, depending on the age of the visitor. The cultural memory engendered by the Museum is thus activated through an act of imaginative appropriation performed by the single visitor-consumer, while the historical, critical and philological analysis of each "piece" plays in this respect only a minor role. And since what is exhibited there is a peculiar type of sensitivity—after all we are not at the Louvre, nor at the V&A, where any fantasy of personal ownership would be instantly blocked—cultural memory is finally built on the contact between two forms of sensitivity.

According to Balzac, a collector is the most passionate man in the world: his cousin Pons is the archetype of the asceticism and the sacrificial attitude which characterize the authentically inspired collector. Pons is "un homme-Empire" (an Empire man), he says,[13] and the same could be said of Praz: not because of his style of dressing, but of the identification he achieved with his neoclassical paintings and furniture, whose life he narrated as if it were his own life: an heroic gesture of depersonalization, on his part, where it is still possible to perceive a strain of Surrealism.

At this point, though, a one hundred and eighty degrees revolution imposes itself. We can no longer postpone the question about the real nature of the archival bond the Praz Museum communicates to its visitors. The fact that the original entirety has been infringed cannot, in my opinion, be ignored. All material continuity between the house and the collections has been disrupted with the moving to Palazzo Primoli, and perhaps even before then, through repeated violations from the outside. It is Praz himself to narrate, in the chapter entitled "Venti anni dopo" (Twenty years after)—a title obviously reminiscent of Dumas—which he added to the 1979 edition of *La casa della vita*,[14] how the first housebreaking, in 1969, had a decisive influence towards his decision to abandon the apartment on the Via Giulia, even if at that time the moving could still be postponed for some years. In fact only a chair had been damaged. No other piece of furniture had been contaminated and the general atmosphere still kept its charm intact. But the external walls did no longer offer a secure shelter to the collections: "il guscio stesso della mia residenza era stato intaccato dall'effrazione; gli oggetti tuttavia restavano" (the very shell of my existence had been cracked by the effraction; the objects, nevertheless, remained in their place).[15] And the "objects" were to be saved, without delay, from impending danger. They would be his last citadel. Like Mrs Gereth in *The Spoils of Poynton*, he then flies away with his treasures and relocates them in the new apartment, which had become available just at the time of the first housebreaking: literally a breaking of the solidarity between the external eggshell and the vital yolk within.

After such a violation, no recovering of the former archival integrity would be even thinkable. Many years before, Praz himself had pointed out how those collectors whose aim it is to reproduce the original environment in which the things they collect were originally set, appear to him but amateurs whose work is comparable, in the field of furniture, to that of translators in the field of literature and the arts: at best, they can only hope to see their puzzle completed.[16] And now it is his turn to do the work of the collectors who are but translators: himself an eminent translator of literary texts, the professor now translates his whole idea of domesticity to neutral ground, one not marked by previous experiences.

To the collector's sensitivity things evade time; or rather, they live in the privileged, and much beloved time, which is the product of his, or her, own oneiric fantasies. The moment Praz decides to relocate his Things, this happy condition of atemporality ends both for the things and for himself. The change must have been no less painful than the one dramatized by Baudelaire in *La Chambre Double*.[17] A knocking at the door and the room aromatized with desire and regret, which so far, immersed as it was in the delightful darkness of harmony, has been the perfect set for a heavenly rêverie, while the unimpeded soul indulged in abandon and self-forgetfulness, is suddenly plunged into the ordinary time of everyday life. From now on there will be this chasm, this open wound, in the still time in which the things had so far appeared immerse. They will be the same things, after that knocking; yet how differently they will look!

It should not be forgotten, here, that for the professor the move from one house to the other coincided with the moment of retirement: an event which, more than any other, triggers the count-down of time. Praz enters then the secrets of collecting as translating. From now on, he will not *write* nor *invent* the Things: he will just edit them. On the occasion of the moving, the pieces come all at the same time: none of them has been looked for and bought for that wall, for that perspective. Therefore they will have to be adapted, and relocated. The Via Giulia apartment had been a casket of memory even before Praz had gone to live in it: the sixteenth-century palazzo had been the Roman home of the unfortunate couple Isabel-Osmond in the Jamesian *Portrait of a Lady*, and Zola too had responded to the appeal of the same building in his novel on Rome. Therefore to Praz's eyes, when he had first moved there in 1934, the palace itself, not only the apartment and its furnishings, had appeared as a place steeped in literature and in art. Even its façade had a tale to tell: Polidoro da Caravaggio's graffiti were still readable, as they are now, only feebler. They narrated of the rape of the Sabine women, and of Muzio stoically burning his own hand before the Etruscan king.

In the palazzo Primoli apartment—just a floor above the Primoli Foundation, of which the learned professor will be the president till the end of his life—all there is to do is to relocate the things. A good removal firm, extremely accurate measurements of the new rooms, minute evaluations of the possibilities they offer, and the trick is done: it is Praz himself to speak in these terms of this period in his life, in the 1979 edition of *La casa della vita*, which he published with Adelphi, while the old one had been with Mondadori. If the first edition of the book—rich in colour plates—lent itself to be used as a Christmas present, the new one sported a philosophical black and white. The House was already on its way to becoming a Museum.

And as a Museum it will from now on offer itself to other memories. To the visitors who, in taking it with them, transform the site-specific memory inscribed in the place into a living memory. It is ultimately from them that the life which has been spent in the house can expect to be transformed into a "living record". The Shakespearian image of Sonnet 55 is marvellously translated by Giuseppe Ungaretti with the expression "vivi archivi", and this of course brings us back to the idea of the archive.

An archive usually contains books, files and papers, which are taken care of through special funds created for the purpose. A writer's library tells us with whom he, or she, "spoke". In its way, it is an X-ray of his, or her, mind. What is our surprise, then, when we realize that, instead of the books actually owned by Praz, those we see on the shelves and in the bookcases of the Museum are just commercial vintage books. Empty shelves—as the guide says—would not have been nice to see. On the other hand the "original" books had to be put under lock and key, being the legal property of the Fondazione Primoli, by will and testament of their owner. He had to accept this condition in order to obtain the use of the apartment to the end of his days: "offrii la donazione della mia cospicua biblioteca conservandone l'uso vita natural durante" (I donated to them my conspicuous library, only reserving for myself the use of it for the rest of my life).[18] In this way he alienates what we might call the "bare ownership" of his books, while preserving the professional, and, therefore to some extent, the emotional relationship with them. But of this last and surely not a meaningless link with the professor's life the Museum must be amputated.

During the long thirteen years he was still to live, he must have experienced a relation with his books not very dissimilar from the one lived, in relation to their homes, by those old ladies who, approaching the end, suddenly decide to live in style, for the remaining time of their lives, and sell the bare ownership of the house they have lived in till then: that is to say the walls of their abodes, in spite of children's and grandchildren's expectations. And we can imagine that, from that moment on, Death enters those homes and plays the Master in them. Like those old ladies, Praz now alienates his books, which he puts on a par with the external walls of the fabric of his life, but keeps the "objects"—both their ownership and use—for himself. He stresses this point in relation to the first house-breaking, when he was still living in the Via Giulia apartment, when he says that the "objects" remained in their place. Are we to conclude that the books were only partially to be reckoned among the "objects"?

Praz evokes the noble precedent of Petrarch, who in 1362 had transferred his famous library to the Republic of Venice, in order to obtain, in exchange, a house to live in. To all evidence the transaction—a library for a house—was then in the wake of an illustrious tradition. But nothing is ever exactly the same in this world. Unlike Petrarch, Praz exchanges his books with an adequate location for his beloved objects, and not with a shelter for his tired limbs. His real habitation is now with the Things themselves, and the collections are his everyday *habilement*. The house nothing but the "shell of my dwelling", of his *lingering* on the earth. And the alienated books are part and parcel of this shell: the instruments of a professional engagement which has no few points of contact with a high craftsmanship. To read, to catalogue, to collate, to write: all activities one could perform in a well-furnished library. And his library is indeed "conspicuous": something which hits the sight of the eyes. One is reminded of the three Veblenian laws of fashion, which Praz was wont to quote: "conspicuous consumption", "conspicuous ease", "conspicuous waste". The books may well be the photographic image of the life of the one who collected them, but do not coincide with that life, or much less than the "objects", which for no reason could be alienated or exchanged. The little memory invested in them can easily be shed. This is so true that at a certain point Praz will think of using his collections to arrange an annuity in favor of his daughter: as if the "objects" could find their proper location only in the main heritage line, the one founded on biological paternity. But the project was destined to fail. The House would cease to be the living record of personal memory, to become what we now have: a Museum. The instrument of other and different memories.

NOTES

1. Crimp, 2000, 15.
2. Le Goff, 1978.
3. Praz, 1958, and Praz, 1964. The "Victorian" allusion is to Dante Gabriele Rossetti's collection of sonnets with the same title.
4. Praz, 1958, 93.
5. Benjamin, 1966, 104; translation PC.
6. See Praz, 1940; Praz, 1945; Praz, 1964b; Praz, 1971a; Praz, 1971b; and besides a great number of articles in reviews and daily papers.
7. "What sort of diary should I like mine to be? Something loose knit and yet not slovenly, so elastic that it will embrace any thing, solemn, alight or beautiful that comes into my mind. I should like it to resemble some deep old desk, or capacious hold-all, in which one flings a mass of odds and ends without looking them through." *A Writer's Diary, Being Extracts from the Diary of Virginia Woolf*, Frontispiece of Praz, 1958; and Praz, 1979.
8. Praz, 1979.
9. James, 1984, 1144 (*Preface* to the New York Edition of *The Spoils of Poynton, A London Life, The Chaperon*).
10. Benjamin, 1966, 104; translation PC.
11. Pater, 1980, 17; translation PC.
12. Praz, 1945, 36–37; translation PC.
13. Balzac, 1973, 23; translation PC.
14. Praz, 1979, 419–31.

15. Praz, 1979, 424; translation PC.
16. Praz, 1945, 49.
17. Baudelaire, 1958, 22–29.
18. Praz, 1979, 425; translation PC.

Part II
Self-Fashioning

10 Casa Vasari in Arezzo
Writing and Decorating the Artist's House

Ben Thomas

In a letter of 1537 to his landlord Domenico Bolani, the controversial Renaissance writer Pietro Aretino praised the house on the Grand Canal in Venice in which he was living, quoting the opinion of the "famous Giulio Camillo ... who used to say affably that the land entrance of the house I have described, being dark, lop-sided, with nasty stairs, was like the terrible name I have acquired through airing the truth; and then he added that whoever gets to know me intimately finds in my pure, sincere and honest friendship the tranquil contentment experienced on coming out onto the portico and looking out over those balconies."[1] Like the writer, known as "the scourge of princes", Aretino's house had two aspects: one dark and treacherous the other an expansive overview of the vibrant life of the city in which it was situated.

It is suggestive in this context that this dual aspect of the writer's house, and its similarity with the public and private dimensions of Aretino's character, was noted by Giulio Camillo, famous for his invention of a memory theatre, a device that gave the art of memory an architectural form through an array of mythological images displayed within a Vitruvian theatre and viewed from the stage. As Erasmus's correspondent Viglius Zuichemus described it in 1532: "the work is of wood, marked with many images, and full of little boxes; there are various orders and grades in it. He gives place to each individual figure and ornament ... and calls this theatre of his by many names, saying now that it is a built or constructed mind and soul, and now that it is a windowed one."[2] From the stage of his memory theatre, Camillo could recall through the correlation of images the occult connections that allowed him, in the words of Frances Yates, to "develop magical powers as an orator by speaking from a memory organically affiliated to the proportions of the world harmony."[3] By contrast, from the vantage point of his balcony above the Grand Canal, Aretino could survey the passing flux of the "stage play world" whose characters populated his vividly realistic writings: princes, courtiers, merchants of all nations, prostitutes and thieves, and above them all skies worthy of Titian's brush.

In 1541 the artist and later historiographer Giorgio Vasari was called to Venice by Pietro Aretino, his friend and fellow Aretine, to provide the painted decorations for a theatrical performance of one of his comedies (*La Talanta*), staged for the festival by the company of the Calzi. Probably with Aretino's help, Vasari devised a painted scheme for the large room he was to transform into a theatre that recalled Camillo's compartmentalization of knowledge in the memory theatre: square fields for mythological scenes painted in monochrome flanked by niches containing allegorical figures of Prudence, Justice, Charity and so on, while above the ceiling was divided into squares painted with representations of the twenty-four hours of day.[4] The journey to Venice had turned into a research trip for the artist who had already been referred to in Aretino's published correspondence as a historian as early as 1536: "I was summoned to Venice by M. Pietro Aretino, then a poet of renown and my fast friend", Vasari wrote in his autobiography (published in 1568), "As he greatly desired to see me I was obliged to go, and I was glad of the opportunity for seeing the works of Titian and others. In a few days I succeeded in seeing the works of Correggio in Parma and Modena, those of Giulio Romano at Mantua and the antiquities of Verona."[5]

As Vasari was then acquiring for himself a house in his native Arezzo (the contract in the Archivio di Stato in Florence is dated 7 September 1541) (see Figure 10.1), he would also have been interested to see at Mantua the impressive houses of the artists Andrea Mantegna and Giulio Romano.[6] Leaving Venice on 16 August 1542, Vasari returned to Arezzo where "before beginning anything else I painted the ceiling of a chamber I had built in my house with all the arts connected with design. In the middle Fame, seated on a globe, blows a golden trumpet and throws away one of fire, representing slander. About her are all the Arts with their attributes. Not having time to finish, I left eight ovals for portraits from life of our leading artists."[7]

While he was in Venice, Vasari noted that "there are many portraits in all the houses of Venice, and in many gentleman's homes one may see their fathers and grandfathers back to the fourth generation, and in some of the more noble houses back further still." In his biography of Gentile Bellini, Vasari commended "this custom [that] has certainly always been deserving of praise. Who is there who does not feel joy and pleasure, in addition to the honour and adornment which they confer, on seeing the likenesses of his ancestors, and especially if they have been famous and renowned .... And for what other purpose ... did they in the ancient world put the images of the great men with honourable inscriptions in public places than to fire the minds of their successors with the love of achievement and glory?"[8]

The inspirational force of portraits of illustrious antecedents had previously been celebrated in terms of the artist's house in Filarete's treatise on architecture (1460–64), a work which hinges around a neatly circular fantasy of the past valorizing present artistic practice: during the excavation of the foundations for a coastal city, a box is discovered containing an ancient golden book. When this is translated from Greek by the court poet (Filelfo),

Figure 10.1 Casa Vasari, Arezzo, exterior (© Harald Hendrix).

it turns out to contain detailed descriptions and plans of the former port of Plousiapolis, which exactly replicate Filarete's own architectural intentions while also confirming his opinions on the nobility of art. Filarete's lord (Francesco Sforza) orders the city to be constructed exactly according to the account in the golden book, including the house of the architect which the text relates was decorated with images of famous ancient architects, sculptors and painters such as Phidias and Zeuxis: "on the interior of the entrance of this house [there were] all those who have been supreme in architecture, sculpture, figures, or any other science. All were portrayed and their names written below. For the most part the inventors held in their hands a painting of the most noble thing they had done."[9]

Vasari was certainly aware of Filarete's treatise, and as we will see he did decorate the Arezzo house with pictures of ancient artists, however as he considered Filarete to have written "probably the most ridiculous and silly book ever produced" he probably was inspired by other precedents in combining symbolic representations of the arts with portraits of illustrious practitioners.[10] For example, Vasari wrote in his biography of Paolo Uccello about the house of that eccentric and reclusive painter who, obsessed with problems of perspective, lived "like a hermit." Although the house was decorated with "painted representations of birds, cats, dogs and every sort of strange animal of which he could get drawings, as he was too poor to have the living creatures themselves," Uccello also "loved the talent he saw in his fellow-craftsmen; and to preserve their memory for posterity he painted the portraits of five distinguished men with his own hand on a long panel which he kept in his house in memory of them. One was the painter Giotto, standing for the light and origin of painting; the second was Filippo Brunelleschi, for architecture; then Donatello, for sculpture; Uccello himself, for perspective and animal painting; and for mathematics his friend Giovanni Manetti, with whom he often conferred and discoursed on the problems of Euclid."[11] This reads like one of the many passages in the *Lives* where Vasari explains the past in terms of his own personal motivations. Certainly when he came to finally fill the empty ovals in the *Camera della Fama* with portraits of artists (probably c.1568 as they derive from the woodcut portraits included in the second edition of the *Lives*), then the list of those portrayed reflected Vasari's ancestry and personal development as an artist: the Trecento Aretine artist Spinello Aretino, his father Lazzaro Vasari and relative Luca Signorelli, his early mentor Bartolomeo della Gatta, and his teachers Andrea del Sarto and Michelangelo Buonarroti, together with a self-portrait.

A rather grander source of inspiration for Vasari was the villa on Lake Como of the historian Paolo Giovio begun in 1537 and completed in 1543.[12] Although it is now only known through literary descriptions, it is clear that this elaborate structure was arranged like an encomium in praise of history, with frescoed representations of Apollo, Minerva and the Muses inviting the beholder to reflect on the virtuous deeds of the famous figures memorialized in Giovio's impressive collection of portraits. Like Vasari's house, Giovio's villa—which is explicitly referred to as a Museum in the preface to his *Elogia veris clarorum virorum* of 1546—was the product of *otium*, leisure time productively employed to create a temple to virtue. Also like Vasari's house it provided the architectural and visual accompaniment to written history, and—while undeniably advantageous to the writer's status and fame—it was principally intended to have a didactic function, since it was dedicated "ad publicam hilaritatem" (for public enjoyment). [Vasari was to note in his life of the Aretine artist Lappoli that his style improved after he "had seen reliefs and casts of statues by Michelangelo and of antiques brought by Giorgio Vasari to his house in Arezzo."][13]

Paolo Giovio was especially close to Vasari and had recommended him to Cardinal Alessandro Farnese in 1543.[14] He collaborated with Vasari on the frescoes in the Cancelleria in Rome, painted in one hundred days in 1546, celebrating the achievements of Pope Paul III, providing the artist with the iconography and Latin inscriptions. These frescoes function as a visual encomium, employing the rhetorical trope of *synkrisis* to relate modern events to antique precedents, as well as confronting general principles with exemplary narratives, and portraits with allegories. The illusionistic architecture suggests the continuity of real and fictive space, and thereby develops a visual rhetoric invented by Raphael, which served to emphasise the immediate relevance of the past to the beholder. Vasari's correspondence at this time reveals the extent of his dependence on Giovio for advice with his ongoing project of a history of the visual arts.[15] This was a debt which he acknowledged in his autobiography when he located the origin of the *Lives* at a dinner party at the Farnese court attended by Francesco Maria Molza, Annibale Caro, Gandolfo Porrino, Claudio Tolomei, Romolo Amaseo and Paolo Giovio, and it was Giovio who suggested the need for a history of the visual arts (a story made plausible by the existence of short Latin biographies of Leonardo, Michelangelo and Raphael written by Giovio between 1523 and 1527). Whether or not the need for a history of the arts "from the time of Cimabue" was actually first discussed at such a literary symposium, Vasari's account does reveal the importance which he attached to the fact that Giovio had endorsed his historical writings.[16]

In Vasari's frescoes in the Cancelleria present and past are kept in play, but also discretely apart by their organising architecture. When Vasari came to compose his *Lives of the Artists* he was faced with a similar problem of organising disparate material that ranged from the particular fact to the abstract principle, and comparable organisational methods inform the structure of the *Lives* with the biographies of individual artists being framed by a series of explanatory essays. This sequence of introductions and prefaces performs a parallel function to that of the monochrome allegorical figure in the margin of an *istoria,* by drawing general conclusions from the wealth of particularised detail contained in the biographies. By 1547 the writing of the *Lives* was advanced enough for a fair copy to be made in manuscript (by one of the Olivetan monks for whom Vasari was then working in Rimini). Judging by his record books, or *Ricordanze*, Vasari spent the summer of the following year 1548 decorating the principal reception room on the piano nobile of his Arezzo house—so the writing of history was accompanied by the decoration of his house.

The artist's house is a recurring motif in the *Lives*, where it is often indicative either of the individual character of its inhabitant or of the broader theme of the rising social status of Renaissance artists in general (as in the courtly dwellings of Andrea Mantegna, Leonardo da Vinci, Raphael Sanzio, Giulio Romano and Leone Leoni's extravagant Casa degli Omenoni of 1565). In the first case, amusing anecdotes effectively reveal character traits that inform artistic manner (or *maniera*) and also differentiate one vivid personality from another, while at the same time drawing universal lessons that tend to set particularized portraits within a structure of interlocking moral forces framing the trajectory of any artist's existence. We learn therefore that Sebastiano del Piombo's acquisition of a house is indicative of his laziness and lack of application: "Fra Sebastiano had a pleasant house near Popolo [in Rome], which he built and where he lived at ease without thinking of painting or working."[17] We also find that the list of Baccio Bandinelli's expanding portfolio of properties in the Florentine countryside is followed immediately and significantly by a list of unfinished works and neglected projects.[18] Similarly, Pietro Perugino's investment in properties in Florence, Perugia and Castello della Pieve is linked with his early experience of and subsequent fear of poverty, and a general worldliness—symbolized by irreligion and a pretty wife—that informed his repetitive and undiscriminating approach to his art.[19] By contrast, Donatello's lack of worldly concern is vividly conveyed by the domestic detail of the basket hanging from the ceiling in his home, containing all his money, and from which anyone could take what they needed.[20]

Frequently Vasari evokes the artist's house in order to illustrate the eccentricity that he seems both inclined to indulge and also to warn against. Perhaps the most extreme example is the house in Siena of Giovanantonio Vercelli, known as Il Sodoma: "He was an eccentric man, and to please the lower classes he had his house full of parrots, baboons, dwarf asses, Elba ponies, a speaking raven, barbary horses for racing, and such like things, so that everyone was full of his follies."[21] Vasari describes this "Noah's ark" of a house in two separate biographies—that of Domenico Beccafumi, and Sodoma himself. In Sodoma's biography we learn that squirrels, badgers, jackdaws, bantams and turtle-doves also inhabited this menagerie, and that the speaking raven answered the door in the voice of his master. Sodoma raced his horses in the *palio* and won many prizes: "he boasted greatly about them, and would show them to all who visited his house, frequently displaying them at his windows."[22] The consequence of Sodoma's eccentric and libertine lifestyle was that he did not apply himself to his art, he lost his house and ended up impoverished.

The reclusive Jacopo Pontormo displayed a differently orientated eccentricity to that of the extrovert Sodoma. At the time of the Siege of Florence, "after long toil, Jacopo obtained what he had long desired, a house of his own, where he could live as he pleased" (opposite the convent of S. Maria degli Angeli in Florence).[23] By dint of further savings from his artistic commissions, Pontormo was able to repair and expand this house: "he began to build, but he did not do anything of importance. Thus, though some say he intended to spend a great deal for his state and make a convenient and artistic abode, yet it has rather the appearance of the dwelling of a fantastic and solitary man than a well-considered house. The room where he slept and sometimes worked was approached by a wooden ladder which drew up after him, so that no one could come up without his knowledge and permission."[24] Here Pontormo's withdrawal into a strangely proportioned house (with its retractable bedroom) is linked with his solitary development of a peculiar late style in the frescoes of the principal chapel of San Lorenzo in Florence, which Pontormo kept closed and shut up "so that not a living soul entered it except himself" for eleven years.[25] Gifted by nature with innate talent, both Sodoma and Pontormo were able to acquire through art the means to rise above the *bottega* and acquire a house for themselves—however, their eccentricity led to a lack of discretion resulting in the open house of Sodoma's "ark" and with Pontormo the refuge of one indifferent to the world.

Sodoma's biography begins with Vasari musing on how if those who rely solely on fortune are more often than not deceived, the contrary is also true that virtue alone cannot accomplish much if it is not accompanied by good luck. This was the theme that he chose to illustrate at the heart of the Sala del Trionfo della Virtù in his Arezzo house (see [Figure 10.2). As he put it in his autobiography: "[in the ceiling] where the woodwork is very rich, [I did] thirteen large pictures, containing the gods of heaven, the four Seasons in the corners, nude and regarding a large picture in the middle, containing life size paintings of Virtue and Envy under her feet and gripping Fortune by the hair, while she beats both. A circumstance that gave great pleasure at the time is that in going round the room Fortune at one place seems above Envy and Virtue, and at another Virtue is above Envy and Fortune, as is often the case in reality." Vasari then goes on to describe the mural decorations: "On the side walls are Plenty, Liberality, Wisdom, Prudence, Toil, Honour etc., and below them are stories of the ancient painters, Apelles, Zeuxis, Parrasius, Protogenes, with other details which I omit ...."[26]

Figure 10.2 Sala del Trionfo della Virtù, Casa Vasari, Arezzo (Courtesy of the Warburg Institute, London).

For Vasari, therefore, the acquisition and decoration of a house provided a further opportunity for self-fashioning (and not for the indulgence of personal character traits as with Sodoma and Pontormo). An artist standing under the allegory of Fortune in Vasari's house would be framed by allegorical figures and exemplary narratives from antiquity, and find themselves physically located within the explanatory framework that structures each individual biography within the grand narrative of Vasari's history of art. Like Camillo's orator standing on the stage of the memory theatre, the artist can reconfigure the compartmentalized elements of an established system of ethical, allegorical and artistic ideas to discover particular meaning by means of changing their point of view: "a circumstance that gave great pleasure." Like Aretino's house in Venice or Giovo's villa at Como, Vasari's house in Arezzo and its decoration can be taken therefore as an index of the character of the writer who owns it as well as providing a physical accompaniment to his writings. Unlike Sodoma and Pontormo's houses, however, this well-ordered structure is indicative of an equally well-designed self. While "at home" in Arezzo, Vasari found himself in a museum of portraits that integrated him within a constructed genealogy, and on stage in a theatre of memory where his self-performance took place before a perspective scene that located him in history via the mediating figures of allegory.

By means of conclusion some particulars of one wall of the Sala del Trionfo della Virtù can be usefully examined: here we find a fictive piece of sculpture represented, the multi-breasted Diana of Ephesus who, according to the iconographer Vincenzo Cartari, represents Nature. Beneath her in a fictive bronze is represented the story of Zeuxis and the Maidens of Croton from Pliny's *Natural History*, which for the Renaissance writer and artist was emblematic of an eclectic approach to the imitation of multi-faceted nature figured above. The discriminating judgment employed by Zeuxis in selecting the most beautiful features of the maidens to create his composite image of Helen, is comparable to the exercise of prudence, a virtue that is figured allegorically as a female figure above and to the right. Vasari gives Prudence a Janus-head to show that, as Cesare Ripa put it, the prudent person will look both forwards and back, recalling past events in estimating future consequences of decisions to be made; a dual perspective typical also of the historian. Below in the doorway beneath the figure of Prudence, Vasari painted an illusionistic scene opening out onto a fictive room where an artist sitting in a window embrasure studies an architectural plan while beyond the window's grill can be glimpsed a Pantheon-like building. By means of this trompe-l'oeil, Vasari opens up a view beyond the closed system of his artistic memory theatre, but also a backward as well as outward aspect as the figure looks towards the past. The distant figure of the artist is diminished in scale by perspective so that, read horizontally across the wall's surface, an equivalence is established with the figure of Zeuxis to his left. However, perspective separates the two figures as well as equating them; just as Vasari writing as art's historian noted both the similarities and differences between ancient and modern artists.

NOTES

1. Aretino, 1960, 265: "... la cui piacevolezza mi suol dire che l'entrata per terra di si fatta abitazione, per essere oscura, mal destra e di scala bestiale, simiglia a la terribilità del nome acquistatomi ne lo sciorinar del vero; poi soggiugne: che mi pratica punto, trova ne la mia pura, schietta e naturale amicizia quella tranquilla contezza che si sente nel comparir nel portico e ne l'affacciarsi a i balconi sopradetti." Translation from Aretino, 1976, 118.
2. Quoted in Yates, 2001, 136–37.
3. Ibid., 171.
4. Vasari, 1966–87, 5:291–22. Translation from Vasari, 1927, 3:223–25.
5. Vasari, 1966-87, 5:381–82: "Perciò che chiamato a Vinezia da messer Pietro Aretino, poeta allora di chiarissimo nome e mio amicissimo, fui forzato, perché molto disiderava vedermi, andar là; il che feci anco volentieri per vedere l'opere di Tiziano e d'altri pittori in quel viaggio. La qual cosa mi venne fatta, però che in pochi giorni vidi in Modena et in Parma l'opere del Coreggio, quelle di Giulio Romano in Mantoa, e l'antichità di Verona." Translation in Vasari, 1927, 4:268.
6. Corti e.a., 1981, 21. For the Casa Vasari in Arezzo see in this catalogue in particular Alessandro Cecchi, "La Casa del Vasari in Arezzo", (Ibid., 21–34). For the history of the Casa Vasari in Arezzo and iconographical readings of its decorations, see Berti, 1955; Cheney, 1985; Paolucci and Maetzke, 1988; Albrecht, 1985; Rubin, 1995, and Cecchi, 1998. For Vasari's house in Florence and the relation of its decoration to his historical writings, see Jacobs, 1984.
7. Vasari, 1966–87, 5:382: "... dove, anti che ad altro volessi por mano, dipinsi nella volta d'una camera che di mio ordine era stata murata nella già detta mia casa, tutte l'Arti che sono sotto il disegno, o che da lui dependono. Nel mezzo è una Fama, che siede sopra la palla del mondo e suona una tromba d'oro, gettandone via una di fuoco, finta per la Maledicenza; et intorno a lei sono con ordine tutte le dette Arti con i loro strumenti in mano. E perché non ebbi tempo a far il tutto, lascia otto ovali per fare in essi otto ritratti di naturale de' primi delle nostre arti." Translation in Vasari, 1927, 4:268.
8. Vasari, 1966–87, 3:438–39.
9. Filarete, 1965, 259.
10. Vasari, 1966–87, 3:246. See also Albrecht, 1985, 90, for a discussion of the formative influences on Vasari, including Filarete.
11. Vasari, 1966–87, 3:70. For a panel in the Louvre matching this description, sometimes attributed to Uccello, see Emison, 2004, 285–87.
12. On Giovio's villa and collection of portraits, see Rovelli, 1928, and Klinger, 1991.
13. Vasari, 1966–87, 5:185; translation in Vasari, 1927, 3:155. Klinger makes important points about the inspirational role of Giovio's portrait collection and the function of portrait images as representations *for* personal memory (rather than necessarily "likenesses" *of* individuals), and of the role of "imitative geneaologies" within professions where individuals are unrelated by blood, that together with the didactic function of personal "museums" are equally applicable to the case of Vasari. See Klinger, 1991, 99, 108.
14. See Frey and Frey, 1920, 1:124. Vasari's familiarity with Giovio went back more than a decade earlier; for example, he wrote to Niccolò Vespucci in 1531 stating that: "i miei protettori sono monsignore Iovio, messer Claudio Tolomei et il Cesano ...." See Frey and Frey, 1920, 1:2.
15. For example, Giovio suggested the title of the work to Vasari: Frey and Frey, 1920, 1:215. Caro congratulated Vasari on his achievement and suggested stylistic improvements: Ibid., 1:209–10.

16. Vasari 1966–87, VI, p. 389. The fact that Molza died in 1544, two years before the supposed date of this dinner in 1546, has led to doubts about the veracity of Vasari's account. Boase, 1979, 44, for example, redates it to 1543. Barolsky, 1991, 112–15 interprets it as a literary invention. The manuscript of the *Lives* was finished by July 1547 when the Olivetan monks of Rimini began work on a fair copy. It seems impossible that Vasari can have started work on the text in 1546 and finished it by this time. Vasari was already described as "historico, poeta, philosopho e pittore" by Pietro Aretino in a letter dated 7 June 1536 and published in the first volume of *Letters* in 1538, reproduced in Frey and Frey, 1920, 1:70. Similarly, Don Miniato Pitti described him as "pittore, istorico e poeta" in a letter of 1539: Ibid., 1:100–01. In the letter to Duke Cosimo of 8 March 1550 (Frey and Frey, 1920, 1:270), which accompanied the presentation copy of the *Lives*, Vasari described them as "non le fatiche et lo stento di duo mesi, ma quelle di dieci anni ...."

17. Vasari, 1966–87, 5:100: "Aveva fra' Sebastiano vicino al Popolo una assai buona casa, la quale egli si avea murato, et in quello con grandissima contentezza si vivea senza più curarsi di dipignere o lavorare ..." Translation in Vasari, 1927, 3:118.

18. Vasari, 1966–87, 5:268.

19. Ibid., 3:611.

20. Ibid., 3:220.

21. Ibid., 5:166: "Il qual Soddoma, perché come capriccioso, aveva sempre in casa, per sodisfare al popolaccio, papagalli, bertuccie, asini nani, cavalli piccoli dell'Elba, un corbo che parlava, barbari da correr palii, et altre si fatte cose, si aveva acquistato un nome fra il volgo, che non si diceva se non delle sue pazzie." Translation in Vasari, 1927, 3:141 (life of Beccafumi).

22. Vasari, 1966–87, 5:381–85. Translation in Vasari, 1927, 3:285–89.

23. Vasari, 1966–87, 5:325. Translation in Vasari, 1927, 3:248.

24. Vasari, 1966–87, 5:327–28: "Anzi, se bene alcuni affermano che egli aveva animo di spendervi secondo lo stato suo grossamanete e fare una abitazione comoda e che avesse qualche disegno, si vede non dimeno che quello che fece, o venisse cio dal non aver il modo da spendere o da altra cagione, ha più tosto cera di casamento da uomo fantastico e soletario che di ben considerata abitura." Translation in Vasari, 1927,3:250.

25. Vasari, 1966–87, 5:331.

26. Ibid., 6:391–92: "... dove sono gli Dei celesti, et in quattro angoli i quattro Tempi dell'anno, ignudi, i quali stanno a vedere un gran quadro che è in mezzo, dentro al quale sono in figure grandi quanto il vivo, la Virtù che ha sotto i piedi l'Invidia e, presa la Fortuna per i capegli, bastona l'una e l'altra; e quello che molto allora piacque si fu che, in girando la sala attorno, et essendo in mezzo la Fortuna, viene talvolta l'Invidia a esser sopra essa Fortuna e Virtù, e d'altra parte la Virtù sopra l'Invidia e Fortuna, si come si vede che aviene spesse volte veramente. Dintorno nella facciate sono la Copia, la Liberalità, la Sapienza, la Prudenza, la Fatica, l'Onore et altre cose simili; sotto attorno girano storie di pittori antichi, di Apelle, di Zeusi, Parrasio, Protogene et altri, con varii partimenti e minuzie, che lascio per brevità." Translation in Vasari, 1927, 4:276. For an explanation of the iconography of the Sala del Trionfo della Virtù see Corti, 1981, 26–29.

11 In Vasto and in London
The Rossettis' Houses as Mirrors of Dislocated National Identities

Paola Spinozzi

DANTIS TENEBRÆ.
(In Memory of my Father.)

AND did'st thou know indeed, when at the font
Together with thy name thou gav'st me his,
That also on thy son must Beatrice
Decline her eyes according to her wont,
Accepting me to be of those that haunt
The vale of magical dark mysteries
Where to the hills her poet's foot-track lies
And wisdom's living fountain to his chaunt
Trembles in music? This is that steep land
Where he that holds his journey stands at gaze
Tow'rd sunset, when the clouds like a new height
Seem piled to climb. These things I understand:
For here, where day still soothes my lifted face,
On thy bowed head, my father, fell the night.[1]

By dating *Dantis Tenebræ* to 1861,[2] William Michael Rossetti associates it directly with the publication of *The Early Italian Poets*,[3] the anthology of medieval poems his brother translated between his eighteenth and his twenty-second year. Clearly enough, the cultural legacy of Gabriele Rossetti, whose life-long, excruciating journey into Dante Alighieri's figural thought is tinged in the sonnet with the darkness of mysterious hermeneutic paths, bears import on Dante Gabriel's own study and re-working of Italian medieval poetry and painting. While the double national and cultural identity of the Rossetti family has received growing critical attention,[4] Dante Gabriel's and William Michael's different responses to their father's political stances call for closer investigation. Their filial and intellectual bond with an erudite patriot who associated Dante's destiny of *exul immeritus* with his own is fundamental for comprehending the status and the legacy of the Rossettis in Italian and English culture.

149

The places where the Rossettis lived disclose a rich net of Italo-English connections. Focusing on the Rossettis' houses in Vasto and in London involves the retrieval of writings—autobiographical and biographical—in which various dwellings host multi-layered identities and memories. The house in Vasto where Gabriele Rossetti was born, the houses in London where his children were nurtured with Italian literature, and the house where Dante Gabriel lived as an Aesthete can be regarded as objects of narration mediated by memory. Gabriele's sons never saw his native place, but William Michael's narrations about the Rossettis' houses in Vasto and in London are conscientious contributions to the construction of family memories. To such devoted acts of recollection Dante Gabriel opposed amnesia, which marked a cultural distance between their father's Italian house and his own fin de siècle one.

The house where Gabriele Rossetti was born is no longer a dwelling place. Were it not for substantial textual evidence, the presence of the Rossettis in the house would now be very dim. The building in Via Arno, as it was when Nicola Rossetti and Maria Francesca Pietrocola lived there, can only be reconstructed by juxtaposing, or superimposing, visual and verbal pictures of the past. Autobiographical verses by Gabriele Rossetti, excerpts from the biographies written by William Michael, Teodorico Pietrocola Rossetti and Maria Giartosio De Courten will be analysed together with two photographs dating to the early twentieth century and one to the 1980s.

Gabriele Rossetti's recollections of his birthplace are deeply romanticised, above all in the last years of his life, when elegy proves the poetic mode most suited to express an old man's recollection of a lost *locus amœnus*. Sapphire, emerald and pearl constitute the iconic core of his nostalgia for the Adriatic sea and the Pennines. The vividness of his images is pervaded by the sorrowful awareness that remembrance is, and will be, his only mode of vision:

> Scenic seascape, whose reflection, whose whisper
> I can only hear and see as internal image
> Where I glowed with the vivid azure
> Of a beautiful sky, the sapphire of a beautiful sea:
> Beautiful fields where dawn or sunset offer
> Emerald and pearls, grass and dew; ...
> Farewell forever! Before my eyes
> You will come never again: forever farewell![5]

In 1861 Teodorico Pietrocola Rossetti begins the biography of his uncle with precise references to the morphology of the territory. Casa Rossetti is one of the towering houses that look like fortresses and protect Vasto against earthquakes (see Figure 11.1). Five high floors overlooking the sea are the distinctive architectural features of a dwelling which, observed from different angles, arouses contrasting impressions:

Figure 11.1 Casa Rossetti, Vasto, c. 1910, anonymous photograph from Domenico Ciàmpoli, *La famiglia Rossetti* (Rome: Tipografia Artero, 1911).

In the territory around Vasto, shaped by valleys and hills, a city rises in a valley luxuriant with vine and olive trees. The town is surrounded by a ring of towering houses which guard it against upheavals and earth-quakes shaking the valley now and then. Among those houses there is one with five very high floors and a large barn on the ground floor. From a distance, at noon, it gives the impression that the last floor is an eagle's nest, while seen from within the town it looks like a humble abode, because the access from the road is to the last floor. In that modest house ... Nicola Rossetti and Maria Francesca Pietrocola lived ... and there Gabriele Rossetti was born on the 1st of March 1783 .... That outstanding house was finally purchased by G.A. Rulli who years ago was generous enough to donate to the Town Hall in Vasto two rooms where the Rossettis were born, provided that the place would aptly bear remembrance of the great ones who were born there.[6]

Viewed at a distance, the height of the house produces a majestic, dizzy effect, that Pietrocola Rossetti visually renders by comparing the fifth floor to an eagle's nest. Closer inspection, however, reveals that it is a humble abode. The magnifying and diminishing effects that characterise the rhetorical description of the house can be read as allusions to Gabriele Rossetti's existential condition of intellectual fervour and estrangement, of political engagement and dispossession.

Unlike his cousin, William Michael Rossetti's recollects the birth of his father without mentioning the house. Instead, he provides philological and historical details and focuses on the etymology and geo-political location of Vasto Ammone:

> Gabriele Rossetti was born on 28 February 1783, in the city of Vasto, named also (by a corruption from Longobard nomenclature) Vasto Ammone, in the Province of Abruzzo Citeriore, on the Adriatic coast of the then Kingdom of Naples. Vasto is a very ancient place, a municipal town of the Romans, then designated Histonium.[7]

The lack of references to the house where William Michael's grandparents lived must not be fortuitous, if one bears in mind that he never visited it. Why he ignored Vasto is still a puzzlement, above all because he travelled extensively through northern Italy and went to Venice, Pallanza, Genoa, San Remo, to accompany his wife Lucy Madox Brown who suffered from a bronchial disease.

The house will again come out prominently in the family biography published in 1931 by another Italian relative, Maria Luisa Giartosio de Courten. Like Pietrocola Rossetti, she immediately focuses on the Romantic setting:

> Their abode rose high on a steep rock and, due to its severe and outstanding look; it resembled an ancient fortress dominating a very ancient town in Abruzzo, a town that boasts an emerald green sea and an endlessly beautiful sky. And the child was keen on beholding the spectacle before his eyes for hours on end ....[8]

By emphasising the aura of the site, she portrays Gabriele Rossetti as a Romantic Italian son born in a house built as a Gothic fortress and grown in a region where the sublime and the picturesque merge in the steep rocks, emerald sea and azure sky.

Casa Rossetti now hosts the Biblioteca Comunale di Vasto, the town library. Although the interior has been completely altered and the pieces of furniture have been removed, the house is a repository of memories: 132

letters by and to Gabriele Rossetti, the manuscript of his *Comento Analitico* to the *Purgatorio* (Analytical comment on Dante's Purgatory), some original editions of his literary works, five letters in Italian by William Michael Rossetti to the Mayor of Vasto and the *Memorandum*, enclosed to his first letter and consisting of some papers, now not easily legible.[9] The donations to the Town Council testify to a cultural enterprise undertaken not only to commemorate Gabriele Rossetti in his native town, but also to symbolically fulfil his dream to return to Italy.

Yet, William Michael's engagement at a distance expresses his ambivalent attitude towards the Abruzzese matrix of his family. Constant epistolary relationships with Italian parentage did not arouse any desire to visit the places his father had intensely, and vainly, hoped to see again. The Italian roots of the English Rossettis have not been preserved in the house in Vasto. Instead, letters, biographical and autobiographical documents have functioned as primary mediators of memory. The house has been textualised; it has become memory, constructed through writings that bear the signs of inter-cultural exchanges.

Writing, rather than paying visit to someone in another country, was perfectly appropriate, considering that the exchange of letters was a highly codified social ritual. However, writing to relatives in Vasto instead of travelling to meet them in their homes reveals William Michael Rossetti's response to the cultural identity of his family. His effort to find a balance between involvement with and detachment from Abruzzo reveals his awareness that his father's past was a treasured legacy as well as a burden, because it enclosed severed cultural roots.

Verbal and material construction of family memories intertwined, when William Michael strengthened his epistolary relationship with Giuseppe Marchesani by conveying objects from the Rossettis' house in London to the Marchesanis' house in Vasto. Nowadays Palazzo Marchesani, the stately home in Via S. Maria Maggiore, still bears witness to two nationalities and cultural matrices. The letters by William Michael, the photographs and the copies of Talbot daguerreotypes kept at Palazzo Marchesani are vivid, disquieting testimonies of the virtual encounter between the English and Italian members of the family. In fact, the gifts function not only as a surrogate of the journey to Vasto but also as a reunion: itinerant simulacra serve as iconic substitutes for missing physical presences. In particular, the photographs produce disquieting refraction effects. Viewed in Palazzo Marchesani, the picture taken by Lewis Carroll and known as *The Rossetti Family at Cheyne Walk* (see Figure 11.2), together with other ones by Julia Margaret Cameron and by the Elliot & Fry laboratory, are powerful reminders of an English identity that disrupts the stillness of an Abruzzese provincial residence.[10]

The houses of the Rossetti family in London, as William Michael described them in *Some Reminiscences* (1906), are places of dislocation and re-construction of national and cultural identity. Of the first house

Figure 11.2 Lewis Carroll, *The Rossetti Family at 16, Cheyne Walk*, photograph, 1863.

at 38, Charlotte Street, Portland Place, where he was born on the 25th of September 1829, he only remembers the simple façade and small size.[11] The second house at 50, Charlotte Street, where the six family members lived together, revives with childhood recollections.[12] William Michael's visual memory portrays the living space as a repository of two cultures: two small oil paintings, one of the beach of Vasto and the other of the Grotta Azzurra in Capri, received from the local artist Gabriele Smargiassi, and a framed engraving of Queen Victoria seated in her armchair at the theatre are a bizarre collage of typical Southern Italian souvenirs and conventional images of Victorian England.[13] The pictures mirror the Rossettis' will to bear witness to their Italian origins as well as to uphold their newly established English identity.

When the family moved to Mornington Crescent in 1851, Dante Gabriel moved to Chatham Place. While translating early Italian poetry, he assimilated the Stilnovo cult of love in Dante's *Vita Nova*, but was perplexed by his father's interpretation of *The Divine Comedy* and disinclined to read his critical works. Dante Gabriel's deep reverence and subtly disguised self-centeredness permeate two letters to his father, whom he pleased by writing in his native language.

14 Chatham Place, Blackfriars Bridge. Saturday [October 1853].

My Dearest Father,

... I would not have delayed so long in answering your dear and affectionate letter, but that I was wishing to speak somewhat, in my reply, about the *Arpa Evangelica*, and to read it in full before writing to you. Nor have I yet, being much occupied just now, found time for a deliberate reading. I have read the whole second series, the *Solemnities of the Church*, which I liked well; but more perhaps than any of the compositions there I like ... *The Penitent Woman on the Crucifix*, which appeared to me very fine, and which might almost appertain to the argument of the second series. The other evening, in my Grandfather's house, I read with him some of the Arpa.[14]

Replying to his father's letter required reading a ponderous, and often obscure poetical work. Dante Gabriel's will to respond to his father's intellectual enterprise and the lack of interest in his methods and purposes creates a divergence between affection and individual intellectual preferences. Though concealed, his ambivalence emerges from repeated declarations of high regard and apologies for over-commitment and shortness of time.

Thursday evening, 12 January 1854.

Dearest Father,

Excuse me for having so long ago received your dear letter without as yet replying. I heard lately with the greatest sorrow the bad news of your health. But from what I hear now I trust that you find yourself a little better. I would like to say *much*.

I can't yet say that I have read the *Arpa Evangelica* right through; but I have read many compositions in it since I wrote last, and I specially remember that addressed *To the Guardian Angel* as one of the most beautiful, and on an idea which has always seemed to me one of the most poetical that can be treated.[15]

After the death of his wife Lizzie Siddall, in 1862, he found a new dwelling place at 16, Cheyne Walk, Chelsea, a grand historic mansion with a picturesque view on the unembanked river. In *Recollections of Dante Gabriel Rossetti* by T. Hall Caine (1883), *Dante Gabriel Rossetti, An Illustrated Memorial of His Art and Life* (1899) by H.C. Marillier, and *Some Reminiscences* (1906) by William Michael Rossetti, Tudor House is portrayed as a lively, eccentric meeting place, a home to be treasured, embellished and shared with A.C. Swinburne, George Meredith and his brother William Michael.

Tudor House was an aesthetic workshop where Rossetti, endowed with an innate taste for design and interior decoration, innovated English decor. Creativity intended as a need, aesthetic as well as psychological, to be creative, was at the core of a conception of art that Rossetti shared with William Morris. While Morris was concerned about the social implications of the artistic act, Rossetti was fascinated by artistic personality, intended as an aura, an emanation that could permeate with originality, uniqueness and eccentricity the place where it expressed itself. In spite of Rossetti's more conspicuous late Romantic attitude, both regarded furnishing a house as a form of art and art as an antidote to intellectual and spiritual stagnation. Searching for pieces of furniture and *objets d'art* could give a pleasure that healed melancholy and depression.

> He had borne a leading share in the Morris decorative movement; and now he was destined to pave the way for the modern craze for old oak furniture and blue china. Bric-à-brac was not of much account in England when Rossetti first began rummaging the dealers' shops for old and battered cabinets, Chippendale chairs, carved oak panels, "hawthorn" jars (the name was his invention), and an infinite variety of brass implements, chandeliers, sconces, mirrors, and vases of antique and comparatively neglected types. As regards blue china he found a rival in Mr. Whistler, whose acquisitions with his own soon began to send the prices flying up; but it was a purely original idea in those days to buy up old furniture for use, and to enrich the walls of a house with panelled carvings and treasures from Japan. Those who follow the fashion to-day do it in many cases vulgarly and unintelligently, turning their houses into museums of costly and incongruous objects. So far as decoration went Rossetti knew to a hairbreadth what would harmonize and what would not, and however wide the range of his purchases might be he was never guilty of errors of taste. In such matters, it is generally conceded, his judgment was a touchstone.[16]

Rossetti creates a living space marked by valuable, heterogeneous objects that, though made in different countries and with different materials, were neither incompatible with each other nor with Tudor House (see Figure 11.3). The large amounts of money he spent in Japanese prints, engravings and xylographs reveal a compulsive buyer and a collector, and not at all a commercial entrepreneur, like Christopher Dresser or Arthur Liberty. While emphasising the pleasure of inhabiting a spacious, scenic, sophisticated old building,[17] William Michael suggests that "Chinese tables and chairs, Dutch tiles, Flemish, Oriental and African curtains and draperies, and a variety of pieces of furniture"[18] bear the signature of a prodigal, eccentric artist. The non lucrative nature of Rossetti's "Japanese mania" contributed to mythicize his liberal, charismatic personality among Victorian admirers

Figure 11.3 Henry Treffry Dunn, *Rossetti's Dining Room at 16, Cheyne Walk*, from H.C. Marillier. Dante Gabriel Rossetti, *An Illustrated Memorial of His Art and Life* (London: George Bell and Sons, 1899, 227).

and to raise his status among connoisseurs of Japanese art and design, like James McNeill Whistler and the Aesthetes.[19]

In Tudor House, Rossetti the Aesthete and Rossetti the Decadent cohabited. Each room provided ideal settings for late Romantic rites, as can be inferred from the water-colour drawings by his assistant, Mr. Treffry Dunn, which Marillier included in his biography of Rossetti. Thanks to the drawings —the only existing records of the interior as it used to be while Rossetti lived there—Marillier's illustrated memorial acquires the special, dual status of a biographical and iconographic document.

The sophistication and gloominess of Victorian rooms become the symbol of an exquisitely Aesthetic and morbidly Decadent life. The studio (see Figure 11.4]) where the poor lighting damaged Rossetti's gradually failing eyesight, and the bedroom, where the dark, heavy furniture, curtains and hangings created an atmosphere of ghostliness, are places of malaise. Hall Caine's account of his first visit to Rossetti in 1880 shows how the description of a house merges with the narration of a late Romantic life.

> [The bedroom] was entered from another and smaller room, used as a breakfast-room. This outer room was made fairly bright and cheerful by a glittering chandelier ... but the inner room was dark with heavy hangings round the walls as well as the bed, and thick velvet curtains before the windows, so that candles seemed unable to light it and voices sounded thick and muffled.

Figure 11.4 Henry Treffry Dunn, *Rossetti's Studio at 16, Cheyne Walk*, from H.C. Marillier. Dante Gabriel Rossetti, *An Illustrated Memorial of His Art and Life* (London: George Bell and Sons, 1899, 224).

> An enormous black oak chimney-piece of curious design, having an ivory crucifix on the largest of its ledges, covered a part of one side and reached to the ceiling. Cabinets and the usual furniture of a bedroom occupied places about the floor; and in the middle, before a little couch, stood a table on which was a wire lantern containing a candle.... I remarked that he probably burned a light all night. He said that was so. "My curse", he added, "is insomnia ..." It did not escape me that on the table stood two small bottles, sealed and labelled, together with a little measuring glass. Without looking further at it, I asked if that were his medicine. "They say there is a skeleton in every cupboard", he said in a low voice, "and that's mine; it is chloral."[20]

The bed, which Rossetti kept to the end of his life, was sent to him by his mother on his settling at Chelsea, and was the one in which he and his brother and sisters had all been born: a family souvenir treasured for its high symbolic value and surrounded by bizarre bric-à-brac.

Walter Pater was the first among Rossetti's critics and biographers to perceive the correspondence between the house in Chelsea and *The House of Life. A Sonnet Sequence* (1881). Rossetti inhabited his house as intimately as he inhabited his verses:

> The dwelling-place in which one finds oneself by chance or destiny, yet can partly fashion for oneself; never properly one's own at all, if it be changed too lightly; in which every object has its associations—the

dim mirrors, the portraits, the lamps, the books, the hair-tresses of the dead and visionary magic crystals in the secret drawers, the names and words scratched on the windows, windows open upon prospects the saddest or the sweetest; the house one must quit, yet taking perhaps, how much of its quietly active light and colour along with us—grown now to be a kind of raiment to one's body, as the body, according to Swedenborg, is but the raiment of the soul—under that image, the whole of Rossetti's work might count as a *House of Life* ... And it is a "haunted" house. A sense of power in love, defying distance, and those barriers which are so much more than physical distance, of unutterable desire penetrating into the world of sleep, however "lead-bound", was one of those anticipative notes obscurely struck in *The Blessed Damozel*, and, in his later work, makes him speak sometimes almost like a believer in mesmerism. Dream-land ... is to him ... a real country, a veritable expansion of, or addition to, our waking life; and he did well perhaps to wait carefully upon sleep, for the lack of it became mortal disease with him.[21]

The conflation of material place and poetic construction engenders a dwelling, real and mental, where objects coalesce with oneiric activities, metaphysical experiences, and plunges into the self. The relationship between objects and owners is so intimate that, when people pass away, they take the vividness of the house away. The house envelops its dwellers and, since in Symbolist aesthetics body and soul are inextricably connected, the house encloses—and discloses—the soul. Aesthetically experienced as the place where innermost perceptions can be poured out, the house blurs the boundaries between sleep and wake. And since the living space and the self incessantly vibrate with remembrances, thoughts, perceptions, since objects are constantly permeated by mental associations, interiority is a *mise-en-abyme* of the interiors of the house, the inside corresponds with the outside.

Pater's act of sublimation, even of mysticization, is counterbalanced by the irony with which Pre-Raphaelite devotees responded to a house full of exotic animals who died, disappeared, were replaced and took possession of the neighbours' gardens, in spite of the wire cages.[22] Christina Rossetti's hymn in praise of the wombat, Edward Burne-Jones's little sketches and William Bell Scott's drawings of the bizarre marsupial, Dante Gabriel's declaration of affection—"The Wombat is a Joy, a Triumph, a Delight, a Madness!"—[23] which could only be rivalled by his penchant for the seal, drawn at dinner time, are more than *divertissements*. Indeed, the Pre-Raphaelites reveal a deep awareness that the representation of an artist's house is an aesthetic manifesto, since it involves the rendering of a cultural milieu. While deeply enjoying, even magnifying, a living space saturated with the idiosyncrasies and extravagances of a creative mind, they parade their mutual sense of belonging to a circle of artists with multiple talents, but also deflate their extra-ordinariness by performing verbal and visual acts of mockery and self-parody.

Gabriele Rossetti's native house in Vasto became a mental *locus amœnus* tinged with nostalgia; Dante Gabriel Rossetti's historic house in London fostered a late-Romantic cult of personality. However, both the native house of an Italian exile and the eccentric house of an English poet-painter are places of memory. They are autobiographical and biographical repositories of a strong sense of national identity; both grow on textualisation. The house made into text explains why the material preservation of the place was not significant. Instead, "writing" the place allows filling it with meaning, it activates signification, and the houses of the Rossettis proliferate signs of cultural dis-location and re-location. While transferring objects from one country to another, or from one house to another, the Rossettis construe them with deep intercultural significance.

Gabriele Rossetti, his two sons and two daughters created a cultural system of their own, rooted in Gabriele's Italy but raised in Victorian London. It is true, as Domenico Ciàmpoli declared in 1911 with rhetorical emphasis, that the father transfused his strong temperament into his children, who became stronger;[24] but it is also true that such strength nourished different temperaments.

Cheyne Walk, with its bric-à-brac and its menagerie, its sombre atmosphere and lively intellectual life was a "House of Life", and Dante Gabriel, with his love for hospitality and need for seclusion, was its ideal Aesthetic dweller. Patriotism and Italian medieval literature, Gabriele Rossetti's cultural legacy, were fundamental for the poet-painter's self-fashioning as a fourteenth-century Italian artist. However, one can guess at what he meant in *Dantis Tenebræ* with "On thy bowed head, my father, fell the night": he knew that he would not share his father's darkness, that the memory of his own days and troubled nights would be left somewhere else, in a place of intellectual exchange, a secluded, elitist refuge inside, and outside, Victorian London.

NOTES

1. D.G. Rossetti, 1881, 275.
2. W.M. Rossetti, 1911, 668, note.
3. D.G. Rossetti, 1861.
4. Vincent, 1936; Oliva, 1984; Clifford and Roussillon, 2004. On the Abruzzese origins of the Rossetti family see Murolo, 1992, and Oliva, 1997.
5. "Vaghi lidi il cui specchio, il cui sussurro / Sol per interna imago or sento e miro, / Ove in me riflettea vivido azzurro / D'un bel ciel, d'un bel mar l'emul zaffiro: / Bei campi ove offre il dì che sorge o cade, / Quasi smeraldi e perle, erbe e rugiade; ... Addio per sempre! Innanzi al guardo mio / Non verrete mai più: per sempre addio!" The verses are quoted in Giartosio De Courten, 1931, 13–14; translation PS. I thank Gianni Oliva for generously extending to me his hypothesis about "Commiato del poeta cieco", which he identifies as the poem from which the verses are taken. The poem, uncompleted, was included in the third volume of G. Rossetti, 1929.

6. "La pianura del suolo Vastese, or dolcemente avvallata, or di colline adorna, termina colla città che a mezzogiorno si sprofonda in una valle lussureggiante di alberi fruttiferi di vigneti e di ulivi. Ivi una catena di case torreggianti accerchiano la città che come baluardi la difendono dalla frana e da' terremoti che a quando a quando conquassano miseramente la sottostante valle. Fra quelle case havvene una che ha cinque piani elevatissimi e un largo fenile al piano terreno. Se la si vede al mezzodì ei pare che l'ultimo piano sia stanza di aquile, se nell'interno della città sembra umile dimora, perciocché vi si accede per strada livellata al piano estremo. In quella modesta casa dimoravano, verso lo scorcio del secolo passato i coniugi Nicola Rossetti e Maria Francesca Pietrocola ...; —ed ivi nacque al 1° marzo 1783, Gabriele Rossetti .... Quella casa monumentale fu ultimamente acquistata da G.A. Rulli che ne' passati anni non si mostrò alieno di donare al Municipio di Vasto due camere dove nacquero i Rossetti, purché ne avesse fatto luogo atto a rammentare ai posteri i grandi che vi respirarono le prime aure di vita." Pietrocola Rossetti, 2004 (1861), 69–70; translation PS.
7. William Michael Rossetti, *II. Parentage*, in W.M. Rossetti, 1895, 1:4.
8. "La loro dimora si ergeva alta alta su una roccia dirupata, sì da rassomigliare a un antico fortilizio per l'aspetto severo ed imponente, dominando l'antichissima città dell'Abruzzo, città di smeraldo per il mare che la circonda e d'infinita bellezza di cieli. E il piccolo soleva starsene a contemplare da lassù lo spettacolo che si stendeva dinanzi ai suoi occhi ..." Giartosio De Courten, 1931, 13; translation PS.
9. See G. Rossetti, 2004, 30, 247–60.
10. Palazzo Marchesani also hosts portraits by another relative, the Vasto protophotographer Giuseppe De Guglielmo, who, impressed by Carroll's photos, realized one of the most remarkable Italian daguerreotypes of the 1880s, only discovered and reprinted in 1978. See Murolo, 2004, 23.
11. W.M. Rossetti, 1906, 1:1. See Mariani, 2004.
12. Ibid., 1:7, 9.
13. Ibid., 1:13.
14. "14 Chatham Place, Blackfriars Bridge. Sabato [Ottobre 1853] . Mio Carissimo padre, ... Non avrei indugiato tanto nel rispondere alla vostra cara ed affettuosa lettera, se non avessi desiderato di parlare alquanto, nella mia risposta, dell'*Arpa Evangelica,* e di leggerla tutta prima di scrivervi. Né ancora, essendo molto occupato in questo momento, ho io trovato tempo per una lettura accurata. Ho letto intiera la seconda serie delle *Solennità della Chiesa,* la quale mi piace assai, ma forse più ancora ... mi piace l'ultima composizione della quinta serie, *La Penitente sul Crocifisso,* la quale mi è paruta bellissima e che apparterrebbe quasi all'argomento della seconda serie. L'altra sera, a casa di mio avo, ho letto con lui qualche squarcio dell'Arpa ...." W.M. Rossetti, 1895, 2:114–16.
15. "Giovedì sera, 12 *January* [1854]. Carissimo Padre, Scusatemi che da tanto tempo ho ricevuto la vostra cara lettera, senza averci ancora risposto. Ho sentito ultimamente con grandissimo rammarico le cattive nuove della vostra salute. Ma, da quel che sento ora, spero che vi trovate un poco meglio; vorrei dir, *molto.* Non ancora posso dirvi di aver letta in tutto *l'Arpa Evangelica*; ma ne ho lette parecchie composizioni da che vi ho scritto l'ultima volta, e specialmente mi rammento quella diretta *All'Angelo Custode* come una delle più belle, e sopra un'idea che mi è sempre paruta una delle più poetiche che si possa trattare." W.M. Rossetti, 1895, 2:122–24.
16. Marillier, 1899, 121–22.
17. W.M. Rossetti, 1906, 1:272.

18. Ibid., 1:275–76.
19. See Ono, 2003.
20. Hall Caine, 1883.
21. Pater, 1910, 214–15.
22. Marillier, 1899, 228: "... a Pomeranian puppy, an Irish deerhound, a barn-owl named Jessie, another owl named Bobby, rabbits, dormice, hedgehogs, two successive wombats, a Canadian marmot or woodchuck, an ordinary marmot, kangaroos and wallabies, a deer, two or more armadillos, a white mouse with her brood, a raccoon, squirrels, a mole, peacocks, wood-owls, Virginian owls, horned owls, a jackdaw, a raven, parakeets, a talking parrot, chameleons, grey lizards, Japanese salamanders, and a laughing jackass. Besides these there was a certain famous bull, a zebu, which cost Rossetti £20 ..., and which manifested such animosity in confinement that it had to be disposed of at once. The strident voices of the peacocks were so little appreciated in the neighbourhood that Lord Cadogan caused a paragraph to be inserted in all his leases thereafter forbidding these birds to be kept."
23. Marillier, 1899, 229.
24. Ciàmpoli, 1911, 15: "il nocchiero poderoso, onde i rampolli venner su più viridi e fiorenti del vecchio tronco."

12 William Morris's Houses and the Shaping of Aesthetic Socialism

Vita Fortunati

William Morris's houses are cultural constructions, since they are not only places where the choice of materials is charged with a high symbolic value, but also "recipients for ideals"; they are houses embodying a strong tension between the public and the private sphere, between hospitality and separatism. My working hypothesis is that the architecture of both Red House and Kelmscott Manor expresses Morris's utopian thought; more precisely, the two houses are experiments inextricably connected with the development of his socialist ideals. My enquiry into the structural elements of his houses is aimed at pointing out dialectical, even controversial issues connected with his utopian socialism; interestingly enough, such issues come out prominently from his lectures, essays and utopian romance, *News from Nowhere* (1890). The architectural features and planimetry of the two houses can thus be regarded as visualizations of his theoretical views on the living space. Nevertheless, they enclose a series of contradictions, which reveal not only how Morris strenuously attempted to overcome Victorian stereotypes on the concept of the house and on hospitality, but also, and inevitably, how deeply tied his views were to the tradition of vernacular dwellings and country houses.[1] Far from rejecting established notions of the English tradition, Morris tries to revitalize them by injecting his ideas on the Gothic revival and the Arts and Crafts movement.[2] In this perspective, Morris's houses can be re-considered as the embodiment of various cultural memories which he tries to inter-fuse, but which sometimes clash with each other. These two buildings are icons to be decoded, since they no doubt present original elements which mark the development of modern architecture in England,[3] but they also lend themselves to be read as sites that consolidate some conservative views and myths of an eternally medieval, rural England.

Emblematically, Red House and Kelmscott Manor mark two crucial stages in Morris's life and reveal how biographical vicissitudes affect utopian projects.[4] The notion of medieval hospitality at the foundation of the Pre-Raphaelite Brotherhood was tested by the strong individual temperaments of each member and later by the complicated *ménage à trois* involving Morris, Jane Burden and Rossetti. In this sense, the idyllic beauty of these places conceals turmoil and distresses which shed an intriguing, disquieting shadow on their Arcadian quality.

When architect Philip Webb started the building of Red House, Morris was newly married and 23 years old. Dante Gabriel Rossetti's charismatic personality, the ideals of Pre-Raphaelitism and Morris's vivid recollections of 1857 frescoes of the Oxford Union are key elements for comprehending the formation of his intellectual identity and the embryonic stage of his socialism. The discovery of Kelmscott Manor, instead, took place in 1871, when Morris, acquainted with Marx's theories, had become a member of the Socialist League, a commercial entrepreneur and an established writer and artist. His will to conjugate theory and praxis led him to engage himself in a variety of activities ranging from public speeches to Arts and Crafts manufactures.

In spite of the different nature of the two houses, they share specific common elements, since they bear dramatic witness to the gap between Morris's theoretical, ideal assumptions and the practical deficiencies resulting from the construction of Red House and "re-construction" of Kelmscott Manor. In this sense, even though these houses were meant to enhance the quality of life of their dwellers by being shaped as living spaces both beautiful and functional to daily life, they were conceived without taking into account neither practical matters such as the soil and the climatic conditions, nor the complex issues involved in creating a communal house for artists. Red House and Kelmscott Manor are definitely more important as models rather than as places that bear witness to a harmonious relationship between their dwellers and the surrounding nature. They both remain as exemplary models rather than as strictly practical solutions to the problems of alienation and ugliness in an industrial society.

The genesis of Red House is linked to Morris's friendship with Philip Webb and Charles Faulkner, with whom he discussed the project during a boat trip to France. No doubt the house bears witness to a special bond between Webb and Morris; it is a unique work of collaboration between two artists/designers, a client and an architect, and expresses pleasure in labour and in the craftsman's creative freedom. Webb and Morris, both admirers of the English countryside and of medieval buildings, had complementary personalities.[5] Webb's mind was practical, while Morris was a versatile young artist inclined to romance and eager to experiment with various techniques. The ambitious idea of building a house that could host two families, the Morrises and the Burne-Joneses, was sponsored by Morris's recently inherited fortune. Critics have pointed out that the organisation of space in Red House reveals an unsolved tension between the desire to create communal areas where friends and fellow artists could convene, and to retreat from the world by creating a secluded place. In her recent biography on William Morris, Fiona McCarthy has described Red House as a "deeply symbolic building",[6] where Morris's desire to create a beautiful, aesthetic place of retreat contrasts with his will to take leave from it. Red House exemplifies a dialectics between the private and the public dimension, between idyllic privacy and the warmth of hospitality, between "inwardness" and "outwardness".

The Gothic revival promoted by Pugin and Ruskin allows Webb and Morris to retrieve and mingle architectural elements from different historical periods: Red House, though built according to a thirteenth-century style, hosts elements which remind of other epochs, for instance the domestic stained glass typical of fifteenth-century dwellings. In fact, Morris regarded Gothic architecture as a potentially modern style, because it was open to a variety of uses responding to a wide range of needs and adaptable to the specific features of an area which bore witness to vernacular architecture. There are elements which recall monastic buildings and signify seclusion and separateness. The idea of a secluded place is particularly evident in the layout of the grounds of Red House: in fact, the medieval plot garden embodies Morris's views on gardening, as emerges from "Making the Best of It":

> [The garden] should be well fenced from the outside world. It should by no means imitate either the wilfulness or the wildness of Nature, but should look like a thing never to be seen except near a house. It should, in fact, look like a part of the house.[7]

The garden (see Figure 12.1) is the focal centre of the house, in fact the L-shaped plan is tied to it like a quadrangle of an Oxford college. This

Figure 12.1 Red House, Garden (© Vita Fortunati).

structure was intended to stress the fellowship of the inhabitants and the harmony of the building. The windows in the East façade overlook the well, the symbol of sustenance,[8] while in the garden "hedges and wattle fences create a network of enclosures".[9]

In spite of the explicit allusion to the idea of the pilgrimage, drawn from *Canterbury Tales*, the revivalist idea of hospitality passes through an initiation rite that only a few could perform. In this sense, the pointed porch is boldly marked and leads to *Pilgrim's Rest*, a small bench for the visitors: Webb and Morris transform the medieval hall, which functioned as a place of welcome to travellers of different classes, into a smaller room, more typical of Victorian houses, leading to the other rooms on the ground floor as well as to the staircase to the upper floors. Once in the house, a rich network of allusions recalls the lives and ideals of its creators. Far from being a place reviving medieval festivities, it became the embodiment of Tennyson's "Palace of Art", an elitist abode for people sharing intellectual and artistic values.[10]

Morris constantly strove to choose refined and useful everyday objects, which were to be different from the pretentious, uncomfortable pieces of furniture on the market. Such a pervasive idea of beauty and fellowship is emphasised by pieces of furniture made by artists who were friends, and through decorations and mottos—like the Morris family crest, or Morris's personal motto, "Si je Puis"—"If I Can", which establish an inter-textual dialogue among the artists. The motto in French expresses his will to create an environment true to his principles and ideals. Such strong-mindedness, while highlighting his relentless energy and versatility, also reveals the largeness of his financial means: Morris as the host and the owner who proudly presides over his abode. However, and more subtly, the choice of Van Eyck's motto "als ich kan" reveals the awareness of a multiple talent but also of the problematic use of different artistic skills.

Morris wanted to create a deep correspondence between the exterior and the interior. Outside, the use of red brick, a conspicuous material that contrasted with the green-grey colour of the local stone, is associated with the vertical lines of the roof, gable and well, all of them Neo-Gothic. Inside, the extensive use of massive, dark wood for the staircase, ceiling and walls is associated with the thin lines and curves of the pieces of furniture. There is a balance between dramatic effects like the ones produced by the oak staircase looking up to the painted pattern of the ceiling and the huge presence of white paint and light window frames.

The symmetrical, though simple, linear shapes of the first-floor drawing room which Morris wished to be "the most beautiful room in the world" are complemented by some essential pieces of furniture. Burne-Jones's wall painting *The Wedding Breakfast*, originally intended for a series on *The Wedding Procession of Sir Degrevaunt*, portrays William Morris and Jane Burden as King and Queen hosting a banquet: Burne-Jones pays a tribute to the conviviality and sociability of the owners of the house, recollecting the medieval habit of patrons as art commissioners.

A corner of the drawing room on the first floor, where Jane Morris and her friends embroidered decorations for Red House, is lighted by the beautiful oriel window, that reminds of the complex role women played in the Arts and Crafts movement. Morris tried to come to terms with the discrepancy between design, intended as an intellectual, male activity, and embroidery, traditionally considered a manual, female task. Even though Morris himself was proud of his skills in embroidery, such craft remained silent, understated and largely neglected until the 1970s, when scholars like Anthea Callen emphasised the primary female contribution to the Arts and Crafts.[11]

Red House is the fine result of a complex balance between tradition and innovation: it is capped by a steeply pitched tile roof reminiscent of domestic Tudor houses, the very soul of the house, as Ruskin pointed out. In fact the steeple, gabled roof of Red House seems to reflect the importance which Ruskin attached here to symbolism of shelter; but the great innovation, as architects have explained, is in the freedom of fenestration. Windows of various size and shape enliven the massive volumes of the house and bring brilliant clarity into the rooms. The revolutionary element of fenestration was determined by the interior functional requirements.

The unconventional distribution of the rooms testifies to Morris's will to break the hierarchy of the Victorian family. As Girouard remarks, "the original kitchen is down a passage a short way from the dining room."[12] Instead of being separate from each other, the two places communicate and suggest equality rather than hierarchy, and above all make clear that the spaces for work and for leisure are intertwined. The architectural plan of Red House encouraged a combination of working and re-creative activities under the same roof. Indeed, the original, though unaccomplished, idea of a house hosting two families was sustained by the belief that home and workshop could cohabit.[13]

As both Morris's letters and biographies have clearly outlined, in this house he spent a most happy period in his life and week-ends devoted to decorating the rooms and playing games. To Georgiana Burne-Jones Red House looked like a building symbolising the perfect balance between aesthetic and functional qualities. Though the house was not large, purpose and proportion had been so skilfully observed that the visitor had the impression of ample space. Such a utopian interactive community can be regarded as the model for the Bloomsbury group, which used to meet in Vanessa Bell's and Duncan Grant's country house at Charleston Farm.

Morris's project of communal life only lasted a few years and came to an end after Georgiana Burne-Jones's illness, due to psychological tensions and practical matters. The very choice of the place where to build Red House proved problematic. As a matter of fact, a secluded place next to the train station sounds like an oxymoron: Bexleyheath was an orchard in the little hamlet of Upton, very near London and Greenwich railway but also close to the legendary Chaucerian route of the Canterbury pilgrims. Nonetheless, the proximity to the new North Kent Line proved more relevant to

Morris's plans. A young married man of means and of ambitious projects, the medieval Morris actually lived like a modern commuter. This antinomy testifies to the troublesome modernity of his temperament, an inability to stay permanently in one place and to lay roots. It also predicts the collapse of the house as the place of stable memory, where traces of successive generations should be guarded. Morris's desire to preserve family histories—his own and his friends'—are jeopardised by the dissolving, quickening pace of modernity.

According to Mackail, after the collapse of the utopian dream of Red House "Morris never set eyes on it again, confessing that the sight of it would be more than he could bear."[14] Such failure did not anyhow prevent him from pursuing the ideal of a house like a harbour of refuge and in 1871 he found an advertisement for Kelmscott Manor in a London estate agent catalogue. An Elizabethan stone house, set in the picturesque, small rural hamlet of Kelmscott on the edge of the Cotswolds, soon became a powerful source of inspiration. If Red House never stimulated Morris to write about it, Kelmscott Manor, instead, engendered acts of textualization which responded to different needs. Morris wrote vivid, detailed descriptions of the house both in his letters and in a well known article,[15] but the most striking evidence that Kelmscott Manor became the symbol of his socialist ideals can be found in *News from Nowhere*, his utopian romance published in 1890. The pilgrimage of the two protagonists, William Guest and Ellen, travelling by boat from Victorian Hammersmith to Kelmscott, is fulfilled in the last pages, when they reach the old house by the Thames:

> Yes, friend, this is what I came out to see; this many-gabled old house built by the simple country- folk of the long-past times, regardless of all the turmoil that was going on in cities and courts, is lovely still amidst all the beauties that these latter days have created ... It seems to me as if it had waited for these happy days, and held in it the gathered crumbs of happiness of the confused and turbulent past.[16]

In this passage Kelmscott Manor becomes a multi-layered symbolic place: a Golden Age of happiness and friendship among human beings, an Arcadia where life is beautified by the direct contact with Nature. Idealisation, expressed in a simplified, even naïve, vision of the builders as "simple country folk", becomes evident by recalling a basic principle of his communist utopia, namely the absence of hard, mechanical labour which is done by "immensely improved machinery". Nevertheless, the reader retains a vision of an Earthly Paradise, where the land spontaneously brings forth. Eventually, it is almost bewildering to discover that inhabitants of future London are so intensely attracted to a medieval house and, above all, feel a deep nostalgia for an ideal reconstruction of a rural England as a harmonious commonwealth. Thus, Kelmscott Manor becomes an aesthetic and a political ideal, as emerges from the frontispice of *News from Nowhere*, for which Morris choose a view from the entrance (see Figure 12.2).

Figure 12.2 William Morris, *News from Nowhere*, 1890.

As Kelsall has pointed out,[17] Morris's view of the house and especially his communism are in tune with the cultural enterprise launched by the National Trust (1895), because this house deserves to be guarded as a token of history and cultural legacy. Future generations will inherit a simple house, which shuns the Victorian pomp and pride of ostentation, a piece of natural beauty, where, again, the garden acquires a symbolic value.

The garden, divided by old clipped yew hedges, is quite unaffected and very pleasant.[18]

Many a good house both old and new is marred by the vulgarity and stupidity of its garden, so that one is tormented by having to abstract in one's mind the good building from the nightmare of "horticulture" which surrounds it.[19]

The English countryside is seen through Morris's aesthetic eye, whose extreme sensitivity to the harmony of colours, sounds and perfumes, conjures up an idyllic picture. Paradoxically, it is an England both rural and highly civilised: in the meals served in the common halls beautiful, eternally young women dressed in Pre-Raphaelite costumes arouse wonder and desire in Guest. In many passages of *News from Nowhere* Morris re-interprets the medieval concept of hospitality with a late Romantic attitude, in which beauty is crystallised in vividly pictorial scenes. The last moment of conviviality, which takes place in a church turned into a place for festivals, is emblematic:

> We went into the church, which was a simple little building .... It was, however, gaily dressed up for this latter-day festival, with festoons of flowers from arch to arch, and great pitchers of flowers standing about on the floor .... But its best ornament was the crowd of handsome, happy-looking men and women that were set down to table, and who, with their bright faces and rich hair over their gay holiday raiment, looked, as the Persian poet puts it, like a bed of tulips in the sun.[20]

The exterior of Kelmscott Manor (see Figure 12.3) has not undergone relevant restoration, and though built a generation after the close of the Middle Ages, the house follows a recognised medieval plan. In his *Gossip about an Old House on the Upper Thames* (1895) Morris gives a precise description of the architectural elements, which could easily be used as a guide for the visitors, intertwines with a metamorphosis of the building into a late

Figure 12.3 Kelmscott Manor, East front (© Society of Antiquaries of London).

Figure 12.4 Kelmscott Manor, Tapestry Room (© Society of Antiquaries of London).

Romantic place full of charm and romance, especially when he describes the Samson tapestries in the Tapestry Room.

There is a striking contrast between the exterior, which has been left virtually untouched, and the interior, where original architecture coexists with pieces of furniture produced by Morris's firm and with objects collected by himself and Rossetti, the co-tenant. Many pieces were brought from Kelmscott House in London, Hammersmith, where Morris established his firm, and from Red House, both during his life and after his death. Kelmscott Manor can be seen, in Henry James's words, as "a repository of spoils", which creates and strengthens the cultural re-construction of the medieval country house.

The interior exemplifies Morris's approach to the ideal house. The Green Room on the ground floor is a simple and uncluttered space, decorated with objects from different historical periods and pieces of furniture produced by Morris. Each room presents distinctive features characterised by the combination of pieces belonging to the house and Arts and Crafts decorations. In Morris's bedroom a four-poster bed is adorned with hangings embroidered by Jane and May Morris. The Tapestry Room (see Figure 12.4), used by Rossetti as a studio, boasts the famous Samson cycle which Morris described in *News from Nowhere*:

> We sat down at last in a room over the wall which Ellen had caressed, and which was still hung with old tapestry, originally of no artistic value, but now faded into pleasant grey tones which harmonised

thoroughly well with the quiet of the place, and which would have been ill supplanted by brighter and more striking decoration.[21]

As Paola Spinozzi acutely remarks, the inter-textuality between the real place and the fictional one unveils Morris's programmatic construction of an ideological message embedded in an architectural site.[22]

Both Red House and Kelmscott Manor, as reconstructed in the text, can be inscribed in the cultural enterprise launched by the National Trust in 1895 and aiming at the preservation of vernacular architecture, but also with Edwin Lutyens, who built English country houses following and reworking on local tradition. Lutyens's work bridges the divide between the concern for vernacular styles, expressed by the early National Trust, and the greater Houses described and advertised in *Country Life*.

The preservation of such mansions creates controversial issues. Indeed, Morris's houses testify to his search for a communal way of living in a place free from ostentation, where work and leisure could intermingle; but it also testifies to the permanence of certain conventions of the aristocratic landscape. Nonetheless, Kelmscott Manor has become a house treasured and protected; open in restricted periods of the year, it is now a house for antiquaries, for nostalgic radical thinkers but also for amateurs. One can say that there exists a conservative tendency in English radical thought.

But probably these are questions that Morris, who lived in a transitional period, could never have answered. On the one hand, he was involved in a process of commercialisation of English country houses and old artefacts; on the other, he made a strong effort to grasp the "aura", the mystery which pervades certain places and houses. Interestingly enough, in *Country Life* Edward Hudson offered a wide range of items for sale. Though unwilling, Morris himself nourished this hunger for things of beauty to possess. It somehow sounds ironical that Morris poured so much money and emotional drives into an ideal place to live, while he went on changing places. The archaic bond with the mythical rural England dissolves with modern mobility.

NOTES

1. See Kelsall, 1993, in particular 138–47, "Kelmscott House and News from Nowhere".
2. *Arts & crafts houses* I, 1999; see also Miele, 2005.
3. Pevsner, 1936.
4. Fortunati, 2000.
5. Kirk, 1997, 39.
6. MacCarthy, 1994, 156; see also J. Marsh, 2005.
7. Morris, 1882.
8. The image of the well, a recurrent element in symbolist and fin de siècle European painting and literature, is charged with multi-layered meanings. See Hönnighausen, 1971.

9. Waithe, 2004, 573.
10. Ibid., 570.
11. Callen, 1979.
12. Girouard, 1960, 1383. See also Girouard, 1971.
13. Waithe, 2004, 576.
14. Mackail, 1899, 1:165.
15. Morris, 1895.
16. Morris, 1995, 211.
17. Malcolm Kelsall, "Kelmscott House. News from Nowhere", in Kelsall, 1993, 140–141; see also Parry, 1996.
18. Morris, 1995, 211.
19. Morris, 1895, 2.
20. Morris, 1995, 218.
21. Morris, 1995, 212.
22. Spinozzi, 2000, 169.

13 Memories of Exoticism and Empire
Henry Rider Haggard's Wunderkammer at Ditchingham House

Marilena Parlati

The "new cultural geography" seeks to recover an essentially *geographical* dimension: the intimate relationship between people and their environmental setting. Landscape is a way of seeing the world, a codification of social order .... Places encapsulate and communicate identity ....[1]

The "encapsulation" of identities within locations and the construction of locations through myths of identity are processes and practices—both of the everyday and of the literary—at the root of those writers' houses that can be characterised as "programmatic." The empty spaces Greimas referred to in his essay on topological semiotics are translated into places exactly when and because they take on human meaning, both through conscious acts of self-fashioning on the part of their inhabitants and through *post-mortem* acts of reading.[2] While landscape analysis and history have a long tradition in European thought and criticism, a closer attention to interior spaces, to material culture, to monumental and documental memories and their significance is a far fresher field of social and cultural analysis. This step is obviously essential in that it widens horizons and inserts interior design and decoration within the approved and necessary areas of research for scholars of very different background and academic affiliation, ranging from human and cultural geography to literary and cultural studies.

It is also true that the transformation of the residences of famous historical and literary characters into heritage cult is no novelty. And yet, what is being more and more often put to the test, as has been illustrated in the introduction to this volume, is the transformation of literature into matter—or vice versa. These strategies and tactics can and must become also "a critique of literature and an attempt to surpass it." What "matters" in this chapter is the production not simply of housing, but of "dwellings of definite sorts ... in a continuous process of social life in which men reciprocally define objects in terms of themselves and themselves in terms of objects."[3]

The metaphorical lens represented by the expression "programmatic house" and by the objects collected in or dispersed out of it will hopefully

175

serve to survey the house of the British novelist Henry Rider Haggard, who lived through the reigns of Victoria, Edward VII and George V and died on 14 May 1925. The aim of this essay is that of verifying if his Norfolk house can in any way be taken into account as a profitable specimen of a modern and often paradoxical eclecticism very deeply enmeshed with imperial memories and exotic hauntings. Eventually, the cases of both Haggard and his house will be proposed as examples of the slippery nature of cultural memory.

The literary fame of Rider Haggard generally lies with *King Solomon's Mines*, a thrilling African adventure fiction published in 1885, and with *She*, another treasure-hunt adventure whose main character is supernatural immortal Ayesha, the white and extremely beautiful queen of the fictitious black tribe of the Amahagger. This novel was published in 1887 and was received with great enthusiasm, especially because of the imaginative power of femininity later recalled by Freud in his *Interpretation of Dreams*. The novel also profoundly struck Carl Gustav Jung, and his idea of "anima" seems to owe much to Haggard's character. Both novels, and some of his other literary texts, have never gone out of print, and the number of sequels, cinematic versions and parodies that revise and manipulate them is impressive. Furthermore, Haggard's general output has by now become a steady target for critical interventions, due to the rich and complex texture of ideological, sexual, and textual obsessions which crowd his writing and also, as this essay aims to prove, his house. Yet, the extreme popularity Haggard experienced during his lifetime had already started fading in the aftermath of the First World War. In his own view, moreover, his most relevant activities had become those of landowner and of public servant. After his first juvenile experiences in South Africa at the time of the annexation of the Transvaal, his ambition led him first to a literary career, and later on to an ever-growing involvement in Royal Commissions connected with Imperial Affairs and Agriculture. As a result of this, he was knighted in 1912 and created Knight Commander of the British Empire in 1919.

The location referred to is known as Ditchingham House, a Georgian country house standing at the heart of Norfolk, outside the village of Ditchingham, just a few kilometres away from Bungay along the river Waveney. The only source of information available, even if quite rich in details and illustrations, is one of the "Illustrated Interviews" series of *The Strand Magazine*, dating back to January 1892.[4] In a photographic zooming in process, journalist Harry How leads his readers round each significant element of the estate, starting with a perspective view of the house, its most beautiful trees and a distant view of tilled land. Nevertheless, the most relevant element in this introductory visual survey is certainly the writer himself, who plays his proposed role of fit representative of imperial "merry England". Standing straight, his faithful dog at his feet, he wears a country-gentleman outfit and poses with his eyes fixed not straight onto the photographer's camera but on his own property (see Figure 13.1).

Figure 13.1 Henry Rider Haggard looking at Ditchingham House. Illustration from *The Strand Magazine*, January 1892 (Courtesy of Gabinetto Scientifico Letterario G.P. Vieusseux Florence, Italy).

> Ditchingham is a distinctly cosy Norfolk village, small and picturesque. Ditchingham House is a typical Norfolk home. It stands in the middle of a perfect shelter provided by the surrounding elms and beeches ....[5]

Before being allowed in, though, readers must notice the first paradoxical item of Ditchingham House, some giant Mexican ferns brought home by Haggard from his journeys to Northern and Southern America. In the words of How, "some of these ferns are curious." In fact, as a deeper look at Haggard's conservatory would have further proved, this spot of East Anglia was metaphorically "tropicalized" by a number of exotic specimens of plants and flowers from very distant geographical areas: the picturesque countryside, also safely packed full with very typical Norfolk cows, seems either to become prey to foreign botanical power or rather to testify to the strength of an expert whose keen hands could introduce hexogenous species and yet manage to control them and make them reproduce on totally different soil.[6]

The word "curious" and its variants found in the short text which is being here appropriated allows one to take some distance from the mere textual and visual description of the house. Rather, I suggest this house can be read not as a merely casual piling-up of heterogeneous material, but as a truly programmatic location, consciously meant by its owner-author as a repository. This treasure also permitted textual, iconographic, sensual and emotional journeys through a distant past and an equally distant present. In his *History of Curiosity* Justin Stagl defines Renaissance and/or early modern *Wunderkammern*—cabinets of curiosity—as "externalised super-memories, or centres of documentation."[7] Haggard's Ditchingham House seems to be one of these centres, documenting both the writer's continuous oscillations between modernity and primitivism and a specific moment in the history of British culture. If it is true, as Thomas Richards maintains, that "by the 1880s consumerism had fundamentally transformed Victorian culture," one must not look too far to find examples of how exports and imported goods brought to the British citizen and, literally speaking, to the British home the sense that the first were a "magic medium through which English power and influence could be enforced and enlarged in the colonial world,"[8] whereas the second could be domesticated through their exhibitionist nature in the recently institutionalised sites of museum, exhibition, department store.

What Ditchingham House seemed and still seems to provide, though, was no easy access to the experience of neither Victorian consumer nor museum culture; quite the contrary. Haggard's maniac and absolutely anti-categorical collections may prove Ruth Hoberman's statement that in much late-Victorian Gothic fiction "the exhibition is a refuge from commodification ...,"[9] an ambiguous private and yet also public "island of time and space" set in the frame of a *truly*—no matter how fictiously fashioned—British home and countryside experience. The collection, which is implicitly also an exhibition, marks "the place where history is transformed into space, into property."[10] Into literature, one may aptly add at this point, thus rethinking about the unstable connection between object and literary subject matter:

> At home he had created an extraordinary atmosphere .... There was no other house like it ... and the visitor could instantly recognise it as the home of Rider Haggard. Ditchingham House had been built at the end of the eighteenth century but its interior was Victorian and imperial. It was the Victorian fashion for a gentleman's house to be over-furnished and cluttered with booty from the Empire but this clutter and booty was unique since everything prompted a story from its owner .... Everything prompted Haggard to speak the line ... *even as he told the tale, he held the very object it concerned in his hand.*[11]

In surveying Haggard's exhibited and exhibitionist house, it might be worth while to remember Aby Warburg's idea of a "mnemonic energy" connected to the objectivation of culture:

> He tells you nothing but what is worth remembering; his life has been one long chapter of adventure, and every nook and corner of the house, wherever you turn ... has some reminder of a career which has been in many ways remarkable .... The entrance-hall and staircases are crowded with interesting and suggestive mementoes. On the walls are

Arabian shields and swords, lengthy spears, and ugly—though highly decorative—knives ... ancient Egyptian bows and throwing-sticks, and here is an ancient cedar rod believed to be similar to the one which Moses cast before Pharaoh.[12]

... a row of fine ostrich eggs ... chairs from the East Coast of Africa. A lamp ... made of the Royal red wood of Zululand ....[13] (see Figure 13.2 and Figure 13.3)

The house was apparently untouched by the presence of mass-produced goods. Of course, the journalist was only relating upon the *mirabilia* he

Figuer 13.2 Staircase at Ditchingham House. Illustration from *The Strand Magazine*, January 1892 (Courtesy of Gabinetto Scientifico Letterario G.P. Vieusseux Florence, Italy).

Figure 13.3 Entrance Hall at Ditchingham House. Illustration from *The Strand Magazine*, January 1892 (Courtesy of Gabinetto Scientifico Letterario G.P. Vieusseux Florence, Italy).

perused and that were probably carefully chosen by the interviewed celebrity and/or by the smart journalist himself. Thus, a few natural specimens mix with a great majority of handicrafts, with definite or legendary stories and histories behind them. The items which were being remembered are, again unsurprisingly, auratic objects, in the sense Walter Benjamin offers to the term aura: "To perceive the aura of an object we look at means to invest it with the ability to look at us in return."[14]

Obviously, Haggard's objects are also clearly gendered, sometimes unexpectedly: "Here stands a quaint old cabinet. It is exquisitively carved .... It is said to contain forty secret drawers, a score of them yet remain to be discovered."[15] The item referred to is a lady's cabinet, its secrets still inviolate and invisible to the male gazes, which try to pierce through it. If, on the one hand, nineteenth-century myths of gentrification tended to invent an "English" countryside and "English" country-houses which never truly existed, gender declensions are also of great relevance to a dwelling which aimed to embody those myths. Haggard's paragon rooms, packed full of curiosities, can be read in comparison to the typical Victorian middle-class parlour:

> While the taste for *objets d'art* and curiosities is obviously related to the appearance of things in the Victorian parlour, there are at least two

significant differences between the collections [pre-eighteenth-century] and those of a middle-class family .... There is little doubt that the appearance of rooms full of ... decorative objects is a bourgeois appropriation of the aristocratic habit of accumulation and display, but it would be a mistake to assume that the proliferation of objects in the parlour of a Victorian home created effects that served purposes identical to those in a great country house ... the cabinet of curiosities ... was linked to men, and ultimately to public life, while the parlour was clearly marked as feminine, and as private, in contemporary practice and discourse.[16]

As the mere enumeration of the quantity and quality of the mementoes enlisted in the interview makes quite clear, Haggard is no true collector, if a collection is intended as a homogeneous entity, whether in a functional, geographical, or chronological sense. But I argue that he was literally following the path of a Renaissance *Wunderkammer*. His house is a masculinized compendium, a literal encyclopaedia that embodies a desire for a lost—if ever extant—personal and also national totality.

Some of the objects exposed to the inquiring gaze and touch of Harry How are also "recalcitrant" cultural objects—in the sense proposed by Annie Coombes: "... the cultural object was to be the primary signifier of a cultural, national and ethnic identity which proclaimed and celebrated its integrity and "difference" from the centres of Western capitalism."[17] The fruition of some of these objects is mediated by the literal manipulation of the journalist. In the billiard-room lies a little cabinet, covered with a glass door: as in *King Solomon's Mines*, for instance, the narrative treasure hunt is duplicated in the narrated private house (see Figure 13.4). One box contains another vessel, each one surrendering to the eyesight and touch of the two heroes-searchers: on a silver Icelandic Communion cup, How comments:

> a number of rings are put into my open hand. One of the most striking of these is a gold band, thousands of years old, hieroglyphics engraved upon it signifying "Haggard" .... Another gold ring is from the mummy of Queen Taia, the feminine Henry VIII, of Egypt and one of the most fascinating and beautiful women that ever lived. Its inscription reads "Ank Bes, Bes Ank" (the living Bes, Bes the living).[18]

In perfect line with the Victorian cult of personality, Haggard inscribes himself and his own bodily presence in the narration, adding to the list of catalogued objects a signet ring he used to wear: "It was found at Deir-el-Bahari. Its red stone is believed to chronicle the portrait of Rameses the great, the Pharaoh of Oppression, with whose coffin it was discovered."[19]

Apart from exotica, another set of emotional relics collapses personal memory with literary and therefore national memory. Hidden in a niche

Figure 13.4 Billiard Room at Ditchingham House. Illustration from *The Strand Magazine*, January 1892 (Courtesy of Gabinetto Scientifico Letterario G.P. Vieusseux Florence, Italy).

within the billiard-room lies the most revered item, Charles Dickens's writing desk acquired at the Gad's Hill sale of the novelist's properties (see Figure 13.5). The desk is an obvious and highly-treasured relic, meant never to be used for its original function and qualities; it is evidently a spectacular trophy, metonymically and apotropaically representing the Victorian artist-novelist par excellence. In Krystof Pomian's words, this is a very good example of a "semiophore," an object detached from its original use and setting and invested with new, generally very different, meaning, once and if it is allowed to occupy a new position.

> ... knick-knacks in china fill the recesses: more curios from distant climes, amongst which is a little glass photo of a small child [Rider himself] ... Mexican combs, exquisite embroidery and fans are picturesquely scattered about ....[20]

Again, personal stories mingle with curious exotic objects variously linked with a post-Romantic picturesque; they are defined as knick-knacks, and also, repeatedly, as curios—baubles, bibelots, kickshaw, bric-à-brac being equally dense synonyms for this term. They are not art objects but only *objets d'art*, thus demonstrating that they are "amateurish, provi-

Figure 13.5 Charles Dickens's Desk at Ditchingham House. Illustration from *The Strand Magazine*, January 1892 (Courtesy of Gabinetto Scientifico Letterario G.P. Vieusseux Florence, Italy).

sional, personalized, even eroticized."[21] In Haggard's case, objects are very often also textualised, but their authentic and primitive epistemological status is always insecure, stuck in the middle of a never-solved predicament. The most relevant instance of this is the Egyptian ring whose inscription is reproduced on the sherd printed as a pretext to *She*.[22] As in a rhetorical vortex, a fake object—the sherd—is inscribed with fictitious but credible writing made up by experts on Egyptian antiquities, on Greek and Latin, as on medieval Latin and Middle English:

> Here is a Gnostic ring in mediaeval lead setting, and yet another... which will always be associated with his career. It is the scarab that s in *She*. It is a heavy ring, and bears the words "Suten se Ra" ("Royal Son of the Sun").[23]

After the death of the writer, these two objects were donated to the Norwich Castle Museum where they still are today. They are the only truly visible elements still linked to the memory of that writer and of the kind of narrative he was a master of; quite incongruously, these two items are held together, according to a rather peculiar museum category of "writer's objects."

As for his phantasmagoric home, it still exists, but was transformed into independent flats many years ago. Some of his personal properties are still kept by his last direct heir, Mrs Nada Cheyne, who lives at nearby Ditchingham Lodge. As for the Egyptian relics, some were donated to the British Museum, others to Norwich or Liverpool Museum. To sum up, in this case, while the intertextual relations between his fiction and his house were a self-conscious means of self-fashioning (and also of fashioning landscape), the still unsteady canonical and critical position Haggard occupies is a key to the erasure of his memory, his mementoes and to the physical dismembering of his ideal/ideological heritage. In the words of the dangerously enthusiastic editor of a volume on Haggard and Egypt, Shirley Addy, "... I discovered there were many more objects; alas in many cases the trail led nowhere ...."[24]

NOTES

1. Mills, 1993, 150.
2. Greimas, 1986.
3. Sahlins, 1976, 169.
4. Photographs taken by Elliot and Fry, in How, 1892.
5. Addy, 1998, 106.
6. "In 1883 Osborn wrote me a letter concerning some imantophyllum plants that he had collected for me in Zululand, which at this moment, twenty-eight years afterwards, are blooming in the greenhouse, in the course of which letter he makes some rather interesting remarks." See Haggard, 1926, 1: 223–24.
7. Stagl, 1995, 112.
8. Richards, 1990, 26.
9. Hoberman, 2003.
10. Stewart, 1984, xii.
11. T. Pocock, 1993, 89–90.
12. How, 1892, 4, also cited in Addy, 1998, 107.
13. How, 1892, 4.
14. Benjamin, 1969, 188.
15. How, 1892, 5.
16. Logan, 2001, 107.
17. Coombes, 1994a, 89. See also Coombes, 1994b.
18. How, 1892, 5–6.
19. Ibid., 6.
20. Ibid.
21. Daly, 1994, 57.

22. "... the elaborate sherd compounded by my sister-in-law, then Miss Barber, and myself being reproduced in two plates at the beginning of the volume .... By the way, the reproduction of this sherd was shown as being from a genuine antique to Mr (afterwards Sir John) Evans, who of course was a great expert on such matters. For a long while he peered at it through his eyeglasses and at last put it down, remarking, "All I can say is that it might *possibly* have been forged"—which I consider great testimony to the excellency of the sherd which now reposes in a cupboard upstairs." Haggard, 1926, 1: 228.
23. How, 1892, 6.
24. Addy, 1998, xv.

14 *La Maison d'un artiste*
The Goncourts, Bibelots and Fin de Siècle Interiority

Claire O'Mahony[1]

The brothers Edmond and Jules de Goncourt are most often remembered for the guilty pleasure of glimpsing "le tout Paris" between the bitchily revealing pages of the *Journals*.[2] Their unerringly detailed gaze scrutinised and critiqued an extraordinary panorama of French cultural exchange throughout the second half of the nineteenth century. In recent years, their novels have also regained currency in post-Clarkian art historical accounts of Realist and Impressionist practice, evidencing the core motifs of painterly identity and the model in *Manette Salomon*, or archetypes of the degenerate Parisienne in *Germinie Lacerteux* and Edmond's *La fille Elisa* (see Figure 14.1). Often overshadowed by the more celebrated narrative formulations within the oeuvres of Balzac, Flaubert and Zola, these texts simultaneously have provided a less heavily excavated seam for theorising the aims and strategies of literary naturalism. For our purposes here, the interpenetrating creative processes and products of the Goncourts' activities as writers, collectors and interior designers will be the sources through which to explore several shifts of paradigm within fin de siècle visual and literary aesthetics. Edmond de Goncourt's engagement with decoration, as both practitioner and as a critic, still offers a highly provocative and instructional case study, especially for design history at the dawn of the twenty-first century, anxiously poised between the rival factions of the history of art and material culture, both desired and despised, much like the contested bibelot which preoccupied Goncourt and his fin de siècle contemporaries.

In 1881 Edmond de Goncourt published his fascinatingly hybrid textual artefact *La Maison d'un artiste* (*The House of an Artist*), which vacillates between a disparate set of tropes, the collection inventory or catalogue, anecdotal autobiography, art criticism.[3] In many ways the writer, his house and his unusual book emerge much as one suspects Goncourt would have liked, inhabiting a visionary, aristocratic, intimate milieu where the ancien régime and its private passions for rococo elegance and Japoniste invention entrance initiates with their heady, synaesthetic charms. However, this aesthetic framework also offered a multivalent, whilst nationally specific paradigm for fin de siècle material and psychological interiority.

Figure 14.1 Caricature of Edmond de Goncourt, *L'Eclipse*, 21 May 1876.

A remarkably eclectic variety of cultural personalities embraced, or at the very least reacted to Goncourt's interventions devoted to decoration. Official and aesthetic arbiters of the Third Republic decorative arts revival recognised the aptness of his beloved Eighteenth century as the vehicle for consolidating national identity. The decadent aesthete Joris Karl Huysmans, a member of Goncourt's Grenier, acknowledged the role of *La Maison d'un artiste* in devising the fin de siècle meditation on interiors and interiority par excellence, *À rebours*. The art nouveau designer Émile Gallé, a fellow aesthetic provincial like the Goncourts a native son of Nancy in Lorraine, not only re-envisioned the Goncourts' twin passions of the rococo and Japan in his oeuvre, but as I hope to suggest deployed their theorisations of psychological trace in his creative process.

However, *La Maison d'un artiste* was also instrumental in forging the success of the anathema of the Goncourts' house-haven: the Department store and its neurotic, consumerist inhabitants, the bibelotiers. The complexities of the Goncourts, their house and texts resonate with the porousness and ineffectuality of the rigid polarities so often declared within and subsequently imposed upon fin de siècle France, where fears of national degeneration and aesthetic strategies of retreat made anxious, yet intimate, bedfellows of Symbolist and commodity culture.

Firstly, one must establish the specificities of the inhabitants, house and collection at 53 Boulevard de Montmorency in Auteuil (see Figure 14.2). Augmented by their literary success, the brothers' financial independence allowed the purchase in August 1868 of a beautiful two-story eighteenth-century house in Auteuil, far from the now more enervating, than inspiring, noise and squalor of central Paris.[4] The house was to be a uniquely intimate and minutely arranged setting for the brothers' ménage, emblematised by the medallion of Louis XV over the front door and the treasure trove within of their carefully honed collection drawn from eighteenth-century France and Japan.[5] However, the idyll was soon shattered in 1870, first by the blow of Jules' horrific and protracted death from syphilis and then by the degradations of the siege and bombardments. After returning from a spell living with Philippe Burty in his central Paris flat, Edmond de Goncourt seems to have found the process of embellishing and re-orchestrating the decoration of the house over the next twenty years of his life a vital help in reclaiming himself from the despair he referred to as his "widowhood". The rebuilding of the second floor in 1884, dismantling the preserved bedroom where Jules died and knocking through the dividing walls to create the famous "grenier" (storehouse) was a dramatically physical manifestation of Edmond's decision to create a new, if lesser, brotherhood of likeminded temperaments, the Sunday afternoon salons which re-ignited the collegiality of the Magny dinners begun in 1862 and foretold of the Drouot dinners of the Académie Goncourt.

La Maison d'un artiste, after an evocative preamble to which we shall return later, takes the visitor-reader by the hand, literally leading one from the first chapter entitled "Vestibule" through the salle à manger, petit salon, grand salon and escalier chapters in volume I, and the private spaces of the cabinet de travail, cabinet de toilette, chambre à coucher, boudoir and garden in volume II. Each room chapter is subtitled with the carefully selected

Figure 14.2 Exterior of 53 Boulevard de Montmorency, Auteuil, c. 1880 (© Bibliothèque Nationale de France).

grouping of objects which the brothers' arranged there, from the Japanese textiles *(fukusas)* in the vestibule, to the eighteenth-century *objets d'art* and works on paper which are the principal inhabitants of the salons. The book attests to the selectivity of the Goncourts' collecting practice, which was entirely devoted to what William Morris ironically called "the lesser arts", and restricted almost exclusively to the periods of eighteenth-century France and Japan (Gavarni's prints and copies of contemporary novels in the Cabinet de Travail being the notable exception). Edmond de Goncourt's curious text intersperses large sections of description even occasionally in the stark form of catalogue entries listing works by artist, including measurements, with narratively rich recollections of the times experienced in these different spaces. The "Petit Salon" chapter is devoted to the chicken who kept Edmond company during the dark days of 1870, while the "Salle à manger" chapter is evoked through the transportation of a Lorraine woman for a week to the house, brought to cook the ultimate gastronomic experience, a provincial French meal prepared by a woman! In addition to these encyclopaedic and anecdotal rhetorics, Goncourt also includes discursive passages advising his reader-guests on points of decorative strategy, explaining the brothers' selection of contrasting red textiles and luminous black omnibus enamel to create the appropriate colour notes for the walls and ceilings of the Salons (see Figure 14.3). Other chapters offer more wide ranging and provocative meditations on the allure of the objects collected, most notably in the sections on rococo furniture and *objets d'art*.

It should be signalled that this curious hybrid text did not spring fully formed from the head of Zeus. As Dominique Pety has documented, *La Maison d'un artiste* had a number of ancestors as well as a wide-ranging and contested progeny. From Jean François de Bastide's *La petite maison* of 1763 and De Maistre's *Voyage autour de ma chambre* of 1795 to Edgar Alan Poe's *Philosophy of Furnishing* of 1852 and Charles Cousin's *Voyage dans un grenier* 1878, a new visually rich literary genre of what one might call a domestic travelogue had emerged by the 1880s. No doubt to his chagrin, these interventions and Goncourt's book were paralleled within the low culture of the illustrated articles appearing in countless popular journals in the Third Republic describing "the visit to the great author's house" to which Olivier Nora has devoted such an instructive chapter in the "Nation" volume of *Les Lieux de mémoire*. The writer's house and his collection emerge in these texts as lexicons of the authors' talismans, style and identity. Indeed Goncourt's text in many ways insists upon the

Figure 14.3 Grand Salon in the Goncourt House (© Bibliothèque Nationale de France).

formulation of the collection and its arrangement as a marker of the innate superiority of the collector-creator.

Perhaps Goncourt was too persuasive, though issues of precedence are not the object of this study, it suffices to indicate that a cacophony of cultural leaders advised fin de siècle French men, and women in particular, to emulate the care, invention and spending of elite collector/interior designers like Goncourt: Charles Blanc *Grammaire des arts décoratifs. Décoration intérieure de la maison* (Grammar of Decorative Arts. Interior Decoration, 1882); Henry Havard *L'Art dans la maison. Grammaire de l'ameublement* (Art at Home. Grammar of Furnishings, 1884; interestingly written in the room by room structure deployed in *La Maison d'un Artiste*) and Spire Blondel's *L'Art intime et le goût en France. Grammaire de la curiosité* (Intimate Art and Taste in France, 1884). Goncourt's collection and his textual advocacy of decoration as a creative activity helped to dismantle a range of nineteenth-century polar oppositions: between Art and Industry which had barred design from fine art spaces and debates such as the Salon; the valorised gendering of colour and line; female domesticity and masculine public life; private interiority and social collectivity; and so forth. In the forced alliances of the Third Republic, "les arts decoratifs" emerged as a vital tool for negotiating not only the previously distinct worlds of art and of work, but also the audiences for whom art and its elevating consumption were intended. Working class children, artisans and ignorant middle class women were all encouraged not only to learn to draw, but also to regard the decoration of the home as an ennobling and patriotic endeavour. By purchasing French design, the housewife as well as the aesthete-author could revitalise the French economy as well as French taste. As Charles Blanc argues decorating the domestic interior properly was the first step to building a better France:

> The man must initiate himself through private virtues to public ones, it is vital that he not be disgusted by his house, because it is there that his family responsibilities call upon him .... But the house is not just lived in: it is visited, and certain rooms are even especially intended for friends and strangers. These rooms at least, must attest to the effort applied to decorate as best one can and at the level commensurate with one's means. The absence of ornament there would be impolite.[6]

Even in such a passage where the political and economic subtexts of the design revival are so near to the surface, Blanc's rhetoric of courtesy (*politesse*) is also significant of the complex spatial and gender identities within fin de siècle decoration. The domestic sphere is precisely both politically public and privately expressive, and as such this contested domain is both significant of and formulated by both genders. From organisations such as the elite Central Union of Decorative Arts, with its close affiliations with governmental arts administrators, to the window displays and publicity ephemera of the Department stores, the formulations of such injunctions were usually articulated in feminised rhetorics. Blanc, Blondel, Houssaye, Uzanne all use the vocabulary of the feminine toilette such as "parure" to describe the decoration of the domestic interior. [7] However, the Goncourts' interventions demonstrate the reductiveness of therefore arguing that decoration was a feminine activity, rather these feminine formulations became a means by which to allure both genders as consumers, simultaneously through feminine self-identification, but also through the allure of fetishistic otherness for masculine bibelotiers constructing their fairy kingdoms as a retreat from the harsh mercantalism and depravity of the Republic.

The Goncourts' advocacy of the feminised lesser arts of the eighteenth century had provided an ideal vehicle through which to articulate the multivalent appeal of these interventions; delicate Sèvres vases and Louis XV chairs proved resiliently malleable to the disparate identities grating against each other within the Third Republic. The association with the court life of Louis XV was sufficiently resonant with the elitism and monarchical clericalism of the ancien régime to soothe the forces of the Catholic right into less militant anti-Republicanism, whilst the articulation of the rococo as a distinctly French national style and the celebration of the artisan were soon embraced by moderate and leftist alike to help distinguish French luxury goods in the maelstrom of worlds fairs and an increasingly globalised marketplace. The rococo served many masters from state funded reconstruction of the medal room in Labrouste's Bibliothèque Nationale to the entrepreneurial Siegfried Bing's abandonment of internationalist art nouveau ensembles which had been chauvinistically panned as unpatriotic in 1895 for the admirable neo-rococo ensembles of a true French designer Eugène Gaillard in the Pavillion Bing at the 1900 Exposition.

Unsurprisingly the aesthetes were not best pleased about this cohabitation; a comment of the Symbolist Gustav Kahn can adroitly, if unpleasantly, stand for the aesthetes' counter reaction of disgust at the denigration of bibelot-mania, as "the phenomena of cultural appropriation of decorative art, is it would seem a means by which women participated in the cultural bulimia [*boulimie culturelle*] of their era."[8] The bibelots, through which aesthetic arbiters like the Goncourts created both their physical interior and the elite psychological interiority which it claimed to emblematise, provocatively and unfailingly vacillate between the attitudes and rhetorics of the world of mass consumerism and private fetishisation.

A brief consideration of the brothers' own and other commentators' analysis of their mode of collecting may serve to highlight this evocative duality and its importance for a generation of writers and designers. Within the context of this brief study this can be sketchily indicated through the similarity of spectatorial and interpretative mode in Émile Gallé's glass. From Edmond's first purchase of a Boucher drawing at the age of sixteen, the brothers never collected paintings, preferring to have a first rate collection of "lesser" arts rather than a mediocre assemblage of second rate paintings. However, it must be confessed the Goncourts were not universal advocates of material culture, as their critique of Champfleury's passion for Revolutionary stoneware "l'art d'accomoder les pommes de terre" indicates.[9] By the 1860s they refined their criteria even further, selling off over half their works on paper (Dutch, Italian, XVII century pieces) and thenceforward concentrating almost exclusively on eighteenth-century examples. They vehemently abhorred the replacement of passionate amateurs with the encyclopaedic historical positivism typified by Adolphe Thiers's eclectic historicist collecting. Equally they dreaded the materialism of many bibelotiers, typified by the unseemly bidding war by M. de Gallièra and Lord Hertford at Demidoff sale, likened to racing horses against each other, concluding this journal entry: "there are collections of *objets d'art* which show neither passion, nor taste, nor even intelligence, nothing but the brutal victory of wealth."[10]

Eighteenth-century visual culture attracted the Goncourts precisely in its capacity to offer an alternative to these models of worthy Republican erudition or market driven desire, offering a remarkable commingling of sexual and intellectual gratification. Edmond de Goncourt in the late Journals repeatedly and explicitly aligns the *objet d'art* with the feared, yet desired female body. Goncourt delights in a display of *bourdaloue* jugs[11] at the 1892 Exposition des Arts de Femme, writing in his 1 September 1892 Journal entry: "Oh these coquettish and galantes receptacles ... whose form is more tortuous, more serpentine, more voluptuous than the secret parts of woman."[12] Indeed he recognises a direct and proportional relationship between collecting and intellectual as well as libidinous gratification in an early articulation of the precept of "retail therapy":

> I also find in [the passion for collecting] the symptoms of society's *ennui*, a society where women no longer play the alluring role which they did in previous centuries. I have noticed, in my own case, that my purchases are interrupted when my life is very amusing or occupied. My continual, insatiable, pathological buying does not exist except in periods of sadness, loneliness, of inactivity of the heart or mind.[13]

The Goncourts' evocation of the historical moment of the eighteenth century and its material traces upon the objects within their collection should not be limited to simple fetishisation of the bibelot-woman (see Figure 14.4). The Goncourts' celebration of the feminised art of the age of Boucher, evocatively phrased in *L'Art du XVIII siècle* in terms of "le joli", is formulated as much in terms of the evocation of historical memory as sensual delight: "The pretty—here in these gentle hours of history, the sign and seduction of France. The pretty is the essence and the formula of its genius. The pretty is the tone of its customs. The pretty is the school of its fashions. The pretty is the spirit of the age—and it is the genius of Boucher."[14]

Figure 14.4 Bedroom in the Goncourt House (© Bibliothèque Nationale de France).

It is not only sublimated eroticism that led Edmond to extend his collection to a wider range of rococo decorative arts in the 1880s, from tiny perfume bottles to the canopied bed of an ancien régime lady aristocrat. As Edmond signals in his Journal entry for 27 November 1888, these objects hold unique vestigial traces of the women who lived with them during the beloved ancien régime:

> In handling these *jolités* ... in touching and turning these shuttles, holsters, stoppered bottles, scissors, which had for years been the little tools of elegance and gracefulness for the women of the age, one is filled with the desire to find these women to whom they belonged, and

to dream them into being, these women,—the little gold or porcelain object caressed lovingly in the hand.[15]

Unquestionably, the bibelot does supplant sexual contact with the problematic, and as Jules' fate demonstrated, corrupting female body, but it also offers a unique mode of access to a lost historical moment. These women are psychologically and intellectually dreamed into being, as well as erotically handled, by the psychic engagement with the *objet d'art*. As such, the bibelot's complex delight resides both in sheer physical titillation, but also in the aesthetic and intellectual engagement with a lived experience which is so central to the Goncourts' creative evocation of psychological and material reality.

The decorative object, and the myopic physical spectatorship that it requires, lies at the heart of this engagement.[16] Paul Bourget elucidated this relationship in his analysis of the psychological implications of the Goncourts' literary style in *Nouveaux essais de psychologie contemporaine* (*New Essays on Contemporary Psychology*, 1883). Bourget explicitly links the Goncourts writing to their collecting and interior:

> They lived in a little museum which was constantly growing ... from this uninterrupted familiarity with rare and suggestive things, they derived a special way of seeing, which insinuated itself closer and closer to the most intimate aspects of their talent, and to understand this talent, it is this subtle influence which it is necessary to first draw out and then explain.[17]

Bourget contrasts the wholesome, innate relationship of art object, its environment and spectator in the experiences of earlier ages, be they in the medieval chapel or Renaissance palace or Greek temple with the obsessions of the nineteenth century bibelotier, which stand for the highly detailed literary style of the Goncourts. The flaws ascribed to this myopic neurotic personality are what raises the Goncourts' collecting and bibelotmanie into a resonant formulation of a fin de siècle, Symbolist aesthetic of decoration:

> It is firstly a more and more precise apperception of the life of things .... This education of the gaze soon leads to a very particular sort of analysis. Even for persons with only a mediocre artistic sense, the face of a room, the form of an object, its colour, are pretexts for sympathy or equally of antipathy. Men who know how to look, understand the deep reasons for this sympathy or antipathy, and the objects appear to them as signs of an infinity of little facts. Behind a piece of furniture, they see the hand that placed it there, his temperament, his physiognomy. The folds of a garment reveal to them the smallest particularities of a body. They have interminable associations of ideas deriving from each object encountered, handled, contemplated.[18]

Although Bourget's aim ultimately seems to be to underline the unhealthiness of the Goncourts' myopic, yet profound process of observation and decipherment, the analysis is nonetheless helpful to the recognition of the fragility of the distinctions so often ascribed to the strategies of Naturalist detail and Symbolist suggestion. The Goncourts' obsessive attention to the objects which create the décor of the interior does not stop with surface details; it sees into the psychic memory of the object itself, observing the testament not only of its creator, but also its previous owner-collectors. Goncourt's preface to *La Maison d'un artiste* eloquently articulates this suggestive aim:

> In this time where things, of which the Latin poet has noted the latent melancholic life, are associated principally with modern literary description and the History of Humanity, why should one not write a memoire of the life of things in the midst of which a man's existence melts away?[19]

Edmond de Goncourt repeatedly articulates the formulation and display of their house as a creative act, infused with sexual intensity, onanism is the recurrent term, but as a vehicle through which to transport the obsessive collector-observer to a higher aesthetic and intellectual plain:[20]

> In this moment, a life entirely outside of real life and completely filled with the contemplation of the object and the art image, produces a sort of onanism of the retina and of the mind, a physical state of absence and intoxication, where one escapes from the moral irritations and small physical complaints.[21]

Goncourt's evocation of the conjoined aspects of engaging with a decorative object, the discernment of the traces of previous temperaments that have handled the object and the resultant euphoric stimulus in later observer-handlers helped to valorise designed objects with an aesthetic richness traditionally only ascribed to the fine arts of painting and sculpture. The critic Charles Blanc echoes Goncourt's elevation of the decorative arts to discursive interaction:

> When fashioned by the hands of man, things speak to us, they strike us with the turning that a thinking person has given them; it even comes about that once a piece of furniture has long been used, we leave an imprint of our own self within it .... By what mysterious power does the invisible fluid of the human spirit attach itself so intimately, even to inanimate things, like the scent of a vase?[22]

It was this kind of advocacy which helped designed objects to gain a place in the hallowed spaces of the Salon and the art gallery. This concept of psychic trace was certainly vital to Émile Gallé's glass making and its reception (see Figure 14.5). Rêverie was a central element of Gallé's own creative process, he called his works in glass "verreries parlantes". Victor Prouvé's arresting portrait of Gallé eloquently visualises the glassmaker's psychic engagement with the suggestive surfaces and depths of the vase. In an often cited passage from his "Notice sur la production de verres et cristaux de luxe" (Note on the production of luxury glass and crystal) pub-

FIgure 14.5 Victor Prouvé, *Portrait of Émile Gallé*, 1891 (© Musée de l'École de Nancy, cliché Studio Image).

lished for the Exposition Universelle of 1889, Gallé reveals how this prolonged looking and handling inspires the vase's decoration:

> In just such a way the prolonged gaze of the invalid transforms the
> marblings of the wall paper into thousands of strange figures, or the
> clouds at twilight appear to a child like immense sheep folds, while the
> sailor's eye sees in them rolling white caps and beaches ... I sow burn-
> ing flames and then gather up with my spindle paradoxical blossoms
> from the depths of the dark layers where I know they lie waiting.[24]

Gallé, like the Goncourts, advocates a prolonged spectatorial and psychic engagement by viewer-collectors of *objets d'art*. Just as the spontaneous effects of the glass required a trancelike stare from the artist-decorator
to communicate the appropriate symbolic decoration, the prolonged temporal engagement from the spectator-handler would communicate both the
trace of Gallé's psychic presence and trigger the viewer-collectors own corresponding Symbolist subjectivity. Resonant with Goncourt's articulation
of the historical traces of the eighteenth-century ladies upon their little
objects, the critic Louis De Fourcaud claimed that one's appreciation of the
prettiness of Gallé's vases should be deepened to recognise the memory of
the maker and viewer-handler that they can voice:

> A very special art; its every manifestation provokes dreams and
> enchantment! The crystal's translucence is charged with reflections
> where memory of flowering and flowerings of memories palpitate. For
> some, this amounts to nothing more than pleasurable refinements and
> voluptuous eyefuls. Others will find the delights of suggestion, an aban-
> donment to the fluid thread that springs from our interior source.[25]

One of the greatest legacies of the Goncourts literary and collecting practices is the suggestion that objects can be inscribed with traces of human
presence. Mario Praz, standing on the elegant shoulders of the Goncourts,
has more recently affirmed the decorative interior is a "series of mirrors ...
a museum of the soul, the archive of one's lived experience". Design history
has reawakened attentiveness to the ephemera which the Goncourts delight
over in *L'Art du XVIII siècle* (Art of the Eighteenth Century)"these thousands of floating little scraps of paper, which pass from hand to hand in a
society: calling cards, invitations, travel tickets, shop receipts, passeports,
theatre ticket stubs ..."[26] as to the more readily prized contents of the house
in Auteuil. The humblest of objects and their least eminent of users, as well
as collectors, hold a fascinating trace, just as Gallé's exquisite creations or
the Goncourts' beautiful treasures are so much more than "a pretty face."
In an 1884 journal entry Edmond de Goncourt acknowledged:

To make a room in my house: that is, almost always, after the publication of a book and the money it brings, the recreation, the reward that I give myself. Often I have said to myself, if I did not have bread on my plate, the profession which I would have chosen, would have been the creator of interiors for rich people. I would have loved it if a rich banker, allowing me free rein, gave me a palace which had nothing but four walls in which to dream the decoration and furnishing into being for him, from what I would find, restore, commission, with what I would discover in antique shops, modern industrial artists or my own head.[27]

Decoration speaks to history, identity, aesthetics; a dialogue which this anthology explores with such richness, signalling the discursive and historical import of the object and the house, for writers, collectors and commoners alike, with renewed vigour and delight.

NOTES

1. I am grateful to Stephen Bann for suggesting my name to the convenors of the Rome conference from which the volume derives and to Harald Hendrix for his patient and diligent editing of this chapter. The translations are my own and as such any flaws or awkwardness are mine.
2. Edmond 25/5/1822–16/7/1896 and Jules 17/12/1830–20/6/1870.
3. Recently a number of critics have begun to explore the book's equally eclectic impact. Deborah Silverman (1989) broke new ground, demonstrating the Goncourts' pivotal role in articulating the frameworks embraced by the political and aesthetic arbiters of the Third Republic decorative arts revival culminating in the art nouveau extravaganza of the 1900 Exposition Universelle. Janell Watson (1999) argues that it facilitated the literary fin de siècle interior par excellence, Joris Karl Huysmans' *À Rebours* and offers a thoughtful persuasive theorisation of the importance of the bibelot in analysing fin de siècle interiority. The anthology edited by Jacques de Cabanes (1997) and Dominique Pety's wonderful study (2003) are exemplary in their documentary richness, but also in the interdisciplinary methodologies they invent with such subtlety and detail.
4. The brothers had been masters of their own flat in the rue Saint Georges from a relatively young age, having lost their father in childhood and their mother in 1848. Their father Marc Pierre Huot de Goncourt (1787–1834) was a hero of the *Grande armée*; their mother Annette Cécile Guérin (1798–1848). Two sisters were born between Edmond and Jules, but both girls died before the age of three: Nephtalie Jenny Cécile (1824–25) and Émilie Alexandrine (1829–32).
5. For a very useful study of the Goncourt's fascination with Japan see Koyama-Richard, 2001.
6. "L'homme s'initiant par les vertus privées aux vertus publiques, il est essentiel qu'il ne se dégoûte pas de sa maison, parce que c'est là que l'appellent ses devoirs de famille .... Mais la maison n'est pas seulement habitée: elle est visitée, et certaines pièces sont même spécialement destinées aux amis et aux étrangers. Celles-là, du moins, doivent témoigner de l'application qu'on a

mise à les décorer de son mieux et en raison de son fortune. L'absence de tout ornement y serait une impolitesse." cited in Pety, 2003, 109–10.

7. "l'Art intime, cest-à-dire la réunion de ces mille et un objets d'art et de curiosité, qui complètent l'ameublement, lui servent de parure, l'éclairent et l'égatent d'une façon charmante." Spire Blondel, *L'Art intime et le goût en France. Grammaire de la curiosité*, 1884 (avertissement). Pety, 2003, 111, note 169, intriguingly points out that both Blondel and Octave Uzanne in his *Caprices d'un bibliophile* 1878 use the English word *home* to evoke the vision of the interior as refuge.

8. "...une phénomène d'appropriation culturelle par l'art décorative. C'est par lui, semble-t-il, que les femmes ont participé à la boulimie culturelle de leur temps." From J.P. Guillerm, *Les peintures invisibles*, cited in Pety, 2003, 107.

9. Edmond de Goncourt is equally dismissive of Champfleury's cheap editions of books, see Asfour, 2001, and Eudel, 1891.

10. "Il y a des collections d'objets d'art qui ne montrent ni passion, ni un goût ni une intelligence, rien que la victoire brutale de la richesse." Goncourt *Idées et sensations*, 1866 cited in Pety, 2003, 91.

11. The "bourdaloue" chamber pot was named for Louis Bourdaloue, an eighteenth-century designer-commentator who lectured on the hygienic and aesthetic virtues of his jugs.

12. "Oh! Les coquets et galantines réceptacles ... d'une forme plus contournée, plus serpentante, plus amoureuse des parties secrètes de la femme." Goncourt and Goncourt, 1914–18, 3:753 [1 September 1892].

13. "Je trouve aussi là-dedans le symptôme d'une société qui s'ennuie, d'une société où la femme ne joue plus le rôle attrayant qu'elle jouait dans les autres siècles. J'ai remarqué, pour mon compte, que les achats s'interrompent, quand ma vie est très amusée ou très occupée. L'achat continu, insatiable, maladif, n'existe que dans les périodes de tristesse, de vide, d'inoccupation du Coeur ou de la cervelle." Ibid., 2:629 [26 February 1875], also cited in Pety, 2003, 80.

14. "Le joli,—voilà à ces heures d'histoire légère, le signe et la séduction de la France. Le joli est l'essence et la formule de son génie. Le joli est le ton de ses moeurs. Le joli est l'école de ses modes. Le joli, c'est l'âme du temps—et c'est le génie de Boucher." Goncourt and Goncourt, 1914–18, 1:196 (1881).

15. "En maniant ces *jolités* ... en touchant et retournant ces navettes, ces étuis, ces flacons, ces ciseaux, qui ont été pendant des années les petits outils des travaux d'élégance et de grâce des femmes du temps, il vous arrive de vouloir retrouver les femmes auxquelles ils ont appartenue et de les rêver, ces femmes—le petit objet d'or ou de Saxe amoureusement caressé de la main." Ibid., 3:182 [27 November 1888].

16. "Insensibles ou à peu près aux choses de la nature, plus touchés d'un tableau que d'un paysage et de l'homme que de Dieu, n'est-ce point la façon de notre oeil qui nous fait autant aimer l'art, embrassant mieux l'objet, que nous caressons de tout près, que nous touchons presque? Il est à croire que les myopes sont collectionneurs et amateurs d'art de nature." Ibid., 1:233 [2 February 1857], also cited in Pety, 2003, 99.

17. "Ils ont vécu dans un petit musée sans cesse agrandi .... De cette familiarité ininterrompue avec des choses rares et suggestives, ils ont tiré une façon spéciale de voir, qui s'est insinuée de proche en proche jusqu'au plus intime de leur talent; et pour bien comprendre ce talent, c'est cette subtile influence qu'il est nécessaire de démêler d'abord et d'expliquer." Bourget, 1883, 145.

18. "Cette éducation du regard aboutit bientôt à une sorte d'analyse particulière. Pour les personnes meme douées d'un sens artistique médiocre, la face

d'une chambre, la forme d'un objet, sa couleur, sont des prétextes à sympathie ou bien à antipathie. Les hommes qui savant regarder comprennent les causes profondes de cette sympathie ou de cette antipathie, et les objets leur apparaissent comme des signes d'une infinité de petits faits. Derrière un mobilier, ils aperçoivent la main de celui qui l'a disposé, son tempérament, sa physiognomie. Les plis d'un vêtement leur révèlent les moindres particularités d'un corps. Ils ont des associations d'idées interminables à propos de chaque objet rencontré, manié, contemplé." Ibid., 152.

19. "En ce temps où les choses, dont le poète latin a signalé la mélancholique vie latente, sont associées si largement par la description littéraire moderne à l'Histoire de l'Humanité, pourquoi n'écrirait-on pas les mémoires des choses au milieu desquelles s'est écoulée une existence d'homme?" Goncourt, 1881, preface.

20. "La collection est la passion imaginative par excellence, sans aucun mélange d'excitation physique ou de satisfaction des sens matériels. C'est en quel-que sorte l'onanisme idéal du regard." Goncourt and Goncourt, 1914–18, 1:1122 [22 November 1864].

21. "Dans ce moment, une vie absolument en dehors de la vie réelle et toute remplie par la contemplation de l'objet et de l'image d'art, produisant une sorte d'onanisme de la rétine et de la cervelle, un état physique d'absence et de griserie, où l'on échappe aux embêtements moraux et aux petits malaises physiques." Ibid., 3:570 [10 April 1891].

22. "Quand elles sont façonnées de main de l'homme, les choses nous parlent, elles nous saisissent par le tour que leur a donné un être pensant; il arrive même à la longue qu'à force d'user d'un meuble, nous y laissions une empreinte de nous-mêmes.... Par quelle mystérieuse puissance l'invisible fluide de l'âme humaine s'attache-t-il si intimement, même aux choses inertes, comme le parfum au vase?" Blanc, 1882, 154.

23. "Parfois même, je m'amuse à une fabrication d'accidents qui deviennent les objets de jeux piquants, de petits problèmes baroques posés par la matière bigarrée à l'imagination. C'est ainsi que les regards du malade transforment en mille figures étranges les marbures d'un papier de fantaisie, ou que les nuages du couchant apparaissent à l'enfant comme d'immenses bergeries, là où l'oeil du marin voit des caps dentelés et des plages." Gallé, 1908, 350.

24. Louis de Fourcaud, "Les Arts Décoratifs aux Salons de 1894", *Revue des Arts Décoratifs* 15 (1894): 2, cited in Silverman, 1989, 241.

25. Goncourt and Goncourt, 1914–18, 2:235.

26. "Faire une pièce dans ma maison: voilà presque toujours, après la publication d'un livre et l'argent qu'il rapporte, la récréation, la récompense que je me donne. Bien souvent je me suis dit: Si je n'étais pas litterateur, si je n'avais pas mon pain sur la planche, la profession j'aurais choisie, ça aurait été d'être un inventeur d'intérieurs pour des gens riches. J'aurais aimé qu'un banquier, me laissant la bride sur le cou, me donnât plein pouvoir en un palais qui n'aurait eu que les quatre murs pour lui en imaginer la décoration et le moblier avec ce que je découvrirais chez les marchands de vieux, les artistes industriels modernes ou dans ma cervelle." E. Goncourt, 2003, 25.

15 Collecting and Autobiography

A Note on the Origins of *La Casa della vita* by Mario Praz and Its Relation to Edmond de Goncourt's *La Maison d'un artiste*

Patrizia Rosazza Ferraris[1]

In the June 1937 edition of the British periodical *Decoration* Mario Praz published a brief article entitled "An Empire Flat in a Roman Palace"—barely five pages in length with ten or so photographs—in which he described his Rome apartment. Clearly intended for an English readership, the piece opens with a description of central Rome: Via Giulia and Palazzo Ricci, where Praz had been living since 1934, before going on to examine room after room the Empire furnishings that he himself describes as having "started collecting since my Florence days." Several of the most important pieces in the collection, such as the console with the polychrome marble top, the large psyche (reversible mirror) and the bed produced by Jacob were already present in the Palazzo Ricci rooms, while other more modest furnishings were soon replaced with finer pieces. The photographs that accompany the article show the large rooms of Palazzo Ricci almost empty, with the walls particularly striking in that they lack many of the paintings with which they were covered in later years. Certain elements of the collector's taste for assonance are already present, however, such as in "a ladies' sitting-room"—known also as the Love and Psyche Room—that is furnished with a selection of thematically similar subjects, from eighteenth-century pastel reproductions of Raphael's decorations at the Farnesina depicting episodes from the myth of Love and Psyche, to candelabra supported by cherubs, an oil painting with Love tasting the point of an arrow and a Viennese glass with Love behind bars "pour avoir volé des coeurs" (because of his having stolen some hearts). But Praz dwells particularly on the festive colour schemes and lighting throughout the apartment, with the intention of dispelling the widespread perception of the Empire style as "cold," severe and funereal, in favour of highlighting its more pleasing Alexandrian tonalities.

This brief text was the starting point of the collector's lengthy 1958 autobiography *La Casa della vita* (*The House of Life*), which he updated in 1979. The two twenty-year periods, from 1937 to 1958 and from 1959 to 1979, represent the mature and final years of Praz's life. But the drafting of *La Casa della vita* was preceded by two intermediary versions of the

203

same subject: a description by Praz of his home and collection with the title *Un interno (An Interior)*; and with a number of indicative variations in *Gusto neoclassico (Neoclassical Taste)*, a collection of articles and essays published first in 1940 and, once more with certain alterations, in 1959. *Un interno*, in fact, is a broad reworking of the 1937 text, conducted as an ideal conversation with Emilio Cecchi, Praz's master and friend in those years, whom the collector was bent on converting away from the faction of the detractors of the Empire style with a campaign of cultivated quotations and refined comparisons. The photographs reflect the state of the collection at the time, considerably enlarged in the space of just a few years, while the writing key is by now that of *Casa della vita*, lacking only in the sad references to lost time that characterise the highly personal autobiographical style of the author.

A closer look at the variations between the 1940 and 1959 editions of *Un interno* does however reveal a small but enlightening detail: for the second edition of *Gusto neoclassico*, prompted by Sansoni after the success of *La Casa della vita* a year earlier, a copy of the 1940 edition was used, with updates and changes written by Praz directly in the margins by the printed text: all references to the collector's ex-wife Vivyan were furiously cancelled out. Following their tumultuous separation in 1943, it would appear that a kind of ritual homicide in red ink is being perpetrated in the corrections.

Moreover, the library of Mario Praz that has passed to the Primoli Foundation, of which Praz was president and, from 1969 onwards also lodger, contains a copy of Edmond de Goncourt's *Maison d'un artiste (House of an Artist)* which, as indicated by the Ex Libris, was acquired in 1956. This was precisely the moment that Praz began working on *La Casa della vita*, completing the manuscript in April 1957, and the moment in which he acquired the copy of *Maison d'un artiste* with which he was already familiar and that he had liberally quoted in the first modest edition of *Filosofia dell'arredamento (Philosophy of Interior Decoration)* in 1945, republished in 1964 with a rich photographic documentation. A parallel reading of the two texts, particularly in terms of structure, reveals blatant similarities: the organisation of the chapters each dedicated to a room in the house, the meticulous description of the objects accompanied by stories of how they were acquired and woven into the personal life of the narrator, along with a host of other analogies that one would have expected Praz to highlight. In *La Casa della vita*, though, the Goncourt brothers receive only a passing mention in relation to a comment made by them concerning the Zumbo waxes. This omission is particularly surprising in view of the fact that Praz never omitted to quote his sources, to such a degree that in some cases he would even use the same title, such as in *Filosofia dell'arredamento* —a direct quotation from Poe—or his *Scene di conversazione*, taken from Sitwell's *Conversation Pieces* and generously quoted in the introduction.

One therefore wonders why Praz has chosen to ignore his source in a text that has some so obvious similarities with Goncourt's book, particularly in view of the fact that clearly *Maison d'un artiste* made its entry into the Praz library as a useful comparison text the very same year as the drafting of *La Casa della vita*. A clue to the answer of this small but by no means negligible enigma can be found in the many quotations from *Maison d'un artiste* made by Praz in 1945 for the first edition of *Filosofia dell'arredamento*: in one particular quotation, on page 29 of *Filosofia*, Praz criticises Goncourt's affirmation that furniture and objects are a surrogate for the love of a woman. Clearly this phrase touched Praz deeply and he hastened to use every means to disprove it, almost with the same zeal with which he was to erase the memory of his ex-wife in the second edition of *Gusto neoclassico*.

But the writings of Edmond de Goncourt continued to echo strongly in the memory of Praz, so much so that a subtle play of contrasting analogies appears in the quotation from Goncourt's Will on the cover page of the auction catalogue—of which Praz obviously had a copy—when his great collection was dispersed in 1897: "I desire that my drawings, prints, objects ... be spared the lifeless fate of being put on display in a museum for the vacuous gaze of an indifferent passer-by...." And Praz's response in *Filosofia*, "among the many indifferent, distracted or vulgar visitors there will be the sensitive soul who, even for a moment, will feel touched by the warmth that once brought life to all those fine furnishings." With two so sharply contrasting ways of perceiving and living collecting, and of conceiving the future destiny of collections, Praz's eloquent silence on the greater and more precise model for his *Casa della vita—La Maison d'un artiste* by Edmond de Goncourt—would appear to have its justification.

NOTE

1. This brief chapter is the fruit of conversations during the summer of 2006 with Barbara Briganti, responsible for the extremely accurate Italian translation of Edmond de Goncourt's *Maison d'un artiste*, published by Sellerio in 2005, and owes much to the kindness of Clayton C. Kirking of the Public Library of New York. A special thanks goes also to the Primoli Foundation and its President, Massimo Colesanti, for permission to consult the Praz archive that the Foundation keeps so admirably.

16 A Nomadic Investment in History

Pierre Loti's House at Rochefort-sur-Mer

Stephen Bann

I will start with an image (see Figure 16.1). It is a sepia photograph, probably taken in the last decade of the nineteenth century. The light enters the room from a pair of imposing Gothic windows and illuminates a scene that is filled with objects evoking the Middle Ages: elaborate hanging lamps, varieties of wooden furniture including a throne-like chair, and a table with artfully carved legs upon which what appears to be an ivory casket—perhaps in origin a reliquary—has been proudly placed, together with some ancient candle-sticks. It would take a long time to compile an inventory of this space, since even the walls of the room are covered with intricate wooden carvings and hung with cupboards of seeming antiquity. But the effort to itemise the individual objects proves hardly worthwhile, in the end, because the most intriguing aspect of this rich historical milieu is the human presence at the centre of it. A small but undoubtedly impressive male figure is ensconced in the most elaborate, and evidently one of the most uncomfortable of the ancient chairs, positioned in such a way that we cannot fail to take account of his posture. He is seated not symmetrically but in *contraposto*, with his right arm resting on the arm of the chair, his right knee drawn up and his left hand resting on a more relaxed left leg. He is wearing a smart double-breasted suit, not at all in keeping with all these antiquated appurtenances. His face is raised, displaying a forceful expression which might well be intended to convey the message: I am the master of this scene.

This is the writer Pierre Loti, or, to give him his baptismal name, Julien Viaud, photographed in the "Salle gothique" of his house at Rochefort-sur-mer, a room which he inaugurated on 12 April 1888, with ceremonies that will be described further in the course of this chapter. But before plunging into the fascinating story of the creation of this room—and before setting it in the context of Loti's extraordinary life as a writer and a traveller—I want to stress the particular significance of this self-conscious staging of the presence of the writer of the space that he has created, which is of course made possible only by the invention of the photograph. This also enables me to set Loti's house in the context of other writers' houses that are being discussed in this collection. To put it briefly, for writers who lived in a pre-

Figure 16.1 Pierre Loti in his "Salle gothique" at the Maison de Pierre Loti, Roche-fort-sur-mer, c. 1890 (© Maison Pierre Loti, Rochefort-sur-Mer).

photographic age, the photographic image of their house is bound to have, at best, a metonymic relationship to the life that was lived there. For those who lived after the invention of photography, the photograph usually turns out to be our way of eavesdropping on the private events that took place in a particular location, with the protagonists unaware of the ways in which posterity would choose to interpret them. That is the particular attraction of such images. But Loti obliges us to think in different terms. Here, in this image, he designates the "Salle gothique" as his creation, as the fiction of a historical milieu for which he takes all the credit and (we might infer) the authorial responsibility.

Of course, what we see here also has a clear genealogy. The "Salle gothique" derives, in the first place, from nineteenth-century historicism and the cult of the Middle Ages. In a precise sense, it is the outcome of the increasingly detailed knowledge of the history of the furnishings of that previously little studied epoch that reached a culminating point during Loti's own life-time. Viollet-le-Duc published in 1871 his superb history of French furniture which discriminated between the different phases of development in medieval craftsmanship, and graphically represented them in a grand sequence of imaginary rooms each devoted to a single century.[1] Yet these diagrammatic renderings, informed by scrupulous scholarship, clearly provide no direct competition to the rich effect of the photograph. Viollet-le-Duc's careful parsing of the different styles bears no relation to the demonstrably more eclectic array of objects brought together by Loti.

Indeed, we need to look back to a more holistic method of representation, devoted to the aim of recreating the past that was initiated by an earlier generation of painters. The compelling desire to recreate the historical milieu of the Middle Ages and the Renaissance had developed in France during the Empire, in the first decade of the century, and found expression particularly in the paintings of the Lyons School (the so-called "Troubadours"). Works like Pierre Révoil's *Convalescence de Bayard*, first

Figure 16.2 Devilliers âiné, line engraving after Pierre Révoil, *La Convalescence de Bayard*, Salon of 1817.

shown at the Paris Salon of 1817 (see Figure 16.2), gave precise and jewel-like expression to curious antique objects that were incorporated in evocative historical scenes.[2] This process, however, acquired a concrete rather than a purely imaginary form when the collector Alexandre du Sommerard installed his own abundant collections, amassed largely during the 1820s, in the former town-house of the Abbots of Cluny, close to the Collège de France and the Sorbonne. From 1834, this unprecedented collection was open to the public, and after the death of Du Sommerard in 1842 it became a state institution under the title of the Musée de Cluny. Here the visitors were encouraged to imagine that they were stepping back into a remote historical period. Du Sommerard purposely used devices of illusion, like the suits of armour facing one another and ostensibly playing chess in the window of the so-called Salle de François 1ᵉʳ, to stress the incentive to suspend disbelief.[3]

Yet Du Sommerard's strategy was to efface himself behind the spectacle that he presented. He was painted in 1826 by Charles-Caïus Renoux as *L'Antiquaire*—The Antiquary—but this portrait displayed him at an early stage, when his collection was not yet installed. At this stage, his objects were evidently in a state of some disarray and required the personal narrative of the collector engaging a visitor in conversation to provide them with a history. Yet the very choice of the title, *The Antiquary*, for Renoux's painting betrayed the avowed indebtedness of Du Sommerard to the stimulus that he had received from Sir Walter Scott. This internationally celebrated author had himself already succeeded in making the transition from being a collector of antique objects to sponsoring the neo-medieval milieu of Abbotsford. In creating an environment that sustained and supported his activity as a writer of imaginative fiction, Scott had taken a decisive step in ensuring that the writer's house would be accepted as an indissoluble feature of his public persona.

So, in order to set Loti's recreation of the past in context, we need to revisit Scott. Loti's "Salle gothique" is assuredly not a museum room, nor is it a dictionary entry intended as a lesson in discriminating between the periods of medieval furnishing. As the presence in the photograph suggests, it is designed to advance and support Loti's identity as an author. But an important comparison emerges, where Scott is concerned. Scott built Abbotsford to fulfil a complex personal and psychological agenda. There can be no doubt about this.[4] But where the image of Scott appears at Abbotsford in the form of a representation, it is as if he had stepped with alacrity into a pre-assigned role that transcended his hard and impecunious life as a writer. We see Scott at Abbotsford in the guise of a country gentleman, painted like many of his fellow Scottish gentry and aristocracy by Sir Henry Raeburn, or presented in the form of a bust in the classic style used for commemorating of great men, as sculpted by Sir Francis Chantrey. Sir John Watson Gordon's posthumous painting of Scott as a writer, seated at his working desk, does not show him in his study at Abbotsford, but in the more modest premises that he occupied in Queen Street, Edinburgh, before building his neogothic pile.[5] Loti, likewise, does not present himself in the guise of a writer. There is no study, or personal library, installed in the house at Rochefort to commemorate what one might imagine to have been this important feature of his everyday activity. Loti is anxious to mark his presence as an author in the family house that he has reconstructed. He does so in this photograph, and he repeats the exercise in others dating from the same period. But he exploits the photograph to effect a kind of elision between the image of the author and the finished product of the author's imagination as it has taken on a concrete and spectacular form. This is all of a piece with the continuing story of Loti's life in general, in which the threads of fictional narrative and personal adventure are so intimately intertwined that it appears impossible to make a hard and fast distinction between the two.

This is the reason why my chapter bears the title "A Nomadic Investment in History". Scott employed the medieval alias of Abbotsford as a way of reclaiming his inheritance as the descendant of a noble but dispossessed Border family, and of centering a fictional opus whose imaginative source lay in the rediscovery of the Middle Ages. Loti never saw himself specifically as a historical novelist, intent though he was on opening up the virtually obsolescent milieu of the Breton fishing communities. For the most part he concentrated his attention on the far-away and fascinating domains of oriental culture that he was able to explore in the course of his career as a marine officer. Yet within his house at Rochefort he cultivated the historical and the exotic with equal passion, privileging neither but leaving them to bear witness alternately to the vicissitudes of an Ego that was prone to an enduring ordeal of identity. Even more vividly than the novels themselves, the juxtaposed rooms of the Maison Pierre Loti testify through their unresolved heterogeneity to the multiple roles through which the author's identity was invested.

Before this bizarre and yet undoubtedly productive tension in Loti's life and work is addressed, I should draw one further comparison with the Romantic tradition to which Loti was attached, in the very process of distancing himself from it. When the American writer Washington Irving visited Britain in 1817, he determined to visit and write about the homes of the two most famous and productive writers that the English-speaking world had contributed to the mature flowering of European Romanticism: Sir Walter Scott and Lord Byron. Scott he was able to visit at Abbotsford, and the resultant memoir is a brilliant record of the writer in the house that was then coming into being. Byron he could not pin down so easily, since the ancestral home of the Byrons, Newstead Abbey in Nottinghamshire, was untenanted, and hardly recovered from the extreme dilapidation to which the poet's improvident grandfather had condemned it. Abbotsford was, at the time of Irving's visit, "just emerging into existence" from the scaffolding[6]—a new building, however much the design was steeped in Scott's awareness of the history of the Scottish Borders. Newstead was a true historic seat, whose visible features immediately recalled the distinctively English event of the Dissolution of the Monasteries by Henry VIII, when many English gentry had been granted the lands and buildings of former monastic houses. It was, indeed, a house that still exhibited a stark contrast between the remains of the old monastery church, an impressive ruin, and the more recent dwelling house, itself (because of its origin in monastic buildings) a medley of assorted spaces. As Byron himself remarked of its "mix'd Gothic" in Canto XIII of *Don Juan*:

> Huge halls, long galleries, spacious chambers join'd
> By no quite lawful marriage of the arts,
> Might shock a connoisseur ....[7]

The conclusions of this line of comparison can be stated briefly. Where Scott centres his life, and his fiction, upon a recreated medieval site, Byron views his ancestral home from a position of exile, not only because he cannot afford to live there, but also because its heterogeneous construction—part authentic medieval ruin and part oddly assorted domestic dwelling—cannot be appreciated as a unified plan. Loti, I would suggest, puts together elements of both these approaches, although his ultimate creation of a writer's house belongs to a period in which both Romantic irony and Romantic nostalgia for the past were perceived as features of a world that had irremediably vanished. Loti's constellation of differently themed rooms is, in a sense, the necessary supplement to his fiction, which itself results from the scattering of his authorial identity across a panorama of different temporal and cultural scenes. Viewed against the Romantic context, then, the house enacts the splitting of the authorial self, and offers a public representation of that splitting, in a fashion that appears distinctively modern.

Pierre Loti was born Julien Viaud in the parental home at the French port of Rochefort in 1850. Rochefort on the mouth of the Charente River was a historic town and stronghold whose naval base had served for the production of cordage for the fleet since the time of Louis XIV. Numerous expeditions to all parts of the world had originated from Rochefort in the early modern period, and it was still, in the nineteenth century, a hub of marine activity. Loti's parental home was a modest building, faced in the yellowish Charente stone, and situated in one of the long straight streets that betray the town's military origins. Young Julien made his first sea voyage in 1868 at the age of eighteen, and over the next two years, for his first practical experience in the merchant marine, he covered a large part of globe, sailing in the Mediterranean, off the coast of Africa, across the Atlantic and to the countries of South America. On his return to Rochefort, where his father had died in 1870 leaving his family in debt, he was able to purchase the family home from his mother, no doubt in part from the earnings as a writer which he had begun to receive during those years. This dual career as a future marine officer and a journalist, soon also become a highly successful writer of novels, continued to be the determining feature of his life, and remarkably enough proved a source of strength rather than a cause of conflict. This became amply clear in 1883 when he was serving as a marine officer in French Indo-China, and published articles in the *Figaro* which were highly critical of French colonial policy. Although he was summoned home as a result of the political furore provoked by his opinions, the issue soon evaporated in the face of his literary celebrity.[8] The subsequent success of his novels was crowned by increasing official, as well as popular, recognition. He became Chevalier de la légion d'honneur in 1887 and a member of the French Academy in 1892.

Although Loti's achievement has recently become a bone of contention in the context of the debate about "Orientalism", it must surely be seen as distinctive in the degree to which it involved stages of immersion in non-Western cultures, and a compellingly direct manner of signalling the results of this immersive process. Loti's period of six months or so spent in Constantinople in 1876–7 involved a close relationship with a young Turkish girl which was to be the basis of his novel *Aziyade*, published anonymously in 1879. When he determined to return to the Turkish capital in 1890, his work was by that stage so well known in Turkish official circles—and indeed appreciated by the Sultan himself—that he was given facilities denied to virtually all foreign visitors, such as the opportunity to inspect the extraordinary display of costumes and jewels of the former Ottoman rulers in the palace of the Seraglio.[9] As far as the present topic is concerned, however, it is the desire to plant a token of the environment of Constantinople in the parental house at Rochefort that is specially noteworthy. Already on his return from his first journey to Turkey in 1877 Loti had decided to create a Turkish room, but of this first installation no trace remains. In 1884, on his return from Indo-China, he installed another so-called "Arab Room", and finally, in 1894, a much more ambitious Turkish salon entitled "La Mosquée" to take the place of both the earlier installations (see Figure 16.3). It goes without saying that Loti's increasingly ambitious projects over these years were largely dependent on the success of his books, which in turn led to him having more resources to acquire the objects that he discovered in the course of his repeated voyages. Eventually, after 1895, he gained precious additional space with the purchase of the adjacent house, and undertook extensive architectural modifications in the pursuit of his chosen themes.

It would be impossible to sum up the combined history of all the installations in the Maison Pierre Loti in this brief chapter. There were Chinese and Japanese as well as Turkish rooms, not to mention those devoted to the Gothic and the Renaissance. The process was, in every sense, an ongoing one, involving successive modifications of the limited space available, and invariably reflecting his passions and his voyages of the moment. The culminating achievement of the Turkish room will be mentioned at the end of this chapter. The "Gothic Room", with which this account began, presents perhaps the clearest visual evidence of Loti's compulsive engagement with the experience of historical otherness. This is not only because the photographic documentation is more extensive, but also, perhaps, because the project gained an added attraction from being founded upon an impossibility. Japan and Turkey could be visited at leisure, and their spoils brought back to Rochefort. But in the final resort the medieval period—despite all that might be done in the way of historical research and the purchase of suitable objects—was a domain accessible only to the imagination.[10] The prospect of nurturing and even sharing that imaginative vision of the past was a mirage that excited Loti to his most ambitious feat of historical mimicry.

Loti chose an upper room in the original parental home to contain this medieval installation. The side elevation of the decorous eighteenth-century building clearly shows the range of Gothic windows with pointed arches, derived from a medieval church that was awaiting demolition, and marks the clear contrast with the simple rectangular fenestration on the ground floor. In fact, Loti was obliged to turn the windows round, so that the deep ledges originally on the outside of the church were transferred to the inside of the house, in order to keep the new range flush with the rest of the façade. He also anticipated the possibility that a visitor to the "Gothic Room" might glimpse through those windows an adjacent building which looked very unlike a medieval church, and arranged for his neighbour's roof to sport a splendid gargoyle!

Loti's sophisticated play with the mechanisms of illusion can be compared and contrasted—in this respect as in others—with the devices of the earlier Romantic tradition. Significantly, one commentator had discussed the experience of the Musée de Cluny in relation to the *Tales of Hoffmann*, pointing to the way in which what is now termed the literature of the "fantastic" solicits a pleasurable suspension of disbelief.[11] For Loti, one might feel, the stakes invested in the possibility of illusion are much higher. Indeed they are impossibly high. But that is what makes the whole exercise of imaginative recreation so compelling. To create a frisson of illusion in fictional writing is one thing, but the real challenge, which certainly borders on the impossible, is to make that illusion palpable in terms of the very plenitude of the environment that surrounds us: in other words, to transform the everyday scene through a ceremonial reenactment of the experience of another temporal dimension. Du Sommerard just waited for his visitors to turn up, and then charmed them with his eloquent narrative voice and his ingenious elements of artifice—such as the notorious figure of cowled monk which caused surprise, and, on occasions, severe shock when they entered the medieval chapel of the Hôtel de Cluny. Loti, having elaborately fitted up his Gothic room, needed to inaugurate it with a sumptuous medieval banquet at which sundry relatives, local acquaintances and friends from Paris would garb themselves in an assortment of medieval dresses, and feast on capons, lampreys, geese and squirrels, washed down with hypocras and hydromel, not to mention the sound Gascon wines that probably came from the family properties of his long-suffering wife, Blanche Franc de Ferrière.

This whole episode pertains, no doubt, as much to the history of publicity as to that of literature. It is clear that the opening of the "Salle Gothique" on 12 April 1888 was widely reported. Local people who were not invited to the meal were allowed to troop past, by way of the convenient upper gallery, as long as they made concessions to the Gothic period as far as dress above the waist was concerned (what went on below the belt was invisible to Loti and his guests). Even the Parisian press was galvanised, since Loti had received acceptances from celebrities like the popular novelist Juliette Adam, and the man-about-town and scion of the Serbian royal family Prince Bojidar Karageorgevitch, transmuted for the evening into a rather implausible troubadour, under the alias of René de Hyalange. All of this, however, was not just for the guests' benefit, but for the delectation of Loti himself, who of course foresaw in advance that it was bound to be a disappointment. Or very nearly so. The photographs that survive as a record of the inaugural feast were not taken on the day itself, but on the subsequent morning which proved, as Loti wrote in his journal "a radiant spring day after the resumption of winter".[12] For the great day itself, Loti makes a brief but significant entry:

The day of the Louis XI dinner.

For two fleeting instants, I have the total impression of the Middle Ages: on arrival, when I am the first to enter the room lit with the red light of torches held by valets with long hair, the bag-pipes moaning softly from below us,—the long procession of the guests following on behind.

And also, at the arrival of the peacock, carried on a stretcher with its wings outstretched, preceded by bag-pipes and the escort (Fressac) fully armed,—followed by valets carrying resin torches .... [13]

The desired role of Loti's house, and its "Salle gothique" specifically, is epitomised in this evocative passage. It has been brought into existence in order for the writer to lose himself as near completely as possible in the experience of otherness: to enable him to be so comprehensively assaulted in respect of all the senses as to achieve a momentary release from the banal identity of a late nineteenth-century petit-bourgeois. The lengthy preparation of the scene and the "fleeting" nature of the satisfaction can only be compared, one would imagine, with the act of love, and it is no coincidence that Loti was carrying on an extremely active and unconventional career as a lover at the same time as he was writing his novels and installing his historical rooms. In fact, the private journals incorporate six-pointed stars—which Loti's editors identify tactfully as denoting "amorous performances"—on virtually every night of the week when the "Louis XI dinner" was held. But it would be inept to try and hierarchise these different aspects of Loti's waking activity. Indeed his whole career seems of a piece in being driven by the insatiable desire for the palpable experience of being taken out of himself. It was once said of him that he was passionately in love with persons of both sexes—and if there had been a third sex, he would have valued the opportunity of being in no way less enthusiastic about that! From such a point of view, his incessant journeyings around the world, and bizarre adventures such as the protracted period in which he posed as a Breton sailor, and became engaged to a Breton peasant girl, find a direct correlative in the fitting up of his house as a series of plunges into an alien domain. Home is no home for the sailor Pierre Loti. It is a contrived suspension of multiple fictional possibilities, outside of which there is nothing, or little else. The small bedroom in which he would have spent at least his sleeping hours is as sparsely furnished as the cell of a monk.

What finally set the seal on Loti's comprehensive reconstruction of the family home was the increased space that became available when the adjoining property was purchased. Where the "Salle gothique" was a room on the first floor, somewhat isolated from the rest, the "Salle Renaissance" (begun after 1895) was at the core of the building. Loti succeeded in achieving a spectacular dislocation of the expected proportions of the interior, by allowing the new room to rise over two floors and almost to the roofline. Indeed the space was really not quite adequate for such a grand overall effect, and the stone staircases that lead down from the gallery level had to be made excessively, even dangerously, steep. But the result remains the grandest demonstration of Loti's ingenious redeployment of the architectural fragments that he had salvaged throughout South-West France and Northern Spain.

As with its medieval predecessor, expediency dominated the choice of period furnishings in the "Salle Renaissance". There was no chance of a purist selection as illustrated by Viollet-le-Duc. Thus, the lower part of the magnificent fire-place that dominates the room is in true Renaissance style, but the upper part is in the flamboyant Gothic that Loti greatly admired. The Rochefort masons who worked under his supervision have effectively smoothed over the transition, and also installed a sixteenth-century Spanish St Theresa within an elaborate niche. It is also worth recalling that this large and ponderously furnished dining room provides direct access to a small drawing room, the Salon Louis XVI, where in 1897 Loti installed his elegant inherited furniture—the only relatively modern feature of the house. By the very end of the nineteenth century, the previous century, which had culminated in the French Revolution, had probably acquired just the requisite degree of historicity to make its recreation worthwhile.

I have laid some stress throughout this chapter on the vein of scepticism that underlies all of Loti's constructions, which is so far removed from the full-blooded confidence in the ability to recreate the ambiance of the past that we find in Scott and Du Sommerard. Yet, in Loti's case, this should not be regarded just as a return to the irony of an earlier period. The point is that the "Salle gothique" and the "Salle Renaissance" do indeed carry conviction. But at the same time they encourage visitors to be fairly sophisticated in gauging the degree of authenticity in the scene to which they are being exposed. In the "Salle Renaissance", Loti has even included a little reminder to the curious in the form of a fine seventeenth-century Brussels tapestry that shows the Empress Helena in the process of selecting the True Cross. Nothing could be more wittily analogical to the process of viewing and appraising the furnishings of this particular room, where careful attention is needed to ensure the necessary discrimination between the "true" and the "false".

However my final point deals not with the epistemological aspect of Loti's historical rooms, but with the way in which these installations were represented in his own period. Unlike the holdings of the Musée de Cluny, which were popularised by the new technique of lithography, the rooms of the Maison Pierre Loti came at a stage when they could be recorded by its triumphant successor: wet-plate photography. Loti indeed seems to have particularly relished the opportunity to photograph the rooms in their turn, and to put on record ceremonies that taken place in them, such as the medieval dinner that inaugurated the "Salle gothique". When he chooses to be photographed in the "Salle gothique", he appears acutely conscious of the way in which the brilliant daylight will catch every intricate surface and illuminate every rich and ornamental texture, for the benefit of the camera. He himself is enshrined in the midst of all this intensely realised visual detail.

Such a degree of self-consciousness surely marks a decisive stage in the development of the notion of the writer's house, and though the photograph reproduced in this chapter may have been confined to a limited circulation, there were certainly others that were destined for a wider public. I have recently acquired a postcard that was sent by Loti to a female admirer in 1916 (see Figure 16.3). The card is obviously part of a commercially marketed series, since it bears the legend "Collection G. Gozzi—Déposé" in the left-hand corner of the image. What is shown is the elaborate architectural setting of the Turkish "Mosque" that had been installed on the top floor of the house. As if to stake his proprietary claim, Loti has added his own signature in the right-hand corner, endorsing the caption: "Maison de Pierre Loti—la Mosquée, à Rochefort." Appropriately enough, the postcard carries on its reverse side a delicate message of appreciation to the young lady who has sent the master an "exquisite work" of her own composition: a song bearing an intimate connection to the theme of his first Turkish novel, *Aziyadé*. What better way to reply to this correspondent

Figure 16.3 "La Mosquée", Maison de Pierre Loti, Rochefort-sur-Mer, postcard with original signature of Pierre Loti, 1917.

than by demonstrating the material evidence of Loti's infatuation with the East! Such an image of the metamorphosis of the writer's house implies a gentle compliment to the sender as well as to the receiver.

NOTES

1. See Viollet-le-Duc, 1871, xii–xv. Each print represents a "Chambre de château" from the relevant century.
2. See Bann, 1996, and Bann, 2001, where the link between this type of historical recreation through pictures and the more concrete form of the historical museum is explored.
3. For a general account of Du Sommerard's work, see Bann, 1995, 145–50.
4. Ibid., 99–101, 152–53; see also Bann, 1984, 93–111. The argument of this chapter was deeply influenced by my discovery of the remarkable book published by Washington Irving in 1835, which recounted his experiences of a visit to Abbotsford in 1817, and compared and contrasted Scott's house with Byron's Newstead Abbey. I know of no text which so compellingly anticipates the interest in memory, self-fashioning and tourism that is developed in the current collection of essays; see [Irving], 1835. In view of the comparative rarity of the work, I have referred the reader to the quotations used in my own book in the first instance.
5. See Bann, 1995, cover and 99.
6. Quoted in Bann, 1984, 95.
7. Quoted in Ibid., 98.
8. See Loti, 1997, 118, diary entry for 6 February 1884. His appointment with the minister resulted in no disciplinary action. On the contrary, he was treated

as a celebrity and his return became a "triumph", so that he was confirmed in his desire to combine his marine career and his work as a writer.

9. See my discussion of this visit in Bann, 1998. The extraordinary spectacle included the ceremonial kaftans of the former sultans dating back to the sixteenth century, mounted as if their wearers were still alive. In recent years, these gorgeous robes have travelled to the West with exhibitions of Turkish art and culture. The stark contrast between Loti's exceptionally privileged access, and the opportunity of viewing them made available to an international public hardly more than a century later, remains an instructive one.

10. In this respect, Loti is the successor not of Scott, but of Flaubert, whose intensive research for his historical novel *Salammbô* was accompanied by a declared scepticism on the possibility of "resuscitating" the past. See Bann, 1984, 6.

11. See Bann, 1995, 145–50, for the remarks of Mme de Saint-Surin, originally published in 1835. Of the spectacle of the two knights in armour engaged in a chess game, she writes: "certainly with less imagination than Hoffmann had when he wrote his fantastic tales, it appears as if you are present at this game" (146).

12. Loti, 1997, 254.

13. Ibid.

17 Une Chambre Mentale
Proust's Solitude

Jon Kear

The relationship of literature to the place in which it is produced has generally been a neglected issue in literary studies. This matter immediately raises a number of questions about how we conceive of such a relationship. What connection exists between the space in which an author writes and the work he or she creates, and how do ideas about literature current at the time shape the environment an author constructs in order to write in? To what extent does an author's studio need to be seen not simply as a private space but as a space of literary self-fashioning? These issues seem important for Proust's work. Few writer's rooms are so emblematic as Proust's cork-lined bedchamber at his second storey apartment at no. 102 Boulevard Haussmann. Proust moved into the apartment on the fashionable new Parisian boulevard, in 1906, and it was here he began *À la recherche du temps perdu*. It might be said that it was while he was at this address that he first became a novelist, for despite a prolific output of short stories, literary sketches and criticism for newspapers and symbolist reviews, his early aspirations as a novelist had resulted in only the aborted *Jean Santeuil*.[1] Proust was to stay at the Boulevard Haussmann for the next thirteen years semi-invalided for much of the time due to the gradual worsening of the severe asthma he had contracted as a child, and it was in the apartment's bedroom that doubled as a studio, he wrote most of the manuscript of his novel.[2]

The apartment on Boulevard Haussmann, however, no longer exists; Proust's study is now the boardroom of a commercial bank's headquarters. Nevertheless, the bedroom has been reconstructed at the Musée Carnavalet, albeit in the form it took after Proust had been evicted to a small apartment Rue Hamelin, where he spent the last months before his death in 1922. Preserved with its original furniture, this fragment of Proust's room is presented like a pristine time capsule located among a group of other historical reliquaries, that include Marie Antoinette's slipper, Robespierre's shaving bowl, pottery from the revolution and the cork lined bedroom of the poet the Comtesse Anne de Noailles, who like Proust, shared her friend's preference for writing while semi-recumbent in bed.[3] The Carnavalet exhibit displays Proust's heavy wooden furniture, offset by delicate

Oriental decoration and fabrics (including a Chinese screen depicting an exterior scene), set against the famous pale blond cork-lined tiled walls, an ensemble whose combination of Occidental and Oriental furnishings is typical of the eclectic rococo revival style of the Second Empire, in which the French style of domestic interior was relieved by the taste for exotic fantasy that alluded to the colonial spaces far beyond the boundaries of Europe.

Few exhibits better illustrate the powers of the museum to transform the objects in its collection. Contemporary visitors to Proust's apartment record a very different impression of his living quarters, portraying them as a more austere and theatricalised space. Though the large second storey apartment contained eleven rooms, Proust generally confined his move-ments to the bedroom, the adjoining rooms of which included the main salon and a private dressing room and bathroom, the doorway leading to which was located immediately next to the bed. Unlike in his family home in the rue de Courcelles, Proust excluded all images from the walls of his bedroom at the Boulevard Haussmann, though portraits were hung in other parts of the apartment, notably in the main salon where the portraits of his father and mother were displayed and the small adjacent salon where the famous portrait of Proust as a young man by Jacques Émile Blanche, was placed.[4] The only concessions to the visual arts in his bedroom were a small white statuette of the infant Jesus, which he placed on the marble top of his mother's rosewood chest where he kept the black leather notebooks of the manuscript of his novel, his rosary and a cache of photographs of relatives, friends and actresses that served as aides memoirs for his novel, and a photograph of himself and his brother Robert as children, which he always kept on view.[5] In this sequestered room Proust would lie in bed writing in the multiple black bound notebooks that together contained the unfinished manuscript of *À la recherche du temps perdu*, working generally in the evening and through the night.[6]

The memoirs of his housekeeper and *bonne à tout*, Céleste Albaret, recall his bedchamber as a dark, cramped room placed at the very end of the apartment.[7] Proust's bed was placed at the furthest distance from the windows. From the vantage point of his bed Proust could survey the three entrances into the room but was himself partially screened from view from the entrance of the main salon doorway by the densely arranged furniture. The predominant colour scheme of the room, consistent with the apart-ment as a whole, was bronze and black with parquet floors. The reminis-cences of Proust's *habitués* mention that the blonde cork-lined tiles Proust had installed to reduce the noise from his neighbours and the boulevard, but which he never got around to covering with wallpaper, had become discoloured due to the daily fumigations of Legras powder. And that the dimly lit interior, whose windows were covered by the always drawn shut-ters and curtains, took on the curious ambience of an austere stage set.[8] This impression would have been enhanced by the heavy velvet curtains inside the doorways that gave on to the darkened space, illuminated only by the small green lamp on the bedside table (despite the presence of a large electric chandelier); the lamplight like a spotlight picked out the author tucked in his bed at the end of the room. Arranged next to the bed were three small tables on which were placed Proust's pens, inkwell, notebooks, his watch, an assortment of books, handkerchiefs and hot water bottles, and a copious supply of coffee and Evian water.[9]

The memoirs of those close to Proust emphasise the secluded and eccentric existence he led for the last half of his life, an existence that has accordingly acquired its own mythic dimensions.[10] While the distance Proust took from society was in part as a result of his declining health, it was also a conscious decision to devote himself henceforth to writing, for, according to Proust, his early literary ambitions had been frustrated and compromised by the busy social life he led in fashionable Parisian society. Whether this was true or not the idea took on great explanatory force for the author and his later more solitary life absorbed by writing became a way of redeeming his own sense of time lost. The organising theme of *À la recherche du temps perdu* of the struggle of the young protagonist, also named Marcel, who having tasted the pleasures of love and society devotes himself to becoming a writer, mirrors the course of Proust's own life, encouraging too readily a view of the book as a fictionalised memoir. The biographical circumstances that led to Proust's later reclusion present a more complex psychological picture than his own account paints but one that again finds its mirror image in the novel Proust wrote. *À la recherche du temps perdu* begins and ends under the shadow of death, a death that hovers over the narrator; the search for lost time is in essence a search also for the lost objects of the past and the apartment at the boulevard Haussmann was a space over which the spectre of death hung heavily.[11]

Proust moved into the apartment at the boulevard Haussmann following the deaths in short succession of his father and mother.[12] The death of his mother in 1905, to whom he had remained inordinately devoted to since childhood, greatly distressed him and profoundly shaped the course of his future. Proust, who had remained alone in his bedroom rather than face his mother on her deathbed, lay for almost two months in sleepless seclusion in the parental apartment obsessively writing letters of condolence to anyone he discovered had experienced bereavement, even perfect strangers. In the aftermath he spent six weeks in a private clinic. During this time his nocturnal and neurotic behaviour, which had long estranged him from his family, became more pronounced. Traumatic as this experience was it also served to make him financially independent for the first time and released him from the burden of a parental expectation that weighed heavily upon him. The mother's death may indeed be said to have released him to become a writer and her death, which finds expression in the novel in the narrator's mourning of his grandmother in *Sodome et Gomorrhe*, clarified for him the great preoccupation with the theme of love and loss that prevails within his work, a theme which he had previously failed to conceptualise in his earlier writing.

Although Proust's decision to leave the family home in the rue de Courcelles suggests an intention to move away from the memories of the past, he quickly set about re-constructing a space where those memories would be embedded. Proust's choice of the second floor apartment at the Boulevard Haussmann was probably motivated by sentimental reasons. The apartment had previously been occupied by his great-uncle Louis Weil, who had died a few years earlier; Proust accompanied by his mother had watched Weil die in the very bedroom he would later occupy. Most of the furnishings that adorned Proust's bedchamber were heirlooms from his deceased mother. These included a Boulle worktable inscribed with her initials and the lacquered black grand piano that was placed at the centre of the room.[13] These inanimate objects, mute witnesses invested with vestigial memories of Proust's childhood and lost relatives, functioned as memorial icons that bore the presence of time past. The apartment thus in one respect became a space of memory and mourning filled with the signs of the presence of the lost object of the mother. Are we to see Proust's regression into a dependent bedridden state as in some degree a regression to a primary state of narcissistic identification with the lost body of the mother? The dark, womb-like space of the almost hermetically sealed bedroom might suggest so.

In his essay *Mourning and Melancholy* Freud explored the similarity between two states of mind that share in common traits of psychical conflict that may express themselves variously through all consuming forms of exclusion, inhibition, illness, sleeplessness and the cessation of interest in the outside world combined with self-reproach, self-reviling and delusional expectations of punishment, all of which serve to psychically prolong the existence of the lost object.[14] In both instances Freud describes two kinds of narcissistic identification with the lost object, whether actual in the case of mourning or delusional in the case of melancholia, and suggests that a subject's desire to prolong the act of mourning can lead to forms of regression or forms of anticathexes in which the subject may seek to incorporate or internalise the lost object or in which the lost object is experienced as overwhelming the subject's ego. The notion of a reversion to a primary narcissistic identification with the lost object may perhaps shed some light on the particular form of mourning that Proust underwent and the peculiar living arrangements he created for himself at the apartment at the boulevard Haussmann.

The explanatory force of such biographical observations are important in explaining Proust's secluded existence in the latter part of his short life and the impression it makes upon his writing, but the preoccupation with Proust's life has threatened to overshadow the actual work he produced or at least to reduce it to a literary memoir. Recent interpretation has sought to redress this and counter some of the legends that have arisen about the author. The portrayal of Proust as literary *isolé* has been challenged by recent accounts, that have questioned the terms of this characterisation and the tendency to read *À la recherche du temps perdu* as a thinly veiled biography.[15]

These lines of critique have usefully served to revise our understanding of the relationship Proust had to the outside world. The relationship of Proust to his society was, as Shattuck has written, a more complex and contradictory one than supposed.[16] Yet, to emphasise Proust's self-absorbed preoccupation with interior experience, both in his living arrangements and in his novel, is not to say the author's isolationism marked a simple disengagement with the historical context in which he lived or calls for a mode of interpretation that disentangles the author's relationship to his times. On the contrary Proust's solitary conception of writing belongs to a wider, as yet still largely unwritten history of private life.[17] As historians have recently argued, the preoccupation with interiority in late nineteenth-century France, far from simply being a flight from society reflected historical changes in the conception of the urban scene and in particular a new accent on privacy and the private interior that emerged out of the rebuilding of Paris in the period of the Second Empire and early Third Republic. While Jules and Edmond de Goncourt saw the massive transformation of the urban structure of Paris, begun under Baron Haussmann during the period of the Second Empire, as regrettably marking the death of the interior and the birth of a life increasingly lived out in the new public spaces of the refashioned Paris, spaces they regarded as given over to spectacle, promenading and commodified public leisure, arguably the reverse was actually transpiring.[18]

As Sharon Marcus has stated Haussmannisation was as much about private as public arenas, about the creation of new interior spaces and enclosures as it was about a new transparent urban space.[19] This "interiorisation of Paris" grew in momentum towards the end of the century with the collapse of radical republicanism in the 1880s. Deborah Silverman in her book *Art Nouveau in Fin-de-Siècle France*, traces the conversion of *art nouveau* from a new monumental public art aligned to the bold radical liberalism of the Third Republic under Jules Ferry, with its accent on social progress through technological modernity to an art conceived as decoration for the private interior.[20] A shift that, she argues, saw the replacement of a rationalist paradigm of modern art focused on the architect engineer's bold futuristic public monuments constructed from modern industrial materials, whose most overt symbols were the steel colossus of the Eiffel Tower and functionalist glass and iron ensemble of enormous *Galerie des machines*, for that of the visionary artisan's miniaturised variants of art nouveau statuary, private ornamentation made for private apartments.

This shift within art nouveau from a bold technological public art to an art of purely subjective experience that Silverman traces, marked a wider morphology that saw the redefinition of modernity as it had been defined in the Second Empire and first two decades of the Third Republic from a culture focused on the public spaces of the new Parisian boulevards to a decorative conception of modern art, aligned to the elegantly adorned private interior, an interior seen as a space that preserved subjectivity from what were seen as the detrimental effects of modern life.[21] By the end of the nineteenth century discourses on metropolitan life had become increasingly focused on alarmist fears about the depleting effect of the conditions of modern urban existence, which was widely regarded as producing neurasthenia. Such concerns spurred on new psychiatric research into neurosis and scientific investigations into various forms of perceptual and attention deficit disorders, of which the synaesthesia so often cultivated by writers associated with Symbolism, was taken to be one example. Charcot's investigations into the suggestibility of patients under hypnosis seemed to offer evidence of just such influence operating below the threshold of consciousness. His research provided a conception of the subject as neither really defined, permanent or stationary but rather as illusive and floating, multiple and intermittent and as such continually subject to the febrile suggestive power of the external environment.[22] Charcot's characterisation of the furtive influence of external factors and unconscious forces on the subject's psyche profoundly compromised the idea of the bourgeois subject as an autonomous individual with a clearly defined personality and the ability to exercise free will.

The new modern interior was conceived as a soothing, regenerative and appropriately vitalising *envelopment* to counter the perceived anxieties, exhausting pace, spatially de-natured and the over stimulating sensory barrage of the modern city that pacified mental will, eroded nerve fibres and penetrated deep into the subject's psyche. The modern interior thus became seen as an alternative self-sufficient realm, emblematic of self-fashioning, a space at once removed from the contingencies of modernity but whose decor combining evocations of natural imagery, dreams and allusive fantasy constructed an alternative realm of the virtual, that substituted for the frenetic and depleting public realm. In short the modern interior became a place where a form of self-fashioned subjecthood reasserted itself over the divided self that inhabited the public domain.[23]

Such ideas provide a general context in which to understand Proust's secluded living arrangements. However, in contrast to the new modern interior filled with *objets luxe* designed either for aesthetic contemplation or revitalising visual stimulation, Proust's apartment seems by comparison remarkably spare and minimalist. Visitors frequently remarked on the drabness of his cell like bedroom, of Proust's apparent indifference to the aesthetics of interior design and the lack of taste of his furnishings, which Proust himself mockingly described as a "triumph of bourgeois bad taste". Unlike the Goncourts whose apartment was constructed as an intimate, nostalgic space of rêverie that provided an alternative world to the modernity of Haussmanisation, or the fictional Des Esseintes' elaborate and visually palpitating interiors in Huysmans *À rebours* (1883), Proust's apartment was arranged as a space that restricted not only visual and aural stimulus from the outside world but visual, aural and even olfactory distractions from within. As Albaret's memoir details, the hypersensitive Proust went to exceptional lengths to control the sights, smells and most particularly the sounds he was subjected to. This sensory inhibition became more extensive as time wore on. The telephone and *théatrophone,* on which Proust used to listen to music and plays piped directly into his bedroom, were removed toward the end of 1914.[24]

The radical restriction of visual and aural sensation within the writer's studio stands in direct contrast to the importance of these sensations in the novel itself and the privileged place the senses occupy in provoking the involuntary memories that retrieve the past (most especially taste and touch which Proust described as containing "in the tiny and almost palpable drop of their essence, the vast structure of recollection."[25] An extraordinary division exists between the detailed sensory description of *À la recherche du temps perdu* and the withdrawn consciousness that self-reflexively recalls, meticulously analyses and reflects upon its meanings. Despite Proust's professed Cartesian denigration of the senses, particularly sight and sound, as deceptive, few writers have written so unremittingly from the senses. *À la recherche du temps perdu* could be described as an observatory of visual constellations in which the pleasures of a conscientious *curiosité* are ever present and the pleasures of visual description take centre stage.[26] As Malcolm Bowie has written, the seizing of every opportunity for enlarging, multiplying, clarifying, analysing and deepening perception of the succession of images, sensations and appearances that make up the narrator's field of perception articulates a desiring optics, that imitates scientific scrutiny in its quest for precision.[27] The array of optical instruments and contraptions and the various forms of visual representation, transmission and projection, from painting, to photography, to magic lantern shows, constitutes a forceful presence in the novel. A similar point can be made about sound. The inhibition of sound in Proust's studio similarly contrasts with the emphasis on sounds and in particular on music in the novel, as well as the particular savour Proust took in representing the rhythms and intonation of speech.[28]

It is as though this restriction of sensory perception had become the precondition of Proust's productivity, that the force of the representation of sensation in *À la recherche du temps perdu* had for Proust become founded on its exclusion from his existence as a writer, as if Proust was aspiring to a condition of innocence from which sensation could be experienced purely cerebrally and entirely afresh and thus, experienced as such, become the powerful vehicle of involuntary memory. As Diana Fuss has remarked, it is significant that in *Le Coté de Guermantes* the narrator, in a series of synaesthetic passages, twice invokes the image of deafness as a paradigm of creativity and rebirth: "take away for a moment from the sick man the cotton-wool that has been stopping his ears and in a flash the broad day-light, the dazzling sun of sound dawns afresh, blinding him" and later dreams of "an Eden, in which sound has not yet been created."[29] This episode parallels the statement by the painter Monet, who Proust much admired, of wishing to see afresh as though he had been born blind and suddenly regained sight.[30]

As this suggests Proust's preoccupation with inhibiting sensation associated with the social and environmental distractions of the modern urban milieu in his living arrangements, reflected more than a desire to create a secluded space in which to write. His attempts to exert greater and greater control over his physical environment and to isolate himself from the social world he depicts were intricately connected to the particular understanding of the conditions of literary production that was emerging in his writing. The conception of the interior as a sanctuary was a disciplinary mechanism of sorts, a place to conserve his fragile energy, protect his nerves in order to focus his attention on the great novel he had as yet failed to realise, certainly, but it also implied a theory of literary production. Proust constantly reflected on the conditions he regarded as necessary for him to write. While these reflections were by no means unprecedented (they emerge out of a Symbolist intellectual milieu that, rejecting the empiricism of realism, saw the ostensible disengagement with modern life as a prerequisite of true artistic creation), the importance Proust placed on solitary reflection takes on a deeper and more complex meaning in relation to the distinction he drew between the "moi social" and the "moi profond" he regarded as essential to creative processes of writing and able to be materialized only through and in the act of writing.[31]

This distinction is first properly elaborated in his essay *Contre Sainte-Beuve*, one of a series of pieces in which he takes issue with the positivism of France's then leading literary critic, where he writes: "A book is the product of a different self from the one we manifest in our habits, our social life and our vices."[32] The act of writing thus conceived becomes a matter of making contact with the "deep self which is rediscovered only by abstracting oneself from other people and the self that knows other people, the self that has been waiting while one was with other people, the self one feels is the only real self; artists end up by living for this alone."[33] For Proust the *social self* lacked depth and unity, being comprised of only the momentary expressions of a public persona, a surface or superficial selfhood that is conditioned by the company or circumstances the subject finds itself in. It is only when the self is no longer at the mercy of others, Proust argues, when we are solitary and isolated from the words and voices of others that we find ourselves again. This distinction is mirrored in *Contre Sainte-Beuve* in Proust's distinction between two distinct kinds of language use, conversation and literature.[34]

Proust's anxiety about the detrimental influence of social life on the consciousness of the writer permeates even Proust's reflections on the nature of reading. In the longer of the two versions of his article *Days of Reading,* Proust takes issue with Ruskin's conception of reading as a conversation with the great minds of civilisation, offering instead a view of reading that emphasises instead the role of the reader, and the subjective nature of reading.[35] But even reading, essential though it might be for edification, is presented as to some degree a distraction from the communion with this deeper self. Thus unlike Marx who regarded alienation as an obstacle to the constitution of authentic subjecthood, in Proust alienation is regarded as essential to preserving a deeper uncontaminated consciousness divorced from the superficialities, influences and distractions of social intercourse.

Given this emphasis on an essential originary individuality in Proust's reflections on literature, it is no coincidence that *À la recherche du temps perdu* was immediately preceded by a series of literary pieces which served to define and distinguish himself in relationship to leading contemporary writers, enacting a series of little oedipal dramas in which he asserted his identity as a writer; these include the aforementioned *Contre Sainte-Beuve* and a series of extraordinary and highly entertaining pastiches in the style of leading writers including the Goncourts, Zola and Flaubert. It is as though before beginning his novel he had to both analyse and master the style of these writers and cleanse his own prose and his underlying conception of literature of any indebtedness to them.

This preoccupation with a deeper stream of reflective selfhood is omnipresent in *À la recherche du temps perdu*, where it acquires a far more intricate formulation than the opposition of surface and deep self might suggest. The book's most insistent theme might be understood as the intricacies, problematics and vicissitudes of personal identity, of how a self comes to recognise itself as such, to maintain identity in time and in spite of time.[36] Arguably even the themes of memory, death and art that form the leitmotifs of Proust's work might be seen as ultimately aspects of a larger enveloping question of identity for the writer. The narrator obsessively returns to the structure and concreteness of human agency providing philosophical and psychological reflections on the question of how a self is construed; whether it is to be ultimately to be understood as concentrated and indivisible or multiple, nomadic and dispersed, continuous or discontinuous, found or constructed, autonomous or an effect of the play of language, material or an abstraction.[37]

The quest for self-knowledge reaches a moment of revelation in *Le temps retrouvé*, the final volume and ontological telos of *À la recherche du temps perdu*, in which the narrator's search for the rediscovery of the past is ostensibly fulfilled and the endless series of scattered reflections on self-identity that make up the previous volumes is resolved in a sudden epiphanic rediscovery of a past he thought forever lost. In *Le temps retrouvé* all the varieties and sub-varieties of the passions of the human subject are accommodated and assigned a place in, as Malcolm Bowie has put it, "a temporal architecture of the self," integrated into an overarching artistic design, that the narrator describes allusively as "like a cathedral, ... like a medical regime, ... like a new world" and which ultimately gives purpose to the artistic quest the narrator has embarked upon.[38] Yet the certainty and moral purpose of *Le temps retrouvé* does little to offset the accumulation of perplexing impressions, doubts, anxious speculations, misrecognitions, and paradoxes that make up so much of the preceding volumes and which at some level cannot help but cast doubt on the foundations on which the final volume is constructed. Proust's self is ultimately not the transcendent self represented in *Le temps retrouvé* but one only discovered and continually rediscovered in and through language, a textual self that is written and constantly rewritten in the solitary act of writing itself.

As I have already argued to re-emphasise the importance of solitariness for Proust's conception of literature is not to divorce the author from the social context in which he wrote or to suggest that the exterior world does not leave its imprint on the writer's consciousness. The relationship of *À la recherche du temps perdu* to the environment in which it was written, is a complex one and it is not out of the question that being at the heart of the new Paris may have exerted a powerful unconsciously role in shaping the author's preoccupation with recapturing lost time. In taking up residence in the heart of the new Paris, as Benjamin observed, Proust was occupying a space that had undergone violent disruption, a transformation which had in effect eradicated the past, that had entirely effaced the streets of the old Paris, whose passing the Goncourts so lamented, and with the destruction of the *vieux quartier,* a salient part of its history.[39]

Diana Fuss in *The Sense of an Interior,* has characterised Proust's writing as "a kind of literary Haussmanisation", comparing its long sentences, expanded chapters and reordering of the novel to the extensive new vistas, monumentality and reorganisation of urban space of Haussmann's Paris.[40] However, Proust's writing far more resembles the structure of the old medieval Paris, with its winding roads and ever burgeoning spaces growing slowly expanding, redefining and spiralling outwards, and the design of his novel seems closer to the grand polyphonic and ornamental architectural style of Gothic cathedral, an analogy Proust himself was fond of making in discussing his work, than the rational uniformity of the new Parisian apartment buildings. The regularity, transparency and uniformity of both the new boulevards and the modern apartment dwellings that occupied its highly rationalised spaces seem far removed from the densely intricate ornamental sentences, intransitivity and labyrinthine structure of Proust's prose, sentences that Anatole France amusingly described as "interminable enough to make you consumptive."[41]

Likewise, the dimly lit and curiously labyrinthine arrangement of furnishings in the interior of Proust's bedroom also seems almost deliberately to contravene the organisational plan of the modern apartment's interior space with its emphasis on breadth, light, symmetry and functionality. There is much evidence to suggest that Proust consciously fashioned his novel after the example of the Cathedral, reaching back into the medieval as a source for his literary endeavours and thus explicitly away from the ultra modernity of Haussmannisation. It was during the period in which Proust had undertaken his translations of Ruskin that he discovered the structural conception of narrative that ultimately informed his epic novel.[42] Through Ruskin he had encountered the idea of reading a Cathedral like a book. Reversing the analogy allowed Proust to establish the narrative structure of his great work as a cathedral-novel. Early drafts of *À la recherche du temps perdu* made explicit reference to this, with parts given titles that referred to architectural components, but Proust deleted these titles regarding them as too pretentious and with them also the explicit references to the modes Ruskin had brought to bear on deciphering the intricate structure of the Gothic church.[43] These "veiled" but nevertheless essential references remain imprinted upon the novel on every page, both formally, in terms of the style of Proust's writing and semantically, in terms of how Proust intended the work to be read.[44]

Proust's preoccupation with isolation as the condition of the production of his novel and the creation of a space of all absorbing interiority, may in part be explained by his theories of individual autonomy as the basis of literary production and an almost utopian ideal of self-sufficiency that informs his construction of a pure space of writing. His desire to sublimate his energies and maintain an undistracted attention toward writing *À la recherche du temps perdu* may have led him, whether consciously or not to construct for himself a chamber of pure interiority in which the inhibition of sensation from the exterior world is conceived as necessary for its forceful representation in the parallel world of the novel; the obliteration of all familiarity, the condition of the essential estrangement integral to the interior recovery of involuntary memory. It is in this respect that the bedroom in which Proust wrote his novel might be understood as a curious Cartesian space of sorts, a space of pure interiority that produces a represented world of unfettered sensation.

NOTES

1. On Proust's development toward *À la recherche du temps perdu* see Sturrock, 1988, vii–xi.
2. Though Proust continually complained about the problems the location posed for his health, he appears to have been very attached to it. He remained at the apartment during the German bombing of Paris in the First World War, leaving only due to his forced eviction in 1919, after his aunt, the heir to the Weil estate, sold the building. See Hayman, 1992, 439–42.
3. On Proust's friendship with de Noailles see Carter, 2000, 271–74.
4. Previously at the rue de Courcelles he had at least four pictures on the wall: a watercolour by Marie Nordlinger given to him by the artist, photographic reproductions of Whistler's *Portrait of Thomas Carlyle* and da Vinci's *La Gioconda*, and a photograph of Amiens Cathedral. In discussing the question

of visuality in the arrangement of Proust's bedroom, Fuss, 2004, 82–83 also points out that the room contained two mirrors, which were positioned to be out of view from Proust's vantage point in bed.

5. Fuss, 2004, 195–202.
6. On Proust's work habits see Proust, 1970-93, 5:427, and Hayman, 1992, 294–335.
7. Albaret, 1973, 230.
8. See Cocteau's account of his visits to Proust in Cocteau, 1990, 94-98.
9. Albaret, 1973, 273–75.
10. Hayman, 1992, 327–45.
11. On the theme of death in *À la recherche du temps perdu* see Bowie, 1998, 267–318.
12. Hayman, 1992, 239–47.
13. The furniture in Proust's bedroom also included pieces originally belonging to his father's library (revolving bookcases, an armchair and his father's writing desk) and to Louis Weil as well (the large writing desk placed by the window which Proust never used, preferring to write in bed instead); see Fuss, 2004, 165–75, and Hayman, 1992, 242–47.
14. Sigmund Freud, "Melancholy and Mourning", in Freud, 1984, 245–68. See also Freud's essay "On Narcissism", Ibid., 59–98.
15. While early biographies like George Painter's tended to use Proust's fiction as a source for gleaning biographical information, recent interpreters of Proust like Jean-Yves Tadié have heavily criticised this approach; see Painter, 1959, and Tadié, 1996, 267.
16. Sickly from birth, and experiencing the first serious asthma attack at nine years old, Proust, Shattuck argues, later, came to see the asthma that would progressively govern his health as a means through which he could receive all the attention he could want. In his adulthood, from the seclusion of his sickbed, Proust dominated first his mother and later his various secretaries and servants with "interbedroom memoranda" and his friends with imploring requests for help. Shattuck, 2000, i–xx and Shattuck, 1974, 9–31.
17. An important exception to this is the five volume history of private life edited by Michelle Perrot: Perrot, 1990.
18. Clark, 1984, 69–70.
19. Marcus, 1999, 138–40; see also Loyer, 1988, 238–52.
20. Silverman, 1989, 1–16.
21. Ibid., 48–50.
22. Ibid., 89.
23. Ibid., 75–79.
24. Fuss, 2004, 197.
25. Proust, 1970–93, 1:50–51.
26. On the role of the visual in Proust see Murphy, 1994, and Bal, 1997.
27. Bowie, 1998, 14–16, makes the point that while Proust imitates scientific scrutiny of sense impressions the novel does not share the latter's cumulative marshalling of perception into a reductive regime that yields coherence.
28. Proust's regularly entertained friends with his parodies of those in his circle and in the precise satire of social manners present in *À la recherche du temps perdu*. See Carter, 2000, 144–50.
29. Proust, 1982, 3:74–75.
30. House, 1986, 1.
31. Sturrock, 1988, xxiii–xxv.
32. Proust, 1971, 220.
33. Proust, 1971, 224.

34. Proust, 1988, 147–9.
35. Ibid., 227-33, with both versions of this article.
36. Bowie, 1998, 1–29.
37. Ibid.
38. Ibid.
39. Benjamin, 1969, 215.
40. Fuss, 2004, 162.
41. Quoted in White, 1999, 72. On the "open structure" of the Proustian sentence see Kristeva, 1996, 279–304.
42. Leonard, 2001, 42–57.
43. In a letter to Jean de Gaigeron written in 1919, Proust writes "you read not only the printed book that I have published, but also the unknown book that I would have wished to write. And when you speak to me of cathedrals, I can't help but be moved by your intuition that permits you to divine what I have never said to anyone and am writing here for the first time; that I wished to give to each part of my book the title: Porch I, Stained-Glass Windows of the apse, etc. .... I immediately gave up these architectural titles because I found them too pretentious, but I am touched that you discovered them by a sort of divination of the intellect." Proust, 1970–93, 18:359.
44. In her excellent analysis of the influence of Ruskin's thought on Proust's novel Dianne Leonard discusses the influence of Ruskin's figural modes of reading inscribed in the architecture of the Cathedral. Leonard points to the figuralism or typology leaves its imprint on the semantics of Proust's writing as a kind of "picture-language". Leonard goes on to argue persuasively that the veiling of references to Ruskin was precisely an adaptation of Ruskin's own idea of the veiled reference, or more specifically his idea of the embedded "lost" soul of the medieval architect in the edifice of the Cathedral. A soul able to be "resurrected" or "re-incarnated" by the interpreter's analogical reading of the original ideas underlying the Cathedral's conception; see Leonard, 2001, 44–46, 52–57.

18 Epilogue
The Appeal of Writers' Houses

Harald Hendrix

"It's a pity that I'm a poet. What an architect I would have made."[1] Victor Hugo's bold statement to Viollet-le-Duc was not a provocation. It highlights the poet's inclination to an alternative area of creativity—architecture and interior decoration—and his awareness of an intimate relationship between poetry and space, an insight he was to give spectacular material shape in both his homes on the Isle of Guernsey. During his exile in the years between 1855 and 1870, following his opposition to the prince-president Napoleon Bonaparte, he in fact lived a period of particular creative force, publishing major works like *Les Contemplations* and *Les Miserables*, but also drawing, experimenting with photography and—most notoriously—building and decorating houses, both for his own family (Hauteville House) and for his mistress Juliette Drouet (Hauteville Fairy). The results of his efforts soon became objects of particular attraction to those interested in Hugo: the first illustrated guide *Chez Victor Hugo par un passant* (*A Visit to Victor Hugo at his Home*) was published as early as 1864. This interest however was not primarily directed to Hugo the versatile artist or the man, but to Hugo the writer: "I thought I knew Victor Hugo; in fact, I knew only half of him. Victor Hugo the architect, Victor Hugo the decorator can explain Victor Hugo the author."[2] And because of this interest both houses were turned into museums, Hauteville House *in situ* as it was projected and constructed by the poet himself (1927), and parts of Juliette Drouet's home as of 1903 in the Parisian Maison de Victor Hugo, the apartment on the Place des Vosges where the poet had lived from 1832 to 1848.[3]

The story of the conception and conservation of Hugo's houses presents in a nutshell what this book is about. It shows that writers' houses most often are not neutral spaces but media of expression and self-fashioning for the authors who design, construct and decorate them. In dedicating themselves to architecture and interior design, writers like the Goncourt brothers, Walter Scott, Pierre Loti and Henry Rider Haggard—to name but a few presented earlier in this volume—push beyond the limits of their trade. By experimenting with the arrangement of concrete matter they pursue a dream of materialising the immaterial, of giving tangible shape to their poetic or narrative imagination, driven by curiosity, by an aspiration to versatility, or even out of sheer frustration with those very limits of their trade. In re-mediating their authorship they can create imposing works of art (Hauteville House, Goethe's house in Weimar, Kelmscott Manor, etc.) and build houses that, like the Casa Vasari in Arezzo, Scott's Abbotsford and Mario Praz's "House of Life" in Rome, forge life and art in a construction that easily imposes itself as a monument to its author.

The book therefore also shows how easily these houses tend to become the focuses of memorial practices. They survive as museums because they are able to attract and canalise the respect and admiration the author and his works evoke. Such practices of remembrance can be documented—as we did in the case of Petrarch's houses—as of early modernity with its new interest in the biography of poets and writers. They have not ceased since. Although there certainly were ups and downs in the phenomenon of the literary pilgrimage to writers' houses—illustrated here in the discussion of houses associated with the memory of authors like Shakespeare, Goethe, the Brontë sisters and Keats—it is the continuity of the practice that strikes most. This can only partly be ascribed to its integration in tourism as such. Indeed, from the beginnings of the Grand Tour in the late sixteenth century through the "visit to the great author" propagated by eighteenth-century cult of genius, the visit to writers' houses has always been one of the standard ingredients of cultural tourism, reaching phenomenal proportions in the nineteenth century with its combination of romanticism and nationalism—Scott's Abbotsford and the Brontë Parsonage again can point this out. And once more today: within contemporary cultural tourism writers' houses have actually become one of the main assets, at least in countries like France, Italy, the UK and Germany, where as of the 1990s large numbers of literary houses and literary landscapes have been institutionalised, and an increasing flow of often radiant publications dedicated to the presentation of these sites has come along.[4] But why do literary places, more than other yet comparable sites of remembrance dedicated for example to statesmen or princes, clergymen or artists have such a particular appeal?

To help explore the deeper attraction of writers' houses we may turn to the testimony of one of nowadays' most illustrious literary pilgrims, Julian Barnes, who in 2005 related in what way he was inspired to write his acclaimed 1984 novel *Flauberts Parrot* about such memorial practices:

> In September 1981, on holiday in Normandy, I visited the three main Flaubert sites in Rouen. First, his statue in the intimate and leafy Place des Carmes .... Next, a walk down the Avenue Flaubert ... to the Flaubert Museum at the Hôtel Dieu, where the novelist's father had been head surgeon. Here, I noted antique medical instruments and family memorabilia, and then "most memorably, the bright green, perky-eyed parrot which was lent to him when he was writing *Un coeur simple*, and which irritated him at the same time as giving him an inner sense of parrothood." Finally, a day or two later, I went downstream from

the city centre to Croisset and "the high point of the pilgrimage", the small, square pavilion which was all that remained of the Master's house. My four pages of notebook description of this one-room museum and its haphazard contents end like this: "Then crouched on top of one of the display cabinets, what did we see but Another Parrot. Also bright green, also, according to the gardienne & also a label hung on its perch, the authentic parrot borrowed by GF when he wrote UCS!! I ask the gardienne if I can take it down & photograph it. She concurs, even suggests I take off the glass case. I do ...." Was this just a Curious Fact? Half an Anecdote? A small article for an academic journal? .... It could be the opening—or perhaps clinching—moment in a story about life and art, about France and England, about the pursuit of the writer by the reader, and that moment of contact—practical yet mystical—between the two of them.[5]

The captivating thing about writers' houses is not primarily their architectural quality or their grandeur as monuments that celebrate literary giants. Even more fascinating, Barnes suggests, are the less imposing buildings like Flaubert's one-room pavilion in Croisset, and simple objects that relate to the author's everyday life, whether they are authentic or just pretend to be so. Flaubert's parrot—or Petrarch's cat, being the first of this specimen, as we showed earlier in this book—are not just curious facts or anecdotes, but instances that facilitate "the pursuit of the writer by the reader." They are ingredients in a ritual, in a performance—Barnes takes a tour along three sites—that aims at establishing a "practical but mystical moment of contact between them."

The essence of writers' houses and of the literary pilgrimages that are performed there would thus be the communication between readers and writers, mediated through the house and the objects it contains. But this contact would obviously be something quite different from the visit to the great author that during the eighteenth and early nineteenth century was so popular.[6] It would not be a conversation but "speaking with the dead," and thus a rather one-way communication on matters that still need to be cleared.[7] This interpretation however becomes more persuasive when we relate it to some of the specific characteristics of both the writers' house and the memorial practices surrounding it that have come up in the explorations presented in this book.

Writers that construct houses tend to attribute meaning to space and to objects. Unsurprisingly, they perceive matter—rooms, furnishings, books—in literary terms, whether metonymically—objects are associated with intrinsically related things, like memories of the moment in which they purchased the object—or metaphorically: the space or object evokes associations and imaginations of a totally unbound nature. Some of the most famous writers' houses are eloquent illustrations of this mechanism, particularly the houses of the Goncourt brothers in Paris and the Roman

apartment of Mario Praz. Here we find an interior design completely dedicated to the evocation of associations and notably memories, to such a
degree that the architecture takes precedence over literature. In fact, the
parallel books *La maison d'un artiste (The House of an Artist)* and *La
casa della vita (The House of Life)* are not the foundation but only the
documentation and explanation of the creative work as it had developed
in the building process. But also other writers' houses clearly show the
ambition to "make sense of things". The Rossetti's integrate their family
history and cultural roots in their Cheyne Walk home, Haggard construes
his Ditchingham House on the basis of his travel recollections, as do Pierre
Loti in Rochefort and Goethe in Weimar, and William Morris wants his
homes, both Red House and Kelmscott Manor, to reflect and communicate
his professional and political ideals.

This process of charging spaces and objects with meaning is many-fac-
eted. Its starting point however generally is the appropriation of meaning:
Haggard placing Dickens's writing desk in his home, thus following in the
footsteps of Scott who in Abbotsford had integrated both an original door
from the Tolbooth prison and a chest made of wood taken from a wreck
of the Spanish Armada. Such relocation of meaningful items produces a
kind of sacralisation, and therefore naturally a change of meaning. It also
engenders a fundamental mobility of meaning and of memory. In this process objects and spaces become containers of several layers of meaning, and
thus sometimes need explanation. This accounts for Edmond de Goncourt's
and Mario Praz's urge to write books on their houses, and we also see it
in the motto's some authors like to apply to their homes, from the "Salve"
in Goethe's Weimar house to the motto-mania in D'Annunzio's Vittoriale.
Since this inclination to signification seems predominant in the nineteenth
and early twentieth century, indeed from Scott and the Rossetti's through
Morris, Haggard, the Goncourts to Loti and ultimately Praz, we can easily
relate it to romantic and symbolist aestheticism, and to the bibelot and bric-
à-brac mentality predominant in that age. In fact, Praz, who commandingly
recapitulates and epitomizes this tendency, was an eminent scholar of this
aesthetics, and his Roman apartment is arguably more a tribute to this (late)
Romantic culture of signification than to the man himself.

The urge to charge spaces and objects with meaning can easily be interpreted as a symptom of the "loss of aura" and the nostalgic drive to recu-
perate it that in the wake of Benjamin many scholars have deemed a major
characteristic of exactly the period here under consideration.[8] In the case of
the Goncourt brothers and of Praz there surely has come up much evidence
to support such a view, and our investigation into the connection between
these emblematic figures has shown that even psychological and emotional
issues are relevant here. Surely Luchino Visconti's representation in *Gruppo
di famiglia in un interno (Conversation Pieces,* 1974) of Praz and his apartment has captured the nostalgic mood and despair at the heart of it. However, the simultaneous case of Proust and his apartment on the Boulevard

Hausmann calls for some caution. This was not an environment designed to collect meaning through its objects and their arrangement. It was rather a mental, not a material room—as we have argued before—construed to shape the author's mind and imagination. The space still served as a mnemonic device and thus as an instrument of authorship, but not through a material arrangement of objects reminiscent of the *ars memoriae*, but by it's being neutral and empty of a meaning of its own. Precisely because of this emptiness, of this lack of meaning and aura, the room Proust lived in helped him to evoke what we now call involuntary memory.

Writers' houses therefore are not just "theatres of memory/meaning" but also tools to stimulate one's imagination. They have this function for the authors who design and inhabit them, and it works the same way with the people who later visit them, as literary pilgrims or as tourists. These houses are turned into monuments out of a desire to remember the authors who lived there—like other illustrious persons that became objects of remembrance cults—but also to enable visitors, through "that moment of contact—practical yet mystical—between writer and reader," to come into contact with the imaginative world created by the author, and thus to participate in his imagination. This through-the-looking-glass effect seems a specific quality of writers' houses and of literary places in general. It distinguishes them from yet comparable sites dedicated to the memory of other kinds of persons. Likewise it explains why writers' houses have attracted as of the earliest beginnings of tourist practices in the sixteenth century particular attention, much more than places associated with other illustrious persons. And as we have argued before, it might also explain their success in contemporary cultural tourism.

How in writers' houses real and imagined worlds tend to fuse becomes evident when we look at how the "visit to the great author" transforms into the literary pilgrimage to his no longer inhabited home. While in mid eighteenth-century France people were keen to make long trips in order to personally meet great authors and have conversation with them—Voltaire in his villa Les Délices in Geneva, for instance—at the end of the century they started to visit houses like Les Charmettes in Chambéry, where Rousseau had lived as a young man, between 1736 and 1742. Fifty years after his final departure, his admirer Hérault de Séchelles put up a plaque on the façade of the villa remembering this short but significant stay:

Country home inhabited by Jean Jacques
you remind me of his genius
his loneliness, his pride
and his unhappiness and insanity.
To glory and to truth
he dedicated his life,
and was always haunted
both by himself and by envy.[9]

The text pays tribute not only to Rousseau the great man, but also to his personality full of contradictions, precisely because Rousseau had depicted himself as such in his *Confessions* while giving a detailed account of his life in Les Charmettes. After the publication of the autobiography the house in Chambéry quickly became an attraction for literary pilgrims, who clearly wanted to personally get in touch with the places where Rousseau admittedly had lived his finest years. This contact however was no longer personal. It had become "practical yet mystical," since it was based not only on the material evidence of the house itself, but also, and perhaps foremost, on its imaginative representation Rousseau had given in his *Confessions*.

Exactly the same transformation occurs in Frankfurt, as we have shown earlier in this volume, where until 1775 Goethe himself used to entertain visitors that wanted to pay him their respect. After his departure, first to Weimar, then to Rome, and finally to Weimar again, his family home soon became an attraction for literary pilgrims. This memorial practice gained particular momentum when the first books of Goethe's autobiographical *Dichtung und Wahrheit* (*Poetry and Truth*) with their account of the author's Frankfurt years became available, and when in 1835 Bettina von Arnim published *Goethe's Briefwechsel mit einem Kinde* (*Goethe's Correspondence with a Child*). In the house a special remembrance installation was arranged in what Von Arnim incorrectly had indicated as the poet's bedroom and study. As we know from a contemporary source, the novel *Casa santa* (*Holy House*) dedicated in 1853 to the house by its then inhabitant Virginia Wunderlich, it comprised a few of the poet's autographs under glass, some of the furniture he had used, particularly his desk, and a life-size bust dominating a guest-book where visitors could leave their name and a comment.[10] With this simple arrangement, which anticipates the museological design still dominant in most writers' houses, both the person of the poet and his work are remembered and evoked. These two elements actually tend to fuse in the perception of the literary pilgrim, who in this case was motivated to visit the place because of his knowledge of the poet's autobiographical account of his life in these very rooms and of the works here written, notably *Die Leiden des jungen Werthers* (*The Sorrows of Young Werther*) and *Götz von Berlichingen*.

The fusion of fact and fiction makes writers' houses appealing to various kinds of visitors, as Alphonse de Lamartine perceptively observed in 1849 with respect to Rousseau's Les Charmettes: "All this has a hidden but profound appeal for poets, for philosophers and for lovers alike. We do not acknowledge it, even when we submit to it. For the poets, it's the first page of this soul which was a poem; for the philosophers, it is the cradle of a revolution; for the lovers, it's the nest of a first love."[11] This asset is best exploited in an arrangement where—as in Goethe's birthplace or Flaubert's Croisset room—a combination of *genius loci* and authenticity enhances the suggestion of a virtual communication with the author and his imagination, a "mystical" contact that may even become "practical" through the ritual of the signature or the observation and possibly touching of some curious object allegedly related to the author: Flaubert's parrot, Keats's hair or Shakespeare's mulberry tree. Such rituals are as old as the phenomenon of the literary pilgrimage as such: already in 1544 German students recorded their visit to Petrarch's house in Arquà by leaving their signature on the fireplace of what was then considered the poet's bedroom. And even earlier, in the 1530s, literary walks along the places in Avignon and the Vaucluse associated with the love between Petrarch and Laura came into being. This fact not only confirms the centrality of such performances in this particular form of memorial culture, but also underlines that the element of communicating through contact (the signature) and re-enactment (the literary trail) is at the core of this practice.[12]

Such an interpretation of the writer's house's appeal moreover enables us to better understand its specific nature and function vis-à-vis other yet related institutions. Writers' houses are monuments to authors and their creativity. They are not literary archives. Though obviously related, the two functions of remembrance and documentation should where possibly be kept separate in order to preserve the specific and valuable appeal of writers' houses. This explains why in most of the houses here considered, as well as in many others not presented, curators most often have preferred to distinguish both functions and to locate them separately. The buildings where Goethe is remembered well illustrate this museological notion. When the poet's heirs in 1885 left to the state of Saxony Weimar their grandfather's townhouse and all his extant papers, they made sure that these were administered by separate institutions, the Goethe National Museum and the Goethe Gesellschaft. In Frankfurt such a division was accomplished when in 1897 the Freie Deutsche Hochstift, owner of the poet's birthplace, decided to erect next to it a new building where the related collections of the Goethe Museum could be accommodated. And also in Rome, the most recent institution (1997), this separation of functions is respected, since the library and the documentary collections that have been assembled are placed in a different part of the carefully reconstructed apartment.

The through-the-looking-glass-effect we have detected in writers' houses equally helps to distinguish them from buildings where the memory of other famous persons is cultivated. Also in these other forms of what Zankl in 1972 coined *Personalmuseen* (museums dedicated to single persons) the elements of *genius loci* and authenticity are employed to honor the memory of the persons linked to these buildings.[13] But in the case of houses and palaces where princes and statesmen, inventors and clergymen, artists and musicians are remembered, the primary accent necessarily is on the documentation of their biography and its historical context. Or, in the case of artists, on their material legacy as well. These museums thus primarily have a documentary function. On the other hand, though, precisely because of their immaterial production, writers evoke memorial practices that are not limited to the buildings themselves where they are remembered.

Writers' houses turned into museums therefore not only have—and even not primarily—a documentary function: they also facilitate what Barnes calls the "practical yet mystical contact" with the author and the world of his imagination.

This in turn can explain why writers' houses have such a prominent position in the overall category of *Personalmuseen*.[14] As we have shown before, their success in contemporary cultural tourism makes them arguably the most popular kind of this museum type. This is at least what the imposing and still growing numbers of museums, literary landscapes, walks and travels along literary trails suggest. This success however is not new, as the essays in this book on the houses of Petrarch, Shakespeare, Goethe, Scott, the Brontë sisters and Keats amply testify. And the memorial practices surrounding these houses moreover seem to get established at significantly earlier moments than those related to places where other illustrious persons are remembered. This is what the situation in early modern Italy suggests, which in this field indeed sets the example for the rest of Europe and the Western world. While the cult surrounding Petrarch's houses developed as of the 1530s and was by the end of the century firmly integrated in general tourism, the Grand Tour also encompassed visits to other literary places, related to both classical and modern authors, from the graves of Virgil, Dante and Ariosto to the madhouse in Ferrara where Tasso had been a prisoner from 1579 to 1586.[15] Similar visits to places linked to otherwise famous people are more difficult to identify and certainly were no part of a systematic approach. Vasari's house in Arezzo is a superb example of an artist's house, but never became the focus of a remembrance cult. While Michelangelo's magnificent burial in 1575 was the first occasion ever of such a grand-scale tribute to an artist, it did not give rise to lasting memorial practices. And even though the house he had bought in Florence as a family residence without ever living there was turned into a Michelangelo memorial by his descendants in the first decades of the seventeenth century, it essentially stayed a family home and started to attract public and large-scale manifestations of veneration and remembrance only at the end of the nineteenth century.[16]

The particular appeal of writers' houses, what Bachelard calls "espace saisie par l'imagination" (space taken over by imagination), apparently has a trans-historical dimension.[17] The fusion of matter and imagination motivated the earliest documented literary pilgrims, including the king of France, to visit the places of an imagined love affair. It also marks the profile of nowadays visitors to literary tourist attractions, in whose mind according to market oriented research real and imagined worlds tend to fuse.[18]

NOTES

1. "C'est dommage que je sois poète. Quel architecte j'aurais fait." Statement made to Viollet-le-Duc, reported in Jules Claretie. *Victor Hugo*. Paris: 1882, quoted and translated in Charles, 2003, 13.
2. "Je croyais connaître Victor Hugo; je l'ignorais à demi. Victor Hugo architecte, Victor Hugo décorateur explique Victor Hugo écrivain". Claretie, 1902, 72.
3. On these museums, see Charles, 2003; Grossiord, 1993; Grossiord, 1998, esp. 164–65.
4. See the introduction to this volume, 2.
5. Barnes, 2005.
6. See O. Nora, 1997.
7. See Pieters, 2005.
8. Since MacCannell, 1976, the notion has become a productive though not uncontested interpretative frame for the analysis and explanation of modern tourism.
8. "Réduit par Jean Jacques habité / tu me rappelles son génie / sa solitude, sa fierté / et ses malheurs et sa folie. / A la gloire, à la verité / il osa consacrer sa vie, / et fut toujours persécuté / ou par lui-même, ou par l'envie." Translation HH.
10. "Da stand noch Wolfgangs mit weißer Ölfarbe bestrichener Pult, da waren noch die altertümlichen Stühle, Handzeichnungen und mehrere unter Glas und Rahmen gebrachte Autographen des Dichters. Eine mehr als lebensgroße Büste des Dichters, das Haupt mit einem natürlichen Lorbeerkranz umwunden, stand auf dem Tisch. Vor dieser Büste lag aufgeschlagen das in roten Saffian gebundene Buch, in das die Besucher des Goethezimmers ihre Namen aufzuzeichnen pflegen ...." Wunderlich, Virginia [A. Lacy]. *Santa casa*. Frankfurt, 1853, cited in Maisak and Dewitz, 1999, 114.
11. "Tout cela a pour les poètes, pour les philosophes, et pour les amants un attrait caché mais profond. On ne s'en rend pas raison, même en y cédant. Pour les poètes, c'est la première page de cet âme qui fut un poème, pour les philosophes, c'est le berceau d'une révolution, pour les amants, c'est le nid d'un premier amour." Cited on the website of the Musée des Charmettes (http://www.litterature-lieux.com/EsMaker/index.asp?Clef=24); translation HH.
12. On contemporary versions of such re-enactment rituals and their significance in cultural tourism, see Fine and Speer, 1985, and Torchin, 2002.
13. On the significance and relative weight of *genius loci* and authenticity in writers' houses, see also Hendrix, 2007.
14. Zankl attributes this fact to the high and special status writers enjoyed in Antiquity, where princes particularly cherished poets since they were the ones to guarantee them immortality; Zankl, 1972, 7.
15. On his journey through Italy between 1593 and 1595, Fynes Moryson visited the graves of Aretino, Ariosto, Boccaccio, Dante, Michelangelo and Virgil, as well as the houses and graves of Petrarch and Sannazzaro; cfr. Moryson, 1617, 82, 91–92, 95, 113, 151–52, 164, 174–75.
16. Ragionieri, 2001, 7–15.
17. Bachelard, 1957, 17.
18. Herbert, 2001, 327.

Bibliography

Abbotsford: 12 Photos for your Album. Dundee: Valentine, [1900].

Addy, Shirley M. *Rider Haggard and Egypt.* Accrington: A.L. Publications, 1998.

Adler, Judith. "Origins of Sightseeing." *Annals of Tourism Research. A Social Sciences Journal* 16 (1989): 7–29.

Agamben, Giorgio. *Stanze. La parola e il fantasma nella cultura occidentale.* Turin: Einaudi, 1977.

Albaret, Céleste. *Monsieur Proust.* Ed. George Belmont. New York: McGraw-Hill, 1973.

Alberti, Leandro. *Descrittione di tutta l'Italia.* Venice: Domenico de' Farri, 1557.

Albrecht, Juerg. "Die Häuser von Giorgio Vasari in Arezzo und Florenz." In Hüttinger, 1985, 83–100.

Alewyn, Richard. "Goethe als Alibi?" *Hamburger Akademische Rundschau* 3.8–10 (1948/49): 685–87.

Alexander, Christine, ed. *An Edition of the Early Writings of Charlotte Brontë.* 3 vols. Oxford: Basil Blackwell, 1987–2006.

———. "Charlotte Brontë at Roe Head." In Ch. Brontë, 2001, 394–425.

———. "Elizabeth Gaskell and Victorian Juvenilia." *The Gaskell Society Journal* 18 (2004): 1–15.

Alexander, Christine, and Jane Sellars. *The Art of the Brontës.* Cambridge: Cambridge UP, 1995.

Alexander, Christine, and Margaret Smith. *The Oxford Companion to the Brontës.* Oxford: Oxford UP, 2003.

Allegri, Francesca. *Le case della memoria. Guida alle case di personaggi illustri nella provincia di Firenze.* Florence: Agenzia per il Turismo, [1999].

Allen, Brian. *Francis Hayman.* New Haven and London: Yale UP, 1987.

Allott, Miriam. *The Brontës: The Critical Heritage.* London and Boston: Routledge and Kegan Paul, 1974.

Amerongen, Martin van, and William Rothuizen, eds. *Meneer, dit is heilige grond ... Literaire pelgrimages.* Amsterdam: Van Gennep, 1984.

Ankersmit, Frank. *Sublime Historical Experience.* Stanford: Stanford UP, 2005.

Anon. *The Land of Scott: A Series of Landscape Illustrations, Illustrative of Real Scenes, Described in the Novels and Tales, of the Author of Waverley, from Drawings by the most Distinguished Artists.* London: David Bogue, 1848.

Aretino, Pietro. *Lettere.* Ed. Francesco Flora. Milan: Mondadori, 1960.

———. *Selected Letters.* Trans. George Bull. Harmondsworth: Penguin, 1976.

Arthaud, Claude. *Les maisons du génie.* Grenoble: Arthaud, 1967.

Arts & Crafts Houses I. Philip Webb. Edward Hollamby. William Richard Lethaby. Trevor Garnham. Sir Edwin Lutyens. Brian Edwards. London: Phaidon, 1999.

Asfour, Amal. *Champfleury Meaning in the Popular Arts in 19ᵗʰ century France.* Oxford: Peter Lang, 2001.

Assmann, Aleida. *Erinnerungsräume: Formen und Wandlungen des kulturellen Gedächtnisses.* München: Beck, 1999.

Assmann, Jan. *Das kulturelle Gedächtnis. Schrift, Erinnerung und politische Identität in frühen Hochkulturen.* München: Beck, 1992.

Attanasio, Sergio. *Curzio Malaparte. Casa come me. Punta del Massullo, tel. 160, Capri.* Napoli: Arte Tipografica, 1990.

Bachelard, Gaston. *La poétique de l'espace.* Paris: Presses Universitaires de France, 1957.

——. *The Poetics of Space.* Trans. Maria Jolas. Boston: Beacon Press, 1994.

Bal, Mieke. *The Mottled Screen: Reading Proust Visually.* Trans. Anna-Louise Milne. Stanford: Stanford UP, 1997.

Balzac, Honoré de. *Le cousin Pons.* Paris: Gallimard, 1973.

Bann, Stephen. *The Clothing of Clio: A Study of the Representation of History in Nineteenth-Century Britain and France.* Cambridge, Cambridge UP, 1984.

——. *Romanticism and the Rise of History.* New York: Twayne, 1995.

——. "Old Furniture: the Mobilisation of *milieu* in Romantic Art and Literature." In *Le credibili finzioni della storia.* Ed. Daniela Gallingani. Florence: Centro Editoriale Toscano, 1996, 41–52.

——. "History and the Image: From the Lyons School to Paul Delaroche." In *The Built Surface.* Ed. Christy Anderson. Aldershot: Ashgate, 2001, 2:278–94.

——. "Face to Face with History." *New Literary History* 29.2 (1998): 235–46.

Barbier, Auguste. *Souvenirs personnels et Silhouettes contemporaines.* Paris: Dentu, 1883.

Barilaro, Caterina. *I parchi letterari in Sicilia. Un progetto culturale per la valorizzazione del territorio.* Soveria Mannelli: Rubbettino, 2004.

Barker, Juliet. *The Brontës.* London: Weidenfeld and Nicolson, 1994.

Barnes, Julian. "When Flaubert Took Wing." *The Guardian* (5 March 2005).

Barolsky, Paul. *Why Mona Lisa Smiles and Other Tales Told by Vasari.* Pennsylvania: Pennsylvania State UP, 1991.

Barth, Ilse-Marie. *Literarisches Weimar. Kultur / Literatur / Sozialstruktur im 16.–20. Jahrhundert.* Stuttgart: Metzler, 1971.

Barthel, Wolfgang. *Literaturmuseum. Facetten, Visionen.* Frankfurt an der Oder: Kleist Gedenk- und Forschungsstätte, 1996.

Baudelaire, Charles. *Petits poèmes en prose (Le Spleen de Paris).* Paris: Garnier, 1958.

Bellinati, Claudio. "La casa canonicale di Francesco Petrarca a Padova. Ubicazione e vicende." *Contributi alla storia della Chiesa padovana nell'età medioevale* 1 (1979): 83–224.

Bellinati, Claudio, and Loris Fontana. *Arquà e la casa di Francesco Petrarca.* Padova: Gregoriana, 1988.

Benedetti, Carla. *L'ombra lunga dell'autore. Indagine su una figura cancellata.* Milan: Feltrinelli, 1999.

——. *The Empty Cage. Inquiry into the Mysterious Disappearance of the Author.* Trans. William J. Hartley. Ithaca: Cornell UP, 2005.

Benedict, Clare. *Five Generations (1785–1923), Being Scattered Chapters from the History of the Cooper, Pomeroy, Woolson and Benedict Families: With Extracts from their Letters and Journals, as well as Articles and Poems by Constance Fenimore Woolson.* 3 vols. London: Ellis, [1930].

Bénichou, Paul. *Le sacre de l'écrivain.* Paris: José Corti, 1973.

Benjamin, Walter. "Eduard Fuchs, der Sammler und der Historiker." In *Das Kunstwerk im Zeitalter seiner Technischen Reproduzierbarkeit.* Frankfurt am Main: Suhrkamp, 1966.

————. *Illuminations.* Ed. Hannah Ahrendt, trans. Harry Zohn. New York: Schocken, 1969.

Berry, Nicole. "Portraits de demeures. Un essai psychanalytique." *Revue de littérature comparée 57–53* (1983): 295–302.

Berti, Luciano. *La Casa del Vasari in Arezzo e il suo museo.* Florence: Giuntina, 1955.

Beutler, Ernst. *Das Goethehaus in Frankfurt am Main.* Sixth Ed.. Frankfurt am Main: Freies Deutsches Hochstift/Frankfurter Goethemuseum, 1962.

Bialostocki, Jan. "The Doctus Artifex and the Library of the Artist in the XVIth and XVIIth Centuries." In *The Message of Images. Studies in the History of Art.* Vienna: IRSA, 1988, 150–65.

Biedrzynski, Effi. *Goethes Weimar. Das Lexikon der Personen und Schauplätze.* 2nd ed. Zürich: Artemis and Winkler, 1993.

Billington, Michael. "Crown and Country." *The Guardian Review* (30 April 2005), 19.

Blanc, Charles. *Grammaire des arts décoratifs. Décoration intérieure de la maison.* Paris: Renouard, 1882.

Blason, Mirella et al., eds. *Franciscus. Francesco Petrarca ad Arquà.* Padova: Studio Editoriale Programma, 1995.

Bloch-Dano, Evelyne. *Mes maisons d'écrivains.* Paris: Tallandier, 2005.

Boase, Thomas S.R. *Giorgio Vasari, The Man and the Book.* Princeton: Princeton UP, 1979.

Bollenbeck, Georg. "Normative Höhe und tiefer Fall. Weimar: der deutsche Symbolort." In *Weimar: Archäologie eines Ortes.* Ed. Georg Bollenbeck et al. Weimar: Böhlaus Nachfolger, 2001, 206–15.

————. "Weimar." In François and Schulze, 2001, 1:207–24.

Bongaerts, Ursula. *La Casa di Goethe a Roma.* Rome: Casa di Goethe, 2004.

Bonnet, Jean-Claude. *Naissance du Panthéon. Essai sur le culte des grands hommes.* Paris: Fayard, 1998.

Borchmeyer, Dieter. *Weimarer Klassik. Portrait einer Epoche.* Weinhein: Beltz Athenäum, 1994.

————. "Goethe." In François and Schulze, 2001, 1:187–206.

Bottiglieri, Nicola. *Le case di Neruda.* Milan: Mursia, 2004.

Bourget, Paul. *Nouveaux essais de psychologie contemporaine.* Paris: Lemerre, 1883.

Bowie, Malcolm. *Proust Among the Stars.* London: Harper and Collins, 1998.

Braun, Peter. *Dichterhäuser.* Munich: Deutscher Taschenbuch Verlag, 2002.

Braun, Peter. *Dichterleben–Dichterhäuser.* Munich: Deutscher Taschenbuch Verlag, 2005.

Brendon, Piers. *Thomas Cook: 150 Years of Popular Tourism.* London: Secker and Warburg, 1991.

Brontë, Charlotte. *Jane Eyre.* Ed. Richard Dunn. 3rd ed. New York and London: W.W. Norton & Company, 2001.

Brontë, Emily Jane. *Gondal's Queen: A Novel in Verse.* Ed. Fannie Ratchford. Edinburgh: Austin, 1955.

Brooke, Stopford Augustus. *Dove Cottage. Wordsworth's Home from 1800–1808.* London: Macmillan, 1890.

Brown, Iain G., ed. *Abbotsford and Sir Walter Scott: The Image and the Influence.* Edinburgh: The Society of Antiquaries of Scotland, 2003.

Brown, Ivor, and George Fearon. *Amazing Monument. A Short History of the Shakespeare Industry.* London: Heinemann, 1939.

Brown, Mary Ellen. *Burns and Tradition.* London: Macmillan, 1984.

Brown, Sally. "Suppose Me in Rome." In Payling, 2005b, 15–31.

Bruni, Roberto. "Parodia e plagio nel 'Petrarchista' di Nicolò Franco." *Studi e problemi di critica testuale* 20 (1980): 61–83.

Bryant, William Cullen. *Address on the Unveiling of the Statue of Sir Walter Scott in Central Park, November 4, 1872.* New York: G.P. Putnam's Sons, 1873.

Busch, Angelika, and Hans-Peter Beermeister, eds. *Literaturarchive und Literaturmuseen der Zukunft. Bestandsaufnahme und Perspektiven.* Rehburg-Loccum: Evangelische Akademie Loccum, 1999.

Buzard, James. *The Beaten Track: European Tourism, Literature, and the Ways to Culture, 1800–1918.* Oxford: Clarendon Press, 1993.

Cabanès, Jean-Louis, ed. *Les frères Goncourt. Art et écriture.* Talence: Presses Universitaires de Bordeaux, 1997.

Cabanis, José, and Georges Herscher. *Jardins d'écrivains.* Arles: Actes Sud, 1998.

Cacciatore, Vera. "The House in War-Time." In Payling 2005: 68–71.

Callegari, Adolfo. *Arquà e il Petrarca.* Padova: Ente Provinciale per il Turismo, 1941.

Callen, Anthea. *Angel in the Studio: Women in the Arts and Crafts Movement, 1870–1914.* London: Astragal Books, 1979.

Camus, Dominique. *Le guide des maisons d'artistes et d'écrivains en région parisienne.* Photographs Thibaut de Wurstemberger. Paris: La Manufacture, 1995.

Carletta [= Antonio Valeri]. *Goethe a Roma.* Roma: Società Editrice Dante Alighieri, 1899.

Carter, William. *Marcel Proust.* New Haven and London: Yale UP, 2000.

"Case d'artista. Compenetrare arte e vita: un ideale diffuso tra fine '800 e inizio '900." *Ricerche di storia dell'arte* 36 (1988): 4–67.

Cattaneo, Arturo. *Il trionfo della memoria. La Casa della Vita di Mario Praz.* Milan: Vita e Pensiero Università, 2003.

Cazenave, Michel. *Alexandre Dumas, le château des folies.* Paris: Christian Pirot, 2002.

Cecchi, Alessandro. "Le case del Vasari ad Arezzo e Firenze." In Ciardi, 1998, 29–78.

Cesaretti, Enrico. *Castelli di carta. Retorica della dimora tra Scapigliatura e Surrealismo.* Ravenna: Longo, 2003.

Chambouleyron Lanzmann, Florence. *Maisons d'écrivains au cœur de France.* Photographs Jean Bourgeois. Tours: Éditions Nouvelle République, 1998.

Chandler, Marilyn R. *Dwelling in the Text: Houses in American Fiction.* Berkeley: U of California P, 1991.

Chapple, J. A. V., and Arthur Pollard, eds. *The Letters of Mrs Gaskell.* Manchester: Manchester UP, 1966.

Charles, Corinne. *Victor Hugo. Visions d'intérieurs: du meuble au décor. Victor Hugo, Interior Visions: From Furniture to Decoration.* Paris: Paris Musées, 2003.

Cheney, Liana. *The Paintings of the Casa Vasari.* New York and London: Garland, 1985.

Ciàmpoli, Domenico. *La famiglia Rossetti.* Rome: Tipografia Artero, 1911.

Ciardi, Roberto Paolo, ed., *Case di artisti in Toscana.* Florence: Banca Toscana, 1998.

Claretie, Jules. *Victor Hugo. Souvenirs intimes.* Paris: Maretheux, 1902.

Clark, Timothy J. *The Painting of Modern Life in Manet and His Followers.* New York: Alfred A. Knopf, 1984.

Claussen, Horst. "'Gegen Rondanini über ...' Goethes römische Wohnung." *Goethe-Jahrbuch* 107 (1990): 94–98.

Clifford, David and Laurence Roussillon, eds. *Outsiders Looking in: The Rossettis Then and Now.* London: Anthem Press, 2004.

Clifford, James. *Routes: Travel and Translation in the Late Twentieth Century.* Cambridge, Mass.: Harvard UP, 1997.

Cochrane, J.G. *Catalogue of the Library at Abbotsford.* Edinburgh: Constable, 1838.

Cocteau, Jean. *Opium.* London: Peter Owen, 1990.

Coletto, Gilberto. *Case di scrittori. Guida alle case museo, centri studio, associazioni amici di scrittori d'Italia.* Cremona: Spino d'Adda, 2002.

Colton, Judith. *Monuments to Men of Genius. A Study of Eighteenth-Century English and French Sculptural Works.* Ann Arbor and London, 1976 (PhD New York, 1974).

Compagnon, Antoine. *Le Démon de la théorie. Littérature et sens comun.* Paris: Seuil, 1998.

Coombes, Annie E. "The Recalcitrant Object: Hybridity and the Question of Culture-Contact." In *Colonial Discourse, Post-Colonial Theory.* Ed. F. Barker et al. Manchester: Manchester UP, 1994, 89–114.

———. *Reinventing Africa. Museums, Material Culture and Popular Imagination.* New Haven and London: Yale UP, 1994.

Corti, L. et al., eds. *Giorgio Vasari. Principi, letterati e artisti nelle carte di Giorgio Vasari.* Arezzo: Casa Vasari, 1981.

Couturier, Maurice. *La figure de l'auteur.* Paris: Seuil, 1995.

Crimp, Douglas. *On the Museum's Ruins.* 2nd ed. Cambridge, Mass. and London: MIT Press, 2000.

Crockett, W.S. *Abbotsford, painted by William Smith, Jr., described by W.S. Crockett.* London: Adam and Charles Black, 1905.

Curtis, Vanessa. *The Hidden Houses of Virginia Woolf and Vanessa Bell.* London: Robert Hale, 2005.

Daly, Nicholas. "That Obscure Object of Desire. Victorian Commodity Culture and Fictions of the Mummy." *Novel* 28–1 (1994): 24–51, 57.

Deledda, Grazia. *La casa del poeta.* Milan: Treves, 1930.

Dini-Traversari, Alessandro. *Ambrogio Traversari e i suoi tempi.* Florence: Seeber, 1912.

Dondi dall'Orologio, Giovanni. *Rime.* Ed. A. Daniele. Vicenza: Neri Pozza, 1990.

Duperray, Eve. *L'or des mots. Une lecture de Pétrarque et du mythe littéraire de Vaucluse des origines à l'orée du XXe siècle. Histoire du pétrarquisme en France.* Paris: Publications de la Sorbonne, 1997.

Durie, Alastair. "Tourism in Victorian Scotland: The Case of Abbotsford." *Scottish Economic and Social History* 12 (1992): 42–54.

Eagle, D., and H. Carnell. *The Oxford Literary Guide to the British Isles.* Oxford: Clarendon Press, 1977.

Eckermann, Johann Peter. *Gespräche mit Goethe in den letzten Jahren seines Lebens.* Ed. Heinrich Hubert Houben. 22nd ed. Leipzig: F.A. Brockhaus, 1939.

———. *Gespräche mit Goethe in den letzten Jahren seines Lebens.* 3rd ed. Berlin: Aufbau-Verlag, 1987.

Edvarsen, Erik Henning. *Ibsen museet. The Ibsen museum.* Oslo: Ibsen Museet, 1998.

Ehrlich, Eugene, and Gordon Carruth. *The Oxford Illustrated Literary Guide to the United States.* New York and Oxford: Oxford UP, 1982.

Emison, Patricia E. *Creating the 'Divine' Artist. From Dante to Michelangelo.* Leiden and Boston: Brill, 2004.

Erll, Astrid. *Kollektives Gedächtnis und Erinnerungskulturen. Eine Einführung.* Stuttgart: Metzler, 2005.

Eudel, Paul. *Champfleury, sa vie, son oeuvre et ses collections.* Paris: Sapin, 1891.

Eyre-Todd, George. *To the Homes and Haunts of Scott and Burns by the Caledonian Railway.* 2nd ed. Glasgow: McGorquodale, [1911].

Fawcett, Clara, and Patricia Cormack. "Guarding Authenticity at Literary Tourism Sites." *Annals of Tourism Research. A Social Sciences Journal* 28–3 (2001): 686–704.

Fens, Kees, ed. *Stel dat ik ditmaal hier wil blijven wonen. Schrijvers en hun huizen.* Amsterdam: Meulenhoff, 1998.

Filarete, Antonio Averlino. *Trattato d'architettura.* Trans. J. R. Spencer. New Haven and London: Yale UP, 1965.

Fine, Elizabeth C., and Jean Haskell Speer. "Tour Guide Performances as Sight Sacralization." *Annals of Tourism Research* 12 (1985): 73–95.

Fiorani, Tito. *Le case raccontano. Storie e passioni nelle dimore del mito a Capri.* Capri: La Conchiglia, 1996.

———. *Le dimore del mito. Residenze letterarie a Capri nell'Ottocento e primo Novecento.* Capri: La Conchiglia, 2002.

Floriani, Gianni. *Francesco Petrarca. Memorie e cronache padovane.* Padova: Antenore, 1993.

Fortunati, Vita. "Utopia e biografia: le ragioni di un confronto." In *Vite di utopia.* Eds. Vita Fortunati and Paola Spinozzi. Ravenna: Longo, 2000, 9–18.

Fox, Levi. *The Shakespeare Anniversary Book.* Norwich: Jarrold and Sons, 1964.

Franco, Nicolò. *Il Petrarchista.* Venice: Giovan Giolito de' Ferrari, 1539.

François, Étienne, and Hagen Schulze, eds. *Deutsche Erinnerungsorte.* 3 vols. Munich: C.H. Beck, 2001.

Frank, Ellen Eve. *Literary Architecture: Essays Toward a Tradition. Walter Pater, Gerard Manley Hopkins, Marcel Proust, Henry James.* Berkeley: U of California P, 1979.

Freud, Sigmund. *On Metapsychology: The Theory of Psychanalysis.* Ed. Angela Richards. London: Pelican, 1984.

Frey, Carl, and Hermann Walter Frey, eds. *Giorgio Vasari, der literarische Nachlass.* Munich: Müller, 1920.

Fripp, Edgar I. *Shakespeare's Stratford.* Oxford: Oxford UP, 1928.

———. *Shakespeare's Haunts near Stratford.* Oxford: Oxford UP, 1928.

Fritzsche, Peter. *Stranded in the Present: Modern Time and the Melancholy of History.* Cambridge, Mass.: Harvard UP, 2004.

Fuss, Diana. *The Sense of an Interior: Four Writers and the Rooms that Shaped Them.* New York: Routledge, 2004.

Gallé, Émile. "Notice sur la production de verres et cristaux de luxe." (1908). In *Écrits pour l'Art Floriculture — Art Décoratif — Notice d'Exposition (1884–1889).* Marseille: Lafitte Reprints, 1999, 350–51.

Gaskell, Elizabeth. *The Life of Charlotte Brontë.* London: Smith, Elder and Co, 1857.

Gefen, Gérard. *Maisons de musiciens.* Photographs Christine Bastin, Jacques Evrard. Paris: Éditions du Chêne, 1997.

Genette, Gérard. "La littérature et l'espace." In *Figures II.* Paris: Éditions du Seuil, 1969, 43–49.

Geser, Hans. "'Yours Virtually Forever': Death Memorials and Remembrance Sites in the WWW." *Sociology in Switzerland* (January 1998). Online journal.

Giartosio De Courten, Maria Luisa. *I Rossetti. Storia di una famiglia.* Milan: Alpes, 1931.

Gill, Richard. *Happy Rural Seat: The English Country House and the Literary Imagination.* New Haven and London: Yale UP, 1972.

Giovannini, Ercole. *Il petrarchista*. In *Li due Petrarchisti*. Ed. Barezzo Barezzi. Venice: Barezzi, 1623.

Girouard, Mark. "Red House, Bexleyheath, Kent." *Country Life* (16 June 1960): 1382–85.

———. *The Victorian Country House*. Oxford: Clarendon Press, 1971.

Glendening, John. *The High Road: Romantic Tourism, Scotland, and Literature, 1720–1820*. London: Macmillan, 1997.

Gnoli, Domenico. "Das Goethe-Haus in Rom." *Im Neuen Reich* 2 (1872): 143–48.

Goebel, Gerhard. *Poeta faber. Erdichtete Architektur in der italienischen, spanischen und französischen Literatur der Renaissance und des Barock*. Heidelberg: Winter, 1971.

Goethe, Johann Wolfgang von. *Goethes Werke*. Weimar: Hermann Böhlau, 1891.

———. *Italian Journey [1786–1788]*. Trans. W. H. Auden and Elizabeth Mayer. London: Penguin, 1970.

———. *Goethe's Collected Works*. Vol.Four. *From My Life. Poetry and Truth. Parts One to Three*. Trans. Robert R. Heitner, eds. Thomas P. Saine and Jeffrey L. Sammons. New York: Suhrkamp, 1987.

———. *The Flight to Italy. Diary and Selected Letters*. Trans. T.J. Reed. Oxford, Oxford UP, 1999.

Golz, Jochen. "Das Goethe- und Schiller-Archiv in Geschichte und Gegenwart." In *Das Goethe- und Schiller-Archiv 1896–1996. Beiträge aus dem ältesten deutschen Literaturarchiv*. Ed. Jochen Golz. Weimar, Cologne and Vienna: Böhlau, 1996, 13–70.

Goncourt, Edmond de. *La Maison d'un artiste*. Paris: Charpentier, 1881.

———. *La Maison d'un artiste*. Dijon: L'Échelle de Jacob, 2003.

Goncourt, Edmond de, and Jules de Goncourt. *L'Art du XVIII siècle*. 3 vols. Paris: Bibliothèque Charpentier, 1914–18.

Graham-Campbell, Angus. "Where Byron Stayed in Rome: the 'Torlonia Letter' Rediscovered." *Keats Shelley Review* 18 (2004): 102–03.

Gray, Ezio Maria, and Gabriele de Rosa. *Auf die Spuren Goethes in Italien*. Milan: Treves, [1942].

Greenblatt, Stephen. "The Touch of the Real." In *Practicing New Historicism*. Ed. Catherine Gallagher and Stephen Greenblatt. Chicago: Chicago UP, 2000, 20–48.

Greimas, Algirdas J. "For a Topological Semiotics." In *The City and the Sign. An Introduction to Urban Semiotics*. Ed. Mark Gottdiener and Alexandros P. Lagopoulos. New York: Columbia UP, 1986, 25–54.

Grossiord, Sophie. *Maison de Victor Hugo. General Guide*. Paris: Paris Musées, 1993.

———. *Victor Hugo. 'Et s'il n'en reste qu'un ...'*. Paris: Gallimard, 1998.

Guillery, Peter, and Michael Snodin. "Strawberry Hill: Building and Site." *Architectural History* 38 (1995): 102–28.

Haggard, Henry Rider. *The Days of My Life. An Autobiography*. 2 vols. London: Longmans, Green and Co., 1926.

Halbwachs, Maurice. *La mémoire collective*. Paris: Presses Universitaires de France, 1950.

———. *On Collective Memory*. Trans. Lewis A. Coser. Chicago: U of Chicago P, 1992.

Hall Caine, T. *Recollections of Dante Gabriel Rossetti*. Boston: Roberts Brothers, 1883.

Hardwick, Michael. *Writers' Houses: A Literary Journey in England*. London: Phoenix House, 1968.

———. *A Literary Atlas & Gazeteer of the British Isles.* Newton: Abbot, David and Charles, 1973.

Hayman, Ronald. *Proust: A Biography.* New York: Carroll and Graf, 1992.

Heidegger, Martin. "Building, Dwelling, Thinking." In *Poetry, Language, Thought.* Trans. Albert Hofstädter. New York: Harper and Row, 1971.

Hendrix, Harald. "De kat van Petrarca en de oorsprong van het literair tourisme." *Incontri. Rivista europea di studi italiani* 20 (2005): 85–98.

———. "Philologie, materielle Kultur und Authentizität. Das Dichterhaus zwischen Dokumentation und Imagination." In *Die Herkulesarbeiten der Philologie.* Eds. Sophie Bertho, Bodo Plachta. Würzburg: Königshausen and Neumann, 2007 (forthcoming).

Herbert, David. "Literary Places, Tourism and the Heritage Experience." *Annals of Tourism Research. A Social Sciences Journal* 28–2 (2001): 312–33.

Hewison, Robert. *The Heritage Industry: Britain in a Climate of Decline.* London: Methuen, 1987.

———. *Culture and Consensus. England, Art and Politics since 1960.* London: Methuen, 1997.

Hoberman, Ruth. "In Quest of a Museal Aura: Turn-of-the-century Narratives about Museum-displayed Objects." *Victorian Literature and Culture* 31–2 (2003): 467–82.

Hönnighausen, Lothar. *Präraphaeliten und Fin-de-siècle. Symbolistische Tendenzen in der englischen Spätromantik.* Munich: Fink, 1971.

———. *The Symbolist Tradition in English Literature: A Study of Pre-Raphaelitism and Fin de Siècle.* Trans. Gisela Hönnighausen. Cambridge: Cambridge UP, 1988.

Hoh-Slodczyk, Christine. *Das Künstlerhaus im 19. Jahrhundert. Studien zu den Wohn-/Atelierstätten bildender Künstler.* Munich, 1977. [unpublished PhD thesis]

———. *Das Haus des Künstlers im 19. Jahrhundert.* Munich: Prestel, 1985.

Holderness, Graham. "Bardolatry: Or, The Cultural Materialist's Guide to Stratford-upon-Avon." In *The Shakespeare Myth.* Ed. Graham Holderness. Manchester: Manchester UP, 1988, 2–15.

Horne, Donald. *The Great Museum. The Re-Presentation of History.* London and Sydney: Pluto Books, 1984.

House, John. *Claude Monet: Nature into Art.* New Haven and London: Yale UP, 1986.

How, Harry. "Illustrated Interviews, n. VII: Mr Henry Rider Haggard." *The Strand Magazine* 3 (January 1892): 3–6.

Hüttinger, Eduard, ed. *Künstlerhäuser von der Renaissance bis zur Gegenwart.* Zürich: Waser, 1985.

———. *Case d'artista. Dal Rinascimento a oggi.* Intr. Salvatore Settis. Turin: Bollati Boringhieri, 1992.

Iddon, John. *Horace Walpole's Strawberry Hill, a History & Guide.* London: St. Mary's College, 1996.

Ignasiak, Detlef, ed. *Dichter-Häuser in Thüringen.* Jena: Quartus Verlag, 1996.

Igoe, Vivien. *A Literary Guide to Dublin: Writers in Dublin, Literary Associations and Anecdotes.* London: Methuen, 1994.

Innocenti, L., ed. *Scene, itinerari, dimore. Lo spazio nella narrativa del '700.* Rome: Bulzoni, 1995.

Irace, Erminia. *Itale glorie. La costruzione di un pantheon nazionale.* Bologna: Il Mulino, 2003.

Irving, Washington. *The Adventures of Geoffrey Crayon* (1819–20) http://www.on-lineliterature.com/irving/geoffrey_crayon/26/.

——. [The Author of 'The Sketch-Book'; = Washington Irving]. *Abbotsford and Newstead Abbey*. London: John Murray, 1835.

Isnenghi, Mario, ed. *I luoghi della memoria*. 3 vols. Rome and Bari: Laterza, 1996-97.

Jacobs, F. H. "Vasari's Vision of the History of Painting: Frescoes in the Casa Vasari, Florence." *Art Bulletin* 66 (1984): 399–416.

James, Henry. "The Birthplace." (1902) In *The Novels and Tales of Henry James*. New York: Scribner's, 1907–1917, 17:199–200.

——. *Italian Hours*. Boston: Houghton Mifflin, 1909.

——. *Literary Criticism*. New York: The Library of America, 1984.

Jandolo, Augusto. *Goethe in Rom: Vier Episoden aus dem Leben des Grossen*. Trans. Ludwig Pollack. Rome: W. Modes, 1914.

Johnson, Edgar. *Sir Walter Scott: The Great Unknown*. 2 vols. London: Macmillan, 1970.

Johnson, Robert Underwood. *Remembered Yesterdays*. London: George Allen and Unwin, 1924.

Jor, Finn, and Anne Turner. *Nordic Artists' Homes*. Photographs Jiri Havran. Oslo: Cappelen, 1999.

Kaufelt, Lynn. *Key West Writers and Their Houses*. Sarasota, Fl: Pineapple Press, 1986.

Kellet, Jocelyn. *Haworth Parsonage*. Haworth: The Brontë Society, 1977.

Kelsall, Malcolm Miles. *The Great Good Place: The Country House and English Literature*. New York: Columbia UP, 1993.

Kirk, Sheila. "William Morris, Philip Webb and Architecture." In *William Morris and Architecture*. Ed. Alan Crawford and Colin Cunningham. London: Society of Architectural Historians of Great Britain, 1997.

Kirshenblatt Gimblett, Barbara. *Destination Culture: Tourism, Museums, and Heritage*. Berkeley: U of California P, 1998.

Klein, Erdmute. *Schrijvers en hun huizen*. Photographs Annelies Rigter. Amsterdam: Byblos, 2005.

Klinger, Linda Susan. *The Portrait Collection of Paolo Giovio*. 2 vols. Ann Arbor: University Microfilms International, 1991 (PhD thesis, Princeton University, 1991).

Koyama-Richard, Brigitte. *Japon Rêvé: Edmond de Goncourt et Hayashi Tadamasa*. Paris: Hermann, 2001.

Kristeva, Julia. *Time and Sense: Proust and the Experience of Literature*. Trans. Ross Guberman. New York: Columbia UP, 1996.

Lämmert, Eberhard. "Der Dichterfürst." In *Dichtung, Sprache, Gesellschaft. Akten des IV. internationalen Germanisten-Kongresses Princeton 1970*. eds. Victor Lange and Hans-Gert Roloff. Frankfurt am Main: Lang, 1971, 439–55.

Lees-Milne, James, ed. *Writers at Home*. London: Trefoil Books, 1985.

Lefebvre, Henri. *The Production of Space*. Cambridge, Mass: Blackwell, 1991.

Le Goff, Jacques. "Documento/Monumento." In *Enciclopedia Einaudi*. Turin: Einaudi, 1978, 5:38–48.

Lemaire, Gérard-Georges. *Maisons d'artistes*. Photographs Jean Claude Amiel. Paris: Éditions du Chêne, 2004.

Lemon, Charles. *A Centenary History of the Brontë Society*. Haworth: Brontë Society, 1993.

——. ed. *Early Visitors to Haworth*. Haworth: Brontë Society, 1996.

Leonard, Diane R. "Ruskin and the Cathedral of Lost Souls." In *The Cambridge Companion to Proust*. Ed. Richard Bales. Cambridge: Cambridge UP, 2001, 42–57.

Leoncini, L., and F. Simonetti, eds. *Abitare la storia. Le dimore storiche-museo. Restauro, sicurezza, didattica, comunicazione.* Turin: Allemandi, 1998.

Leopold, Nikia Spelakios Clark. *Artists' Homes in Sixteenth-Century Italy.* 2 vols. Ann Arbor: University Microfilms International, 1981. (PhD thesis, Johns Hopkins University, Baltimore, 1980).

Levinas, Emanuel. "La demeure." In *Totalité et infini.* The Hague: Martinus Nijhoff, 1961, 125–49.

Levine, Miriam. *A Guide to Writers' Homes in New England.* Cambridge, Mass: Applewood Books, 1984.

Liebenwein, Wolfgang. *Studiolo. Die Entstehung eines Raumtyps und seine Entwicklung bis um 1600.* Berlin: Mann, 1977.

Lillie, Amanda. "Memory of Place. Luogo and Lineage in the Fifteenth-Century Italian Countryside." In *Art, Memory and Family in Renaissance Florence.* Ed. Giovanni Ciapelli and Patricia Lee Rubin. Cambridge and New York: Cambridge UP, 2000, 195–214.

Listri, Massimo. *Le dimore del genio.* Milan: Fabbri, 1996.

Lizars, J.H., and James Morton. *Abbotsford: The Seat of Sir Walter Scott, Bart.* Edinburgh: Lizars, 1832.

Logan, Thad, ed. *The Victorian Parlour: A Cultural Study.* Cambridge: Cambridge UP, 2001.

Loti, Pierre. *Cette éternelle nostalgie: Journal intime 1878–1911.* Paris: La Table Ronde, 1997.

Lowenthal, David. *The Past is a Foreign Country.* Cambridge: Cambridge UP, 1985.

Loyer, François. *Paris: Nineteenth-Century Architecture and Urbanism.* Trans. Charles Lynn Clark. New York: Abbeville Press, 1988.

Lüders, Detlef. *Das Goethe-Museum in Rom.* Frankfurt am Main: Freies Deutsches Hochstift, 1973.

Lutwack, Leonard. *The Role of Space in Literature.* Syracuse: Syracuse UP, 1984.

MacCannell, Dean. *The Tourist: A New Theory of the Leisure Class.* Berkeley: U of California P, 1976.

MacCarthy, Fiona. *William Morris. A Life of Our Time.* London: Faber, 1994.

Mackail, J.W. *The Life of William Morris.* 2 vols. London: Longmans, Green and Company, 1899.

[MacVicar]. "Abbotsford." *Dublin Weekly Journal: A Repository of Music, Literature and Entertaining Knowledge* (30 March 1833): 169–74.

Magliani, Mariella, ed. *La Casa di Francesco Petrarca ad Arquà. Guida.* Milan: Skira, 2003.

Maisak, Petra. "Kunst und Literatur im Frankfurter Goethe-Museum. Wiederholte Spiegelungen." In *Gegenwärtige Vergangenheit. Das Freie Deutsche Hochstift hundert Jahre nach der Gründung des Frankfurter Goethe-Museums.* Ed. Petra Hagen Hodgson et al. Frankfurt am Main: Freies Deutsches Hochstift/Frankfurter Goethe-Museum, 1997, 24–51.

———. "Das Haus: Architektur und Geschichte." In Maisak and Dewitz, 1999, 21–35.

Maisak, Petra, and Hans-Georg Dewitz, eds. *Das Frankfurter Goethe Haus.* Frankfurt am Main: Insel Verlag, 1999.

Malipiero, Girolamo. *Il Petrarcha spirituale.* Venice: Marcolini, 1536.

Manguel, Alberto, and Gianni Guadalupi. *The Dictionary of Imaginary Places.* 2nd ed. London: Bloomsbury, 1999 (1st ed. London: Macmillan, 1980).

Marc, Olivier. *Psycanalyse de la maison.* Paris: Éditions du Seuil, 1972.

Marcus, Sharon. *Apartment Stories: City and Home in Nineteenth-Century Paris and London.* Berkeley: U of California P, 1999.

Mariani, Iolanda. "William Michael Rossetti e i *Some Reminiscences.*" In *Le tenebre di Dante. Gabriele Rossetti, i figli, i preraffaelliti.* Vasto: Il Torcoliere, 2004, 153–84.

Marillier, H.C. *Dante Gabriel Rossetti. An Illustrated Memorial of His Art and Life.* London: George Bell and Sons, 1899.

Marsh, Jan, ed. *William Morris and Red House.* London: National Trust Books, 2005.

Marsh, Kate, ed. *Writers and Their Homes. A Guide to the Writers' Houses of England, Scotland, Wales and Ireland.* Photographs Harland Walshaw and Peter Burton. London: Hamish Hamilton, 1993.

Matthews, G.M., ed. *Keats the Critical Heritage.* London: Routledge and Kegan Paul, 1971.

Maul, Gisela, and Margarete Oppel. *Goethes Wohnhaus in Weimar.* 2nd ed. Munich and Vienna: Carl Hanser, 2000.

Maurer, Doris, and Arnold E. Maurer. *Literarischer Führer durch Italien.* Frankfurt am Main: Insel, 1988.

Mazza, Attilio. *Vittoriale. Casa del sogno di Gabriele D'Annunzio.* Brescia: Edizioni del Puntografico, 1988.

McClatchy, J.D. *American Writers at Home.* Photographs Erica Lennard. New York: The Vendome Press, 2004.

Mellon, Thomas. *Thomas Mellon and His Times.* Ed. Mary Louise Briscoe. Pittsburgh: U of Pittsburgh P, 1994.

Miele, Chris, ed. *From William Morris: Building Conservation and the Arts and Crafts Cult of Authenticity, 1877–1939.* New Haven: Yale UP, 2005.

Miller, Norbert. *Der Wanderer. Goethe in Italien.* Munich and Vienna: Carl Hanser, 2002.

Mills, Caroline. "Myths and Meanings of Gentrification." In *Place / Culture / Representation.* Ed. James Duncan, David Ley. London: Routledge, 1993, 149–70.

Mitchell, C. Bradford, ed. *Merchant Steam Vessels of the United States 1790–1868: The Lytle-Holdcamper List.* Staten Island: The Steamship Historical Society of America, 1975.

Montobbio, Luigi. *Arquà Petrarca. Storia e Arte.* Padova and Abano Terme: Edizioni Deganello-Francisci, [1998].

Morris, William. "Making the Best of It." (1882). In *The Collected Works of William Morris.* Ed. May Morris. Vol. 22. London: Longmans, Green and Company, 1914, 81–118.

———. "Gossip about an Old House on the Upper Thames." *The Quest* (4 November 1895).

———. *News from Nowhere.* Ed. Krishan Kumar. Cambridge: Cambridge UP, 1995.

Morris Wright, Catharine. "The Keats-Shelley Association: A Personal History." *Keats-Shelley Journal* 30 (1981): 52–77; 31 (1982): 37–63; 32 (1983): 31–45.

Moryson, Fynes. *An Itinerary vvritten by Fynes Moryson gent. First in the Latine tongue, and then translated by him into English: containing his ten yeeres travel throvgh the tvvelve dominions of Germany, Bohmerland, Sweitzerland, Netherland, Denmarke, Poland, Italy, Turkey, France, England, Scotland, and Ireland. Diuided into III parts.* London: John Beale, 1617. Reprint, New York and Amsterdam: Da Capo Press–Theatrum Orbis Terrarum, 1971.

Müller, Volker. "Den Rest erledigen die Vollstrecker." *Die Zeit* 39 (2004).

Müller, Kanzler von. *Unterhaltungen mit Goethe.* Ed. Ernst Grumach. Weimar: Böhlau, 1956.

Mulvey, Christopher. *Anglo-American Landscapes. A Study of Nineteenth-Century Anglo-American Travel Literature.* Cambridge: Cambridge UP, 1983.

Munthe, Axel. *The Story of San Michele.* London: John Murray, 1929.

Murolo, Luigi. "Inghilterra e terra d'origine nelle riflessioni di Gabriele Rossetti. Un tentativo d'approccio." In *Le muse fra i negozi. Letteratura e cultura in un centro dell'Italia meridionale.* Rome: Bulzoni, 1992, 277–80.

———. ed. *Rossetti. Autobiografie di famiglia.* Vasto: Il Torcoliere, 2004.

Murphy, Jonathan. *Sight or Cite? Aspects of the Visual in Proust.* Cambridge, 1994. (unpublished PhD, University of Cambridge, 1994).

Naldini, Nico, and Fulvio Roiter. *Le case della memoria.* Treviso: Veneto Comunicazione, 1999.

Nestmeyer, Ralf. *Französische Dichter und ihre Häuser.* Frankfurt am Main: Insel, 2005.

Nievo, Stanislao. *I parchi letterari (dal XII al XVI secolo).* Rome: Abete, 1990.

———. *I parchi letterari (dal XVII al XVIII secolo).* Rome: Abete, 1991.

———. *Parchi letterari dell'Ottocento.* Venice: Marsilio, 1998.

———. *I parchi letterari del Novecento.* Rome: Ricciardi, 2000.

Nissim, Liana. *Storia di un tema simbolista: gli interni.* Milan: Vita e Pensiero, 1980.

Noack, Friedrich. "Aus Goethes römischem Kreise." *Goethe-Jahrbuch* 25 (1904).

———. *Deutsches Leben in Rom.* Stuttgart and Berlin: Cotta, 1907.

Nora, Olivier. "La visite au grand écrivain." In Nora, 1997: 2, 2131–55.

Nora, Pierre, ed. *Les lieux de mémoire.* 3 vols. 2nd ed. Paris: Gallimard, 1997. (1st ed. 1984–92).

Nutz, Maximilian. "Das Beispiel Goethe. Zur Konstitution eines nationalen Klassikers." In *Wissenschaftsgeschichte der Germanistik im 19. Jahrhundert.* Eds. Jürgen Fohrmann and Wilhelm Voßkamp. Stuttgart and Weimar: Metzler, 1994, 605–37.

Oliva, Gianni, ed. *I Rossetti tra Italia e Inghilterra.* Roma: Bulzoni, 1984.

———. "'Sbalzato fuori della mia sventurata patria': Gabriele Rossetti 'exul immeritus'." In *Nei paesi dell'utopia. Identità e luoghi della letteratura abruzzese all'estero.* Ed.Vito Moretti. Rome: Bulzoni, 1997, 17–43.

Ono, Ayako. *Japonisme in Britain: Whistler, Menpes, Henry, Hornel and Nineteenth-Century Japan.* London: Routledge Curzon, 2003.

Ousby, Ian. *The Englishman's England.* Cambridge: Cambridge UP, 1990.

Painter, George. *Marcel Proust: A Biography.* London: Chatto and Windus, 1959.

Paolucci, Antonio, and Anna Maria Maetzke. *La Casa del Vasari in Arezzo.* Florence: Cassa di Risparmio di Firenze, 1988.

Papasogli, Benedetta. *Dimore dell'assenza e dell'attesa.* Rome: Bulzoni, 1988.

Parry, Linda, ed. *William Morris: Art and Kelmscott.* Woodbridge: The Boydell Press, 1996.

Pater, Walter. "Dante Gabriel Rossetti." (1883). In *Appreciations.* London: Macmillan, 1910, 214–5.

———. *Ritratti immaginari.* Ed. Mario Praz. Milan: Adelphi, 1980.

Payling, Catherine, ed. *Keats and Italy. A History of the Keats-Shelley House in Rome.* Rome: Il Labirinto, 2005.

———. ed. *Spellbound by Rome. The Anglo-American Community in Rome (1890–1914) and the Founding of the Keats-Shelley House. Incantati da Roma. La comunità americana a Roma (1890–1914) e la fondazione della Keats-Shelley House.* Rome: Palombi Editori, 2005.

Perels, Christoph. "Das Freie Deutsche Hochstift. Frankfurter Goethe-Museum. Memorialstätte, Kulturinstitut, Forschungsstätte." In *Gegenwärtige Vergangenheit. Das Freie Deutsche Hochstift hundert Jahre nach der Gründung des Frankfurter Goethe-Museums*. Ed. Petra Hagen Hodgson et al. Frankfurt am Main: Freies Deutsches Hochstift/Frankfurter Goethe-Museum, 1997, 4–22.

———. "Das Frankfurter Goethe-Museum. Vom Gedenkzimmer zur Galerie der Goethezeit." In Maisak & Dewitz, 1999, 121–32.

Perrot, Michelle, ed. *A History of Private Life*. Vol. 4. *From the Fires of Revolution to the Great War*. Trans. Arthur Goldhammer. Cambridge, Mass: Belknap Press, 1990.

Petrignani, Sandra. *La scrittrice abita qui. Un viaggio nelle case e nella vita sentimentale di Grazia Deledda, Marguerite Yourcenar, Colette, Alexandra David-Néel, Karen Blixen, Virginia Woolf*. Vicenza: Neri Pozza Editore, 2002.

Pettena, Gianni. *Casa Malaparte, Capri*. Florence: Le Lettere, 1999.

Pety, Dominique. *Les Goncourt et la collection: de l'objet d'art à l'art d'écrire*. Geneva: Droz, 2003.

Pevsner, Nikolaus. *Pioneers of the Modern Movement: From William Morris to Walter Gropius*. London: Faber and Faber, 1936.

Pflug, Günther, and Konrad Schürmann. *Goethe-Museum Rom*. Bonn: AsKI, 1989.

Peilmann, Erika. "Goethes Treppenhäuser." *Goethe-Jahrbuch* 115 (1998): 171–81.

Piana, Theo. *Weimar. Stätte klassischer Tradition*. Photographs Günther Beyer and Klaus Beyer. Weimar: Volksverlag, 1955.

Pieters, Jürgen. *Speaking with the Dead. Explorations in Literature and History*. Edinburgh: Edinburgh UP, 2005.

Pietrocola Rossetti, Teodorico. *Gabriele Rossetti*. Turin, Unione tipografico-editrice, 1861.

———. "Gabriele Rossetti" (1861). In Murolo, 2004.

Pocock, Douglas C.D. "Haworth: The Experience of a Literary Place." In *Geography and Literature: A Meeting of the Disciplines*. Eds. William E. Mallory and Paul Simpson-Housley. Syracuse: Syracuse UP, 1987, 135–42.

Pocock, Tom. *Rider Haggard and The Lost Empire. A Biography*. London: Weidenfeld and Nicolson, 1993.

Poisson, Georges. *Guide des maisons d'hommes célèbres: écrivains, artistes, savants, hommes politiques, militaires, saints*. Paris: Pierre Horay, 1982.

———. *Les maisons d'écrivains*. Paris: Presses Universitaires de France, 1997.

Poulet, Georges. *L'espace proustien*. Paris: Gallimard, 1963.

———. *Proustian Space*. Trans. Elliott Coleman. Baltimore and London: Johns Hopkins UP, 1977.

Pratt, Mary-Louise. *Toward a Speech Act Theory of Literary Discourse*. Bloomington: Indiana UP, 1977.

Praz, Mario. *La carne, la morte e il diavolo nella letteratura romantica*. Milan: La Cultura, 1930.

———. "An Empire Flat in a Roman Palace." *Decoration* (June 1937).

———. *Gusto neoclassico*. Florence: Sansoni, 1940.

———. *La filosofia dell'arredamento*. Rome: Documento Libraio Editore, 1945.

———. "Gli interni di Proust." In *La casa della fama*. Milan and Naples: Ricciardi, 1952.

———. *La casa della vita*. Milan: Mondadori, 1958.

———. *Gusto neoclassico.* 2nd revised ed. Naples: Edizioni Scientifiche Italiane, 1959.

———. *The House of Life.* London: Methuen, 1964.

———. *An Illustrated History of Interior Decoration from Pompeii to Art Nouveau.* New York and London: George Braziller and Thames and Hudson, 1964.

———. *Scene di conversazione.* Rome: Ugo Bozzi Editore, 1971.

———. *Conversation Pieces.* London: Methuen, 1971.

———. *La casa della vita.* 2nd revised ed. Milan: Adelphi, 1979.

Premoli-Droulers, Francesca. *Maisons d'écrivains.* Photographs Erica Lennard. Paris: Éditions du Chêne, 1994.

Proust, Marcel. *Correspondance de Marcel Proust.* Ed. Philip Kolb. 21 vols. Paris: Plon, 1970–93.

———. *Contre Sainte-Beuve, précéde de Pastiches et mélanges et suivi de Essais et articles.* Paris: Gallimard, 1971.

———. *Remembrance of Things Past.* Trans. C.K. Moncrieff and Terence Kilmartin. 3 vols. New York: Vintage Books, 1982.

———. *Against Sainte-Beuve and Other Essays.* Trans. John Sturrock. London: Penguin, 1988.

Raabe, Paul. "Dichterverherrlichung im 19. Jahrhundert." In *Bildende Kunst und Literatur. Beiträge zum Problem ihrer Wechselbeziehung im neunzehnten Jahrhundert.* Ed. Wolfdietrich Rasch. Frankfurt am Main: Klostermann, 1970, 79–97.

———. *Spaziergänge durch Goethes Weimar.* 5th ed. Zürich: Arche, 1996.

Ragionieri, Pina. *Casa Buonarroti.* 3rd ed. Milan: Electa, 2001

Reed, Edwin. *The Truth concerning Stratford-upon-Avon, and Shakespeare, with Other Essays.* Boston: Coburn, 1907.

Richards, Thomas. *The Commodity Culture of Victorian Britain. Advertising and Spectacle 1851–1914.* Stanford: Stanford UP, 1990.

Richardson, Joanna. *Fanny Brawne. A Biography.* London: Thames and Hudson, 1952.

Rigney, Ann. *Imperfect Histories: The Elusive Past and the Legacy of Romantic Historicism.* Ithaca: Cornell UP, 2001.

———. "Plenitude, Scarcity and the Circulation of Cultural Memory." *Journal of European Studies* 53.1 (2005): 11–28.

———. "The Movements of Memory: Technologies and Transfers." (forthcoming).

Rochette, Hélène. *Maisons d'écrivains et d'artistes, Paris et ses allentours.* Photographs Pascal Paillardet. Paris: Parigramme, 2004.

Rodd, Rennel. *Social & Diplomatic Memories.* 3 vols. London: Edward Arnold, 1922–25.

Rogers, David. *William Morris at Home.* London: Ebury, 1996.

Rojek, Chris, and John Urry, eds. *Touring Cultures.* London: Routledge, 1997.

Rosazza Ferraris, Patrizia. *Il Museo Mario Praz.* Rome: Edizioni SACS, 1996.

Rosenthal, Michael. *The Art of Thomas Gainsborough: 'a Little Business for the Eye'.* New Haven and London: Yale UP, 1998.

Rossetti, Dante Gabriel. *The Early Italian Poets From Ciullo D'Alcamo to Dante Alighieri (1100–1200–1300).* London: Smith, Elder and Company, 1861.

———. "Dantis Tenebræ (In Memory of My Father)." In *Poems. A New Edition.* London: Ellis and White, 1881, 275.

Rossetti, Gabriele. *Opere inedite e rare: Poesie inedite e rare tratte dagli autografi.* Ed. Domenico Ciampoli. Vasto: Guzzetti, 1929.

———. *La vita mia. Il testamento. Con scritti inediti di William Michael Rossetti.* Ed. Gianni Oliva. Lanciano: Carabba, 2004.

Rossetti, William Michael, ed., *Dante Gabriel Rossetti. His Family Letters with a Memoir*. 2 vols. London: Ellis and Elvey, 1895.
———. *Some Reminiscences*. 2 vols. London: Brown Langham, 1906.
———. *The Works of Dante Gabriel Rossetti*. London: Ellis, 1911.
Rovelli, Luigi. *L'opera storica ed artistica di Paolo Giovio. Il museo dei ritratti*. Como: Cavalleri, 1928.
Rubin, Patricia. *Giorgio Vasari: Art and History*. New Haven and London: Yale UP, 1995.
Rubino, G., and C. Pagetti, eds. *Dimore narrate. Spazio e immaginario nel romanzo contemporaneo*. 2 vols. Rome: Bulzoni, 1988.
Ruzicka, William. *Faulkner's Fictive Architecture*. Ann Arbor: UMI Research Press, 1987.
Rybczynski, Witold. *Home: A Short History of an Idea*. New York: Penguin Books, 1986.
Sabbatino, Pasquale. "In pellegrinaggio alle dimore poetiche del Petrarca. Gli itinerari, le reliquie di Laura e il ritratto di Simone Martini nel 'Petrarchista' di Nicolò Franco." *Studi Rinascimentali* 1 (2003): 61–82.
Sahlins, Marshall. *Culture and Practical Reason*. Chicago: U of Chicago P, 1976.
Salfellner, Harald. *Franz Kafka und Prag*. Prague: Vitalis, 2002.
Samuel, Raphael. *Theatres of Memory: Past and Present in Contemporary Culture*. London: Verso, 1994.
Santesso, Aaron. "The Birth of the Birthplace: Bread Street and Literary Tourism before Stratford." *ELH. A Journal of English Literary History* 71–2 (2004): 377–403.
Saulnier, Verdun-Louis. *Maurice Scève (c. 1500–1560)*. Paris: Klincksieck, 1948-49.
Schauffelen, Thomas, ed. *"... in Dichters Lande ..." Literarische Museen und Gedenkstätten in Baden-Württemberg*. Marbach: Deutsche Schillergesellschaft, 1981.
Schmid, Gerhard. "Das Vermächtnis der Goethe-Enkel." In *Genius huius Loci. Weimar. Kulturelle Entwürfe aus fünf Jahrhunderten*. Weimar: Stiftung Weimarer Klassik, 1992, 101–04.
Schopp, Claude. *Le Château de Monte-Cristo*. Paris: Michel Lafon, 2000.
Schottus, Franciscus. *Itinerarii Italiae rerumq. Romanarum libri tres*. (1600). 2nd ed. Antwerp: Plantijn, 1625.
Schuermann, Konrad and Ursula Bongaerts-Schomer, eds. *"... endlich in dieser Hauptstadt der Welt angelangt!" Goethe in Rom*. 2 vols. Mainz: Philipp von Zabern, 1997.
———. *"... finalmente in questa capitale del mondo!". Goethe a Roma*. 2 vols. Rome: Artemide Edizioni, 1997.
Schulze, Sabine. *Goethe und die Kunst*. Ostfildern: Hatje, 1994.
Schuster, Gerhard, and Caroline Gille, eds. *Wiederholte Spiegelungen. Weimarer Klassik. 1759–1832. Ständige Ausstellung des Goethe-Nationalmuseums*. 2 vols. Munich and Vienna: Hanser, 1999.
Schwarz, Hans-Peter. *"...non visse da pittore ma da principe..." Künstlerhäuser im Spannungsfeld von Hof und Stadt. Versuch einer Typologie*. 2 vols. Marburg, 1981 (PhD thesis, Marburg, 1981).
———. ed. *Künstlerhäuser. Eine Architekturgeschichte des Privaten*. Frankfurt am Main: Deutsches Architekturmuseum, 1989.
———. *Das Künstlerhaus. Anmerkungen zur Sozialgeschichte des Genies*. Braunschweig: Vieweg, 1990.
Scott, Walter. *The Journal of Sir Walter Scott*. Ed. W.E.K. Anderson. Edinburgh: Canongate, 1998.

——. *Reliquiae Trotcosienses, or the Gabions of the Late Jonathan Oldbuck Esq. of Monkbarns.* Edinburgh: Edinburgh UP, 2004.

Seifert, Siegfried. *Weimar. Führer durch eine europäische Kulturstadt.* Leipzig: Edition Leipzig, 1994.

Selmin, Francesco. *Guida ai luoghi letterari dei Colli Euganei.* Milan: Touring Editore, 2004.

Semsek, Hans Günter. *Englische Dichter und ihre Häuser.* Frankfurt am Main: Insel, 2000.

Seng, Joachim. *"Ein Bundestag des Deutschen Geistes." Die Gründung des Freien Deutschen Hochstifts.* Frankfurt am Main, [Freies Deutsches Hochstift], [n.d.].

Settis, Salvatore. "Introduzione." In Hüttinger, 1992, vii-xxiii.

Sharp, William. *The Life & Letters of Joseph Severn.* London: Sampson, Low, Marston and Company, 1892.

Shattuck, Roger. *Proust.* London: Fontana, 1974.

——. *Proust's Way: A Field Guide to In Search of Lost Time.* New York and London: Norton, 2000.

Shelley, Henry C. *Shakespeare and Stratford.* London: Simpkin, Marshall, Hamilton, Kent, 1913.

Silverman, Deborah. *Art Nouveau in Fin-de-Siècle France: Politics, Psychology and Style.* Berkeley: U of California P, 1989.

Siviter, Roger. *Waverley: Portrait of a Famous Route.* Southampton: Kingfisher Railway Productions, 1988.

Smith, Margaret, ed. *The Letters of Charlotte Brontë.* 3 vols. Oxford: Clarendon Press, 1995–2004.

Speroni, Sperone. *Opere.* Venice: Domenico Occhi, 1740. Reprint in 5 vols., Manziana: Vecchiarelli, 1989.

Spinozzi, Paola. "'And in the Dark House Was I Loved.' Writing a Life, Constructing a Utopian Place: William Morris and Kelmscott Manor." In *Vite di utopia.* Ed. Vita Fortunati and Paola Spinozzi. Ravenna: Longo, 2000, 167–77.

Stagl, Justin. *A History of Curiosity. The Theory of Travel 1550–1800.* London: Harwood Academic Publishers, 1995.

Stewart, Susan. *On Longing. Narratives of the Miniature, the Gigantic, the Souvenir, the Collection.* Baltimore: The Johns Hopkins UP, 1984.

Stinger, Charles L. *Humanism and the Church Fathers. Ambrogio Traversari (1386–1439) and Christian Antiquity in the Italian Renaissance.* Albany: State U of New York P, 1977.

Stockholm, Joanne M. *Garrick's Folly. The Shakespeare Jubilee of 1769 at Stratford and Jury Lane.* London: Methuen, 1964.

Sturrock, John. "Introduction." In Proust, 1988: vii–xxix.

Tadié, Jean-Yves. *Marcel Proust.* Paris: Gallimard, 1996.

Talamone, Marida. *Casa Malaparte.* Milan: Clup, 1990.

Tassoni, Alessandro. *La secchia rapita.* Ed. Pietro Papini. Florence: Sansoni, 1962.

Taylor, Gary. *Reinventing Shakespeare. A Cultural History from the Restoration to the Present.* London: Hogarth Press, 1990.

Terraroli, Valerio. *Il Vittoriale. Percorsi simbolici e collezioni d'arte di Gabriele d'Annunzio.* Milan: Skira, 2001.

Thornton, Dora. *The Scholar in His Study. Ownership and Experience in Renaissance Italy.* New Haven and London, Yale UP, 1998.

Tindall, Gillian. *Countries of the Mind. The Meaning of Place to Writers.* London: Hogarth Press, 1991.

Tobia, Bruno. *Una patria per gli italiani. Spazi, itinerari, monumenti nell'Italia unita (1870–1900)*. Bari: Laterza, 1991.

Tomasini, Jacopo Filippo. *Petrarcha redivivus, integram poetae celeberrimi vitam iconibus aere celatis exhibens. Accessit nobilissimae foeminae Laurae brevis historia*. Padova: Pasquati and Bortoli, 1635. Reprint, Pistoia: Libreria dell'Orso, 2004.

Torchin, Leshu. "Location, Location, Location. The Destination of the Manhattan TV Tour." *Tourist Studies* 2 (2002): 247–66.

Tristram, Philippa. *Living Space in Fact and Fiction*. London and New York: Routledge, 1989.

Trunz, Erich. "Das Haus am Frauenplan in Goethes Alter." In *Weimarer Goethe-Studien*. Weimar: Hermann Böhlaus Nachfolger, 1980, 48–76.

Urry, John. *The Tourist Gaze: Leisure and Travel in Contemporary Societies*. London: Sage, 1990.

———. *Consuming Places*. London: Routledge, 1995.

Vasari, Giorgio. *The Lives of the Painters, Sculptors and Architects*. Ed. A.B. Hinds. 4 vols. London and Toronto: Dent, 1927.

Vincent, Eric Reginald Pearce. *Gabriele Rossetti in England*. Oxford: The Clarendon Press, 1936.

Viollet-le-Duc, Emmanuel. *Dictionnaire raisonné du mobilier français de l'époque carlovingienne à la Renaissance, vol. I, Meubles*. Paris: Morel, 1871.

Vogel, Julius. *Aus Goethes Römischen Tagen: kultur- und kunstgeschichtliche Studien zur Lebensgeschichte des Dichters*. Leipzig: Seemann, 1905.

Waithe, Marcus. "The Stranger at the Gate: Privacy, Property, and the Structure of Welcome at William Morris's Red House." *Victorian Studies* 46–4 (Summer 2004): 567–95.

Wang, Ning. "Re-thinking Authenticity." *Tourism Experience. Annals of Tourism Research* 26 (1999): 349–70.

Ward, H. Snowden, and Catherine Weed Ward. *Shakespeare's Town and Times*. New York and London: Truslove and Comba, 1896.

Watson, Janell. *Literature and Material Culture from Balzac to Proust*. Cambridge: Cambridge UP, 1999.

Wehnert, Stefanie. *Literaturmuseen im Zeitalter der neuen Medien. Leseumfeld—Aufgaben—Didaktische Konzepte*. Kiel: Ludwig Verlag, 2000.

Weimar im Urteil der Welt. Stimmen aus drei Jahrhunderten. Berlin and Weimar: Aufbau, 1975.

Wesseling, Henk L., ed., *Plaatsen van herinnering*. 4 vols. Amsterdam: Bert Bakker, 2005–2007.

Wheeler, Robert Bell. *An Historical Account of the Birth-Place of Shakespeare, reprinted from the Edition of 1824, with a Few Prefatory Notes by J.O. Halliwell, Esq., F.R.S*. Stratford: Chiswick Press, 1863.

Wilkins, Ernest Hatch. *Studies in the Life and Works of Petrarch*. Cambridge. Mass: Medieval Academy of America, 1955.

———. *Vita del Petrarca*. Milan: Feltrinelli, 1987.

Winkler, Robert. *Das Haus des Architekten. Architects' Homes. La Maison de l'Architecte*. Zürich: Girsberger, 1955.

Wißkirchen, Hans, ed. *Dichter und ihre Häuser. Die Zukunft der Vergangenheit*. Lübeck: Schmidt-Römhild, 2002.

White, Edmund. *Marcel Proust*. New York: Viking, 1999.

White, Patrick. *On Living in an Old Country*. London: Verso Books, 1985.

———. *Le Vite de' più eccellenti pittori, scultori et architettori nelle redazioni del 1550 e 1565*. Ed. Paola Barocchi and Rosanna Bettarini. Florence: Sansoni, 1966–87.

Woolf, Virginia. "Gas at Abbotsford." (1940). In *The Moment and Other Essays*. New York: Harcourt, Brace and Company, 1948, 56–74.

Yates, Francis. *The Art of Memory*. London: Routledge and Kegan Paul, 1966.

———. *The Art of Memory*. Reprint, London: Routledge, 2001.

Zankl, Franz Rudolf. "Das Personalmuseum. Untersuchung zu einem Museumstypus." *Museumskunde* 41 (1972): 1–132.

Zapperi, Roberto. *Das Inkognito: Goethes ganz andere Existenz in Rom*. Trans. Ingeborg Walter. Munich: Beck, 1999.

Contributors

Christine Alexander is Scientia Professor of English at the University of New South Wales (Sydney), and a Fellow of the Australian Academy of the Humanities. Her critical study on *The Early Writings of Charlotte Brontë* (Blackwell, 1983) won the British Academy Rose Mary Crawshay Prize, and she has edited a multi-volume *Edition of the Early Writings of Charlotte Brontë* (Blackwell, 1987–91). Other publications include *The Art of the Brontës* (co-authored; Cambridge UP, 1995) and the *Oxford Companion to the Brontës* (co-authored; Oxford UP, 2003). She has also published on Gothic literature, Jane Austen, critical editing, literary juvenilia and landscape gardening. She is general editor of the Juvenilia Press and co-editor of *The Child Writer from Austen to Woolf* (Cambridge UP, 2005).

Stephen Bann is professor of History of Art at the University of Bristol. His research interests are museum history and theory (especially curiosity and antiquarianism); historical representation in painting and other visual media (France and Britain); English art criticism (Hazlitt, Pater, Stokes); 20th century avant-garde movements; post-modern media and installation art; land art and landscape theory. He is the author of *Ways About Modernism* (Routledge, 2007), *Jannis Kounellis* (Reaktion Books, 2003); *Parallel Lines: Printmakers, Painters and Photographers in Nineteenth-Century France* (Yale UP, 2001); *Paul Delaroche: History Painted* (Reaktion Books and Princeton UP, 1997); *Romanticism and the Rise of History* (Twayne, 1995); *Under the Sign: John Bargrave as Collector, Traveller and Witness* (University of Michigan Press, 1994); *The Inventions of History: Essays on the Representation of the Past* (Manchester UP and St. Martin's Press, 1990). He serves on the boards of many scholarly periodicals and is a founding member of the editorial board of *Word and Image*. In 2006 a collection of essays, *About Stephen Bann*, was edited by Deborah Cherry (Blackwell), which reflects on the writings of Stephen Bann and his influence on the fields of visual studies, art history and cultural history.

Paola Colaiacomo is professor of English Literature at the University of Rome "La Sapienza." In the field of literary criticism, she has written extensively on the 18th century novel (*Biografia del personaggio nei romanzi di Daniel Defoe;* 1975), on the Romantic poetry and theory of poetic language from Coleridge to Walter Pater, on Shakespeare and the Elizabethan idea of theatre. She translated S.T. Coleridge's *Biographia Literaria* (first complete translation into Italian; 1991). She has also written on the swinging London of the sixties: *La Londra dei Beatles* (with Vittoria C. Caratozzolo; Editori Riuniti, 1996); on British architecture in the sixties (Archigram group), and on serial TV fiction: *Tutto questo è Beautiful. Forme narrative della fine del millennio* (Luca Sossello, 1999). In more recent years she has also been writing and researching in the field of fashion theory: *Cartamodello. Antologia di scrittori e scritture sulla moda* (with Vittoria C. Caratozzolo; Luca Sossello, 2000), *Mercanti di stile. Le culture della moda dagli anni '20 a oggi* (edited with Vittoria C. Caratozzolo; Editori Riuniti, 2002).

Vita Fortunati is professor of English literature at the University of Bologna. Her main areas of research are utopian literature, women's studies and comparative studies. From 1998 to 2001 she co-ordinated COTEPRA, a European Thematic Network on Comparative Studies, since 2002 she has been the co-ordinator of ACUME, a European Thematic Network on Cultural Memory in European Countries. She is the director of the Interdepartmental Centre for Utopian Studies at the University of Bologna and a member of the scientific board of "Forme dell'Utopia," a series of utopian primary texts and critical studies (Longo). She has published on utopia as a literary genre (*La letteratura utopica inglese,* Longo, 1979; *Dictionary of Literary Utopias,* co-edited with Raymond Trousson; Champion, 2000), utopia and biography (*Vite di Utopia,* co-edited with Paola Spinozzi; Longo, 2000), national and cultural identity (*Utopianism / Literary Utopias and National Cultural Identities: a Comparative Perspective,* co-edited with Paola Spinozzi; Compositori, 2001), utopian views of death (*Perfezione e finitudine. La concezione della morte nell'utopia in età moderna e contemporanea,* co-edited with M. Sozzi and Paola Spinozzi; Lindau, 2004). With Raymond Trousson she has co-edited the *Histoire transnationale des utopies littéraires et de l'utopisme* (Champion, 2006).

Harald Hendrix is professor of Italian studies and heads the programme of Renaissance studies at the University of Utrecht. He has published on the European reception of Italian Renaissance and Baroque authors (*Traiano Boccalini fra erudizione e polemica;* Olschki, 1995; the chapter on the 17th century in *Letteratura italiana fuori d'Italia;* Salerno Editrice, 2002) and on the early modern aesthetics of the non-beautiful. He has co-edited six volumes in the series Utrecht Renaissance Studies (Amsterdam UP) and is currently preparing a book on the cultural history of writers' houses in Italy, from Petrarch to the present day.

Dorothee Hock is deputy director of the Casa di Goethe in Rome. Born in 1963 near Cologne, she has been living in Italy since 1982, where she obtained a degree in Translation Studies. A collaborator in the early 1990s at the German Embassy to the Holy See in Rome, she started working for the Goethe house still under construction as of 1996, doing research on the building's history in the Roman archives. Since the museum's opening in May 1997, as its deputy director she has been responsible for its public relations, management and its publication programme.

Jon Kear, MA and PhD (1998) Courtauld Institute London, is a lecturer in history and theory of art at the University of Kent. He has published widely on aspects on 19th and 20th century art and film, including a book and several articles on the French filmmaker Chris Marker, *Sunless: Time and History in the work of Chris Marker* (Flicks Books, 1999). He is currently completing a book on Paul Cézanne, *Reframing Cézanne.*

Claire O'Mahony is lecturer and fellow of Kellogg College, University of Oxford, and director of History of Art Lifelong Learning, University of Bristol. She received her BA from the University of California at Berkeley and a PhD at the Courtauld Institute in London on mural decoration in Third Republic French townhalls. She specialises in the history of art, design and interior decoration around 1900. She contributed to *The Year 1900: Art at the Crossroads (*Royal Academy of Arts, London, 1999), *Degas and America: The Early Collectors* (Minneapolis Institute of Arts, Atlanta, 2001). Other publications include "Modern Muses: representing the life model in fin de siècle France," *Art on the Line* (2003) and "Emile Gallé and la Lorraine artiste," *Art on the Line* (2007).

Marilena Parlati is associate professor of literatures in English at the University of Calabria in Cosenza. She published various essays on Jacobean theatre and early modern English and Italian literatures, plus a monograph on John Webster's tragedies in connection with conduct and courtly literature of the 16th century (*Infezione dell'arte, paralisi della memoria nelle tragedie di John Webster,* 1998). Her other fields of research include late-Victorian popular fiction and theatre. She is currently writing a monograph entitled *Beyond Modernity,* in which she tries to survey authors such as Haggard, Stoker, Doyle and Hope through the lens of the anthropological and archaeological discourses of the time. She co-edited, with Nicholas Daly, the first issue of *Textus,* the scholarly journal of the AIA (Italian Association for English Studies), on *The Cultural Object. Maps, Memories, Icons* (2006), and with Eleonora Federici the proceedings of *Locating Subjects. Views on Identity and Difference* (2006).

Catherine Payling has been the curator of the Keats Shelley House in Rome since 1997. She has a degree in English Literature and Language from

Oxford University and is a Chartered Accountant. She has also worked in Great Britain at the National Maritime Museum, the Royal Opera House and Royal Philharmonic Orchestra. She is the editor of *Spellbound by Rome. The Anglo-American Community in Rome (1890–1914) and the Founding of the Keats-Shelley House / Incantati da Roma. La comunità anglo-americana a Roma (1890–1914) e la fondazione della Keats-Shelley House* (Palombi Editori, 2005) and of *Keats and Italy. A History of the Keats-Shelley House in Rome* (Il Labirinto, 2005).

Bodo Plachta is professor of German Literature at the Free University of Amsterdam. He completed his doctorate with a thesis on *Der handschriftliche Nachlaß der Annette von Droste-Hülshoff* (1988) and his teaching and research interests are in the fields of German literature since the 18th century and scholarly editing. He is president of the "Arbeitsgemeinschaft für germanistische Edition", and co-editor of the *International Yearbook of Scholarly Editing, editio*. His publications include the following monographs, editions and anthologies: *Damnatur—Toleratur—Admittitur. Studien und Dokumente zur literarischen Zensur im 18. Jahrhundert* (1994), *Annette von Droste-Hülshoff: Sämtliche Werke in zwei Bänden* (with W. Woesler, 1994), '*Sturm und Drang'—Geistiger Aufbruch 1770–1790 im Spiegel der Literatur* (with W. Woesler, 1997), *Editionswissenschaft. Eine Einführung in Methode und Praxis der Edition neuerer Texte* (1997), *Text und Edition. Positionen und Perspektiven* (with R. Nutt-Kofoth, H.T.M. van Vliet, H. Zwerschina, 2000), *Literarische Zusammenarbeit* (2001), *Vincent van Gogh: Briefe* (2001), *Perspectives of Scholarly Editing. Perspektiven der Textedition* (with H.T.M. van Vliet, 2002), *Edition und Übersetzung* (with W. Woesler, 2002), *Ein 'Tyrann der Schaubühne'? Stationen und Positionen einer literatur- und kulturkritischen Debatte über Oper und Operntext im 18. Jahrhundert* (2003), *Literatur als Erinnerung* (2004), *Editionen zu deutschsprachigen Autoren als Spiegel der Editionsgeschichte* (with Rüdiger Nutt-Kofoth, 2005) *Varianten — Variants — Variantes* (with Christa Jansohn, 2005), *Thomas Mann, 1875–1955* (with Walter Delabar, 2005), *Zensur* (2006), *Die Herkulesarbeiten der Philologie* (with Sophie Bertho, 2007).

Ann Rigney is professor of Comparative Literature and heads the programme in Literary Studies at the University of Utrecht. She is a Fellow of the Royal Dutch Academy of Sciences. Her research deals primarily with the intersections between literature and historiography, and she has published widely on topics relating to narrative theory, historical representation, and cultural memory. She is author of *The Rhetoric of Historical Representation: Three Narrative Histories of the French Revolution* (Cambridge UP, 1990, 2002[2]) and *Imperfect Histories: The Elusive Past and the Legacy of Romantic Historicism* (Cornell UP, 2001; winner of the John-Pierre Barricelli Award 2001). She is co-editor (with Joep Leerssen) of *Historians and Social Values* (Amsterdam UP, 2000) and (with Kiene Brillenburg Wurth) of *Het leven van teksten. Een inleiding in de literatuurwetenschap* (Amsterdam UP, 2006). Her most recent project involves a study of the cultural afterlife of the work of Walter Scott.

Patrizia Rosazza Ferraris is director and curator of the Museo Mario Praz in Rome. She is the author of *Il museo Mario Praz* (Edizioni SACS, 1996, 2000²), and is currently preparing a comprehensive catalogue of the museum's holdings.

Michael Rosenthal, BA, PhD London, MA Cantab, is professor in the History of Art at the University of Warwick. Principal publications: *British Landscape Painting* (Phaidon, 1982), *Constable. The Painter and his Landscape* (Yale UP, 1983), *The Art of Thomas Gainsborough: 'a little business for the Eye'* (Yale UP, 1999), and with Martin Myrone, *Gainsborough* (exhibition catalogue Tate Britain 2003). His current research is on early colonial Australia.

Paola Spinozzi is lecturer in English literature at the University of Ferrara. Her research on interart studies focuses on the theories and methodologies of comparatism between literature and the visual arts, and on verbal/visual aesthetics in the Victorian age and in Pre-Raphaelitism. She is the author if *Sopra il reale. Osmosi interartistiche nel preraffaellitismo e nel simbolismo inglese* (Alinea, 2005), and has published on late Victorian ekphrasis, Ford Madox Ford's reception of D.G. Rossetti and A.S. Byatt's re-writing of the Victorian scientific debate. Her research on utopian literature covers art and aesthetics, science and technology, imperialism and urban imagery in writings by W. Morris, S. Butler, A. Trollope, W. Hudson, R. Jefferies, P. Greg. She contributed to the *Dictionary of Literary Utopias* (Champion, 2000). She has edited *Utopianism / Literary Utopias and National Cultural Identities. A Comparative Approach* (Compositori, 2001), and co-edited, with Vita Fortunati, *Vite di Utopia* (Longo, 2000), and with Vita Fortunati and M. Sozzi, *Perfezione e finitudine. La concezione della morte nell'utopia in età moderna e contemporanea* (Lindau, 2004).

Ben Thomas is a lecturer in history and theory of art at the University of Kent. His research interests include Renaissance art and art theory, prints and the history of collecting. He is the author of several articles on Italian Renaissance art, and the editor (with Timothy Wilson) of *C. D. E. Fortnum and the collecting and study of applied arts and sculpture in Victorian England* (Oxford UP, 1999). He is currently working on an interpretive essay on Giovanni Girolamo Savoldo's 'Self-Portrait with Mirrors' (Paris, Louvre) and on a book entitled *The Better Art? The Problem of Sculpture in Renaissance Art Theory*.

Index